915.9704 Borton, Lady.
BOR
        After sorrow.

$23.95   22916

DATE			

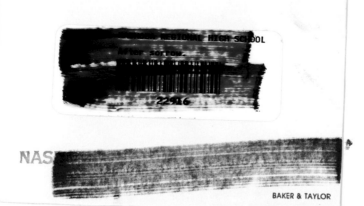

After Sorrow

LADY BORTON

After Sorrow

An
American
Among the
Vietnamese

VIKING

VIKING
Published by the Penguin Group
Penguin Books USA Inc., 375 Hudson Street,
New York, New York 10014, U.S.A.
Penguin Books Ltd, 27 Wrights Lane, London W8 5TZ, England
Penguin Books Australia Ltd, Ringwood, Victoria, Australia
Penguin Books Canada Ltd, 10 Alcorn Avenue, Toronto, Ontario, Canada M4V 3B2
Penguin Books (N.Z.) Ltd, 182–190 Wairau Road, Auckland 10, New Zealand

Penguin Books Ltd, Registered Offices:
Harmondsworth, Middlesex, England

First published in 1995 by Viking Penguin, a division of Penguin Books USA Inc.

10 9 8 7 6 5 4 3 2 1

Grateful acknowledgment is made for permission to use the following works:
Selections from *A Prison Diary* by Ho Chi Minh, *Vietnamese Literature:
Historical Background and Texts*, edited by Nguyen Khac Vien and Huu Ngoc,
and issues of *Vietnamese Studies*. By permission of The Gion Publishing House, Ha Noi.
Poem on page 53 by Nguyen thi Minh Khai, translated by Lady Borton.
By permission of the Viet Nam Women's Union.
Song lyric on page 149 by Han Ngoc Bich. Used by permission.
"Last Night I Dreamed I Met Uncle Ho" by Xuan Giao. Used by permission.
"My Son's Childhood" by Xuan Quynh, translated by Phan Thanh Hao.
Reprinted by permission.

All photographs courtesy of the author unless otherwise indicated

Maps by the author

LIBRARY OF CONGRESS CATALOGING IN PUBLICATION DATA
Borton, Lady.
After sorrow : an American among the Vietnamese / Lady Borton.
p.   cm.
ISBN 0-670-84332-6
1. Vietnam—Description and travel.   2. Borton, Lady—Journeys—Vietnam.   I. Title.
DS556.39.B68   1995
915.9704'44—dc20   94-39146

This book is printed on acid-free paper.
∞

Printed in the United States of America
Set in Adobe Minion
Designed by Kathryn Parise

for
all our
children

The wheel of the law turns.
After the rain, good weather.
. . . .
What could be more natural?
After sorrow comes joy.

FROM "The Weather Clears"
A Prison Diary
HO CHI MINH
1890–1969

AUTHOR'S NOTE

"We have never before told these stories," Second Harvest once said to me. "Not to each other. Not to anyone."

Vietnamese peasants—regardless of religious or political affiliation—share a Confucian background that defines their place in human and spiritual relationships. The modesty that grows from the Confucian legacy of Right Relationship often charms Westerners; however, at the same time, its focus away from the individual and onto the community can seem disconcerting.

For a Vietnamese peasant, telling her story as if it had some worth of its own is the epitome of arrogance. This is the reason the villagers with whom I lived asked that I change their names. Although they remain recognizable to each other, these villagers feel that with their names changed they no longer call attention to themselves.

"Everyone in the world shares the same longings," Second Harvest said. "But the details of our lives are as individual as faces."

HA NOI, VIET NAM
September 1994

CONTENTS

Book III: Ha Noi
Viet Nam's Largest Village

Epilogue

FOREWORD

*I*n August 1969, with six other Americans, I traveled down National Highway 1, a mostly dirt road from Ha Noi south to the Ben Hai River, close to the DMZ. We stopped at the last little battered village, Vinh Linh. A young man, exhausted, distressed, looked up, talked to our guides a moment. He wondered why he had to speak to Americans, why the Fatherland Front had asked him to speak to us. We asked only one question: How are you able to remain here? "If we leave, who will defend this land?" He said this in Vietnamese to our guides, angrier at them than at us.

At the very river bank an old woman had planted a small field of cassava in view of the bare South Viet Nam shore. The United States defended the southern province Quang Tri with almost total destruction. The old woman wanted the Americans to see her green field.

Lady Borton was working that day (and until 1971) on the other side of the river in Quang Ngai, working with Vietnamese civilian amputees. That's when she learned to speak Vietnamese. "Most important," she said, "I learned to listen. The Vietnamese peasants I came to know changed my life."

The war in Viet Nam probably changed my life, but a lot more modestly of course. I tried the language. "Grace, you must get the tune. You don't have it," Nien, our translator, said.

But I do have head-changing pictures in my mind—that good picture-saving place—and greenness washes them all. A green that must have been observed from above by our American high fliers, who were, our guides said, great creators of fish ponds. Many of those pilots were brought down, shot back to earth, became POWs. Some became MIAs, their large bones snagging in the roots of trees, crowding the hundred thousand smaller limbs of the Vietnamese MIAs.

When we landed at the little Ha Noi airport, having flown in a small plane from Phnom Penh, our hosts greeted us with flowers and asked, "Could you see from up there how green our Ha Noi is?"

In a 1980 flight to Minneapolis, I sat beside a Vietnamese woman from Sai Gon. After some easy conversation, I told her I'd been to the North during the war. She turned to look at me. "Really!" I expected a political remark. Instead, she said, "Ha Noi! We were children. In 1954 the sisters took us in trainloads to the South—so we shouldn't become Communists, you know. I was so young but I remember the green."

This is how we traveled in our two jeeps. We were four peace movement Americans whose task it was to bring three American POWs home, which we did at the end of August. There were three filmmakers, several translators, a nurse who carried the responsibility of our health and would not allow us one aspirin unless we ate two bananas, a couple of political bosses as well who unusually enough encouraged conversation. On our long journey we often came to a stream or river whose bridge had been completely destroyed three or four times. A decision must once have been made that it would be wiser to raise the river than rebuild a bridge. Three women had just finished piling stones high and wide enough for us to pass in our jeeps; they had stood with brooms, staring at us. Their eyes had widened into absolute roundness. Then they began to sweep the road before us. Not only our jeep but many bicycles with old tires would carry arms, food, information over those dirt roads. Later we learned a slogan. "We will patch our roads as we patch our sweetheart's trousers."

In *After Sorrow*, the rivers are once again the main highways, and as Lady Borton writes about the farming traffic and the communal visiting in small river boats, I thought of these women and how finally, after the French Wars and American War, they were able to go home. I also remember them when giant yellow earth-moving machines heave and tremble and sigh in order to smooth our narrow Vermont roads.

One more green remembrance. There had been no bombing for a couple of months—the Christmas bombing lay ahead. But grass had grown over the broken houses, the torn amphitheater of a beautiful little city, Dong Hoi. You could hardly see the entrances to the underground tunnels and rooms in which people had lived for years. "Does nobody live here now?" we asked.

"Not so many. This city was bombed again and again so fiercely. We don't know why. But we've built a new Dong Hoi in the mountains, well hidden."

Why did they tell us that? Later at a congressional hearing, a pilot said, "I don't know why but we tended to drop all unexpended ordnance on that town."

Lady Borton is probably the only person who lived in South Viet Nam and in North Viet Nam during the war and who also, through Quaker Service and with her facility in Vietnamese, worked among the Boat People in the camps of Malaysia. I was surprised that I didn't know until just recently that she was the woman who led the first reporters to My Lai.

I met her a short time before *Sensing the Enemy*, her book about the Boat People, was published. She was beginning her work on *After Sorrow*, the book about the Vietnamese who stayed. I was happy to become her friend. As we talked, I understood that she had sworn herself in love and understanding to the Vietnamese people—*all* the people. But she was not sentimental or neutral. She would not play our liberal national game called "on-the-one-hand and on-the-other."

I often think of how good works on the political right or left fall before the required assertion of faith. When you're old you think now and then about how you've lived your life (when you're not too busy). I'm not angry at the way I've lived mine, not even the hard parts. But I believe I would have liked to have done good on that Lady Borton scale with political understanding, offering knowledge and labor directly to those whose suffering was in some way my responsibility. I truthfully can't think of a better, more intelligently useful person than Lady Borton.

Leaning gently but steadfastly against Vietnamese ideological fears, bad authoritarian habits, and intransigent American self-love, she finally persuaded the Vietnamese that she should be able to live in an ordinary way among the village peasants, working beside them in the fields and paddies, talking in their language, listening to their stories. She longed to tell these stories to us—to Americans who for thirty years have not been listening.

—Grace Paley

Book I

Ban Long Village
Mekong Delta
Southern Viet Nam

Midnight

All faces have a harmless look in sleep.
Awake, men differ: good and evil show.
No virtue and no vice exist at birth.
Of good and evil, nurture sows the seed.

FROM *A Prison Diary*
HO CHI MINH
1890–1969

I

Arrested

Spring arrives, and a hundred flowers follow;
Spring returns with another hundred blooms.
My eyes watch the passing seasons;
My hair greys with the years.
But this spring not all the flowers faded.
Last night, a plum blossomed near my door.

"Rebirth"
MAN GIAC
1051–1096

"*H*ands up, American!" Second Harvest said in Vietnamese. She poked my spine. "You're under arrest!"

I lifted my sandals, one in each hand, over my head. In the delicate moonlight, cacti along the rice paddy loomed like phantoms with bizarre, prickly limbs.

"Forward, Little Sister!" Second Harvest said in a teasing, laughing voice. "You can't run away now!"

It was the rainy season of 1989. Second Harvest was leading me and Autumn, a friend who had come with me from Ha Noi, into Ban Long, a village of eight thousand people in the waterways of the Mekong Delta seventy miles southwest of Sai Gon. I had first visited Ban Long two years before, in early 1987. That was also when I'd first met and become friends with Second Harvest.

I would make many visits to Ban Long over the next seven years, having chosen it as a village that seemed typical of many in the Mekong Delta. However, by that night in 1989, I had not yet figured out that during the war Ban Long Village had been a Viet Cong base.

The term *Viet Cong*—"Vietnamese Communist"—was originally a pejorative coined by American-backed South Vietnamese President Ngo Dinh Diem in the late 1950s. However, by the late 1980s, Vietnamese in Viet Nam no longer considered the phrase derogatory. Even Second Harvest, a non-Communist nationalist who had worked for the Revolution, used *Viet Cong* and its GI derivative, *VC*, when referring to herself.

During the "American War," as Vietnamese call the Viet Nam War, U.S. bombers had attacked Ban Long persistently, blasting houses into craters, families into corpses. Agent Orange robbed the earth of green. But by now, in 1989, fourteen years after the end of the fighting, the green had returned. Dense foliage obscured the moon. The air smelled sweet with the fragrance of frangipani. An owl called out, *cu cu, cu cu;* two frogs croaked while, all around, cicadas buzzed in an insistent chorus.

As I walked on through the darkness, carrying my flip-flops, I could feel the path of packed mud with my toes. When we came to a moonlit clearing, I stopped. Nearby, gold and white frangipani blooms lifted like trumpets, their fragrance triumphant.

Amazing, I thought: The Earth has forgiven us.

During the war, I had worked in Quang Ngai, South Viet Nam, as an administrator for the American Friends Service Committee (AFSC). Also known as Quaker Service, AFSC had been corecipient of the 1947 Nobel Peace Prize for its work "from the nameless to the nameless" during World War II.

My father, who is old enough to be my grandfather, had worked for AFSC in Germany and Poland after World War I. As I was growing up in suburban Washington during the 1940s and 1950s, he tempered my childhood affluence with stories from his postwar work in a refugee feeding program. He referred to this work—and his attention to its small but crucial details—as a "horseshoe nail."

"There was plenty of food," Pop would tell us over supper. "The problem was distribution. If we provided horseshoe nails, then sledges of food could run all winter." And so, in my family's lexicon, the cliché "horseshoe nail" as in "For want of a nail the horse was lost" has evolved to mean instead a life work of service through small gestures.

My father was deputy director of export control for the Department of Commerce as I was growing up during the Cold War. His conversations with my mother over supper often included stories of people who had attempted to run around the stringent U.S. trade embargo then enforced against the Soviet Union and her allies. My father is an entirely scrupulous man. Although I'm sure it was not his intention to raise an outlaw, my dad's small tales gave me an education in embargo-dodging techniques.

When the United States embargo against North Viet Nam began in 1964, it kept out, among many other things, Western medicine and recent Western medical knowledge. By the 1980s, this included information about AIDS. To my way of thinking, the embargo was unconscionable; and so for most of the thirty years that embargo was in effect, I openly ran around it.

Standing there among Ban Long's frangipani, I thought of my dad and of a story he tells about his younger brother. At the time of the bombing of Pearl Harbor, my uncle Hugh was one of three American scholars of European ethnic background who could read, write, and speak Japanese. He temporarily left academia to work at the U.S. State Department.

At the end of World War II, Hugh served as vice chairman of the State Department committee responsible for recommending policy on postwar Japan. The chairman of the committee announced that Japanese Emperor Hirohito should be tried and executed for war crimes. Hugh understood that the Japanese people regard their emperor as a divine presence deserving their complete obedience. Trying and executing the emperor, Hugh asserted, would precipitate a war the likes of which the United States had never seen. But the chairman held his ground.

By chance, the chairman was absent with the flu the day the committee voted on Japan's postwar fate. Hugh prevailed. Emperor Hirohito was persuaded to support the U.S. occupation of Japan. According to my dad's version of the tale, Emperor Hirohito's cooperation allowed the American occupation to proceed so peacefully that U.S. General Douglas MacArthur stopped wearing a side arm within three weeks of his arrival in Japan.

Thinking of this story as I paused amidst the chatter of Ban Long's cicadas, I felt a recurrent sadness. Over the years, beginning with my time in South Viet Nam during the war, I had struggled to learn the Vietnamese language so I could understand the ordinary people with whom we Americans have been so intimately and devastatingly linked.

Throughout the years, I have felt rueful that history never provided me a one-time opportunity with Viet Nam as it did for my Uncle Hugh with Japan. I remain haunted by this and by the knowledge that, after all the carnage of the "American"/"Viet Nam" War, what I have to say about Viet Nam comes a generation too late.

As Second Harvest, Autumn, and I walked on between two rice paddies, I turned over in my mind how Viet Nam had tested my generation. Much of this contemplation was painful. How could it be otherwise? The war had forced young American men to choose: either fight, complete alternative service, desert, or go to prison. Yet we Americans knew so little about the country that gave the Viet Nam Generation its name. In ignorance, we even compressed *Viet Nam* into one word, *Vietnam,* thereby deflating the country's history.

The Vietnamese language is basically monosyllabic. Sometimes, particularly with words of Chinese origin, two words are joined to create a third. Thus, *Viet Nam* combines *Viet,* the name of the largest of the country's some fifty ethnic groups, and *Nam,* meaning "the South." "South" was used in this context to distinguish Viet Nam from China, which in the ancient times of Chinese domination was called "the North."

However, when the 1954 Geneva Accords provisionally divided Viet Nam after the Vietnamese War of Independence against the French, "the North" and "the South" took on different meanings. Vietnamese soon became reengaged in a civil war and in a nationalist war against the United States, with the U.S. backing South Viet Nam against Communist and nationalist North Viet Nam.

Like most Americans, I watched the war on television. By 1967, I was teaching history in a Quaker high school in Philadelphia. Each evening, Vietnamese refugees streamed across a flickering grey screen and into my living room. The strange tones of their voices haunted me deep into the night; the refugees' anguished faces stayed with me during the day. Perhaps it was my Uncle Hugh's influence, but as I watched the TV war, I felt driven to learn the Vietnamese language so I could listen to those peasants.

Quakers believe that there is "that of God" in each person regardless of race, religion, gender, economic status, or politics. This is the reason Quakers tend to be pacifists, since it follows that killing another person is equivalent to killing "that of God."

Working from a principle of nondiscrimination, Quaker Service assisted Vietnamese civilians on all sides of the Viet Nam War. This included staffing and supplying a rehabilitation center in U.S.-backed South Viet Nam, providing medicine to areas of South Viet Nam controlled by the Viet Cong, and sending medical equipment and educational materials to North Viet Nam.

I helped facilitate the Quaker Service shipments to the North and to Viet Cong areas of the South when I worked in the AFSC national office in Philadelphia during 1968. This was the time of mass antiwar demonstrations in the United States and Europe.

I believed then, as I do still, that women and men should be equal. If the war forced young American men to choose, then I should choose, too. I realized that if I were a man, I would be a conscientious objector. And so, with this in mind, I persuaded AFSC to send me to Viet Nam for what would be equivalent to a conscientious objector's alternative service.

The Quaker Service Rehabilitation Center, where I worked in wartime Quang Ngai from 1969 to 1971, trained Vietnamese to make artificial arms and legs for civilian amputees. The Viet Cong controlled most of Quang Ngai province, which included the village of My Lai, where American soldiers had massacred over four hundred Vietnamese civilians in 1968.

When I arrived in Quang Ngai in 1969, indiscriminate killing of civilians on a smaller scale was common. The war and my white skin kept me from entering ordinary life during those years. I lived on glimpses, yet from those glimpses I saw in the Vietnamese a delicacy and strength I found intriguing. Those wartime experiences compelled me to return to Viet Nam periodically from that time through the 1970s and 1980s.

Soldiers fight and then move on to another battle, but while in wartime Viet Nam I stayed in one place and saw what war left behind. Whatever their politics, our patients came covered with burns and blood. They came without legs, without arms; they were old and young, women and men; they were children and babies.

In 1972, I moved to the small, dilapidated farm in Appalachian Ohio, which remains my home. The starkness of Appalachia and the demands its harsh land puts on those who live there resonate with what I have come to feel about Viet Nam. For more than twenty years I have tried to create a whole life by being a semi-immigrant in both places.

In early 1975 I returned to Viet Nam, accompanying one of the AFSC shipments to Ha Noi and becoming one of the few Americans to visit North Viet Nam during the war. Later, in 1980, I lived and worked in Pulau Bidong, Malaysia's largest refugee camp for Boat People who had fled post-war Viet Nam. From the Bidong jetty I saw swamping boats arrive with men recently released from Communist reeducation camps, with women whom Thai pirates had raped en route, with children dying from thirst.

But while on Bidong I wondered, too, about the huge majority of Viet-namese who remained behind, struggling to rebuild their war-ravaged country. They were shunned by the United States and its allies. To what purpose? I felt compelled to know those people who had chosen to stay. And so I made a short trip to Viet Nam in 1983, when I first met Autumn, and then I made other visits in 1987 and 1988. Now, on a moonlit night in 1989, the Vietnamese had sufficient trust in me that I was allowed at last to stay with a family in a village.

The spine of a tiger-tongue cactus pricked my forearm. I stepped away from the hedge, which separated a rice paddy from a mud house. The aroma of wood smoke and cooked rice was comforting, but the laughter of children made me shrink. If those kids spot me, I thought, they'll rouse the whole village.

My rational mind told me I was perfectly safe. But everything felt so strange. My bare feet didn't fit the footprints embedded in the path's mud. The night air with its eerie noises and exotic perfumes seemed alive with spirits whispering news of an intruder. Suddenly I longed to be home on my farm in the hills of Appalachian Ohio. No one would notice me there. I could listen without apprehension to the cicadas in the huge elm in front of my house and could delight in the whimsical sighs of the goats.

We were passing another house. In the moonlight, I could make out its thatch roof.

"Where will we stay?" I whispered in Vietnamese to Second Harvest.

"With an old man." Her voice carried respect.

"Who is he?"

"Just an old man." She spoke with that tone older sisters reserve for inquisitive siblings.

Grass underfoot tickled my arches, telling me I had strayed from the path. With my toes, I searched for packed earth. I felt annoyed by Second Harvest's lack of explanation. During previous visits, I had been allowed to stay only a few hours in Ban Long and then only under close supervision. Everything had seemed so formal, constrained, oblique. Now I worried that this visit would also feel the same.

"Won't we disrupt the old man's family?" Autumn asked. She was a northern intellectual. Over the two years we three had been working together, she and Second Harvest, a southern peasant, had become good friends.

"No," Second Harvest answered. "He lives alone. Here. Turn. There's his house."

We turned, and my toes gripped the path. I felt I couldn't move. Frail kerosene light defined a welcoming doorway and the shadowy outline of a wooden house in a grove of trees. But between me and that doorway stood a creek and, spanning the creek, one last *cau khi*—monkey bridge.

I had already teetered across a dozen monkey bridges. Some had been two logs set side by side, others a single log with a flimsy handrail. But this last monkey bridge was a lone and graceless palm trunk. Muddy footprints greased its bark. *"Chet roi,"* I muttered, using Vietnamese slang for the insurmountable, literally "dead already."

Second Harvest stepped onto the moonlit bridge. She was stocky for a Vietnamese and wore her peasant blouse and loose black trousers with the ease of middle age. Her round face was open like a lotus blossom at midday.

During the war, peasants like Second Harvest had fled from American soldiers. Now, after so many years lurking in the shadows and slipping away from American GIs, Second Harvest could at last linger in the moonlight, in full view of an American. She must have chuckled to herself as she watched me cower before a monkey bridge.

"You can do it, Last Child," Second Harvest said, using my Vietnamese name.

In ancient times, particularly in southern Viet Nam, peasants never revealed a child's name because it might summon the spirit of any deceased person with the same name. To this day parents tend to call children by birth order rather than risk evoking unknown spirits. Parents further confound evil spirits likely to covet a firstborn by calling their first child "Second." They then name subsequent children by number until they come to "Last Child" or "Little One." Since I'm the youngest in my family, I now had a new name.

"Step up, Last Child," Second Harvest said. As I climbed onto the log, she took my hand. I could feel the calluses on her palm and the roughness of her fingertips. Tensing my arches, I spread my toes as if they were fingers and dug them through the mud into the rough bark.

In the moonlit darkness, balanced by this former Viet Cong woman, I edged across.

As soon as we reached the old man's house, Second Harvest showed me where to stow my bag. Taking a kerosene lamp made from a tin can and a piece of string for a wick, she guided me along the woodshed to the privy perched like a miniature duck blind over a small pond. I grimaced at the privy's two-foot tin skirting designed for people shorter than I. I would need extra grace to step backwards over the miniskirt and squat on the two flimsy slats inside. Later in the evening, I did manage this feat.

Suggesting I would want to wash up after our trip, Second Harvest led me to the tin bathhouse by the creek and left me there with the tiny lamp. Inside, I hung the lamp on one nail and my clean clothes on the other. A sliver of moonlight fell on the soiled clothes I tossed over the door. I reached for the dipper floating in an earthen crock of creek water and yelped as cold water struck my shoulders and cascaded down my back. The water had a rich smell like damp leaves, yet it was so soft that even the hard lye soap lathered into a rich foam. I doused myself again and again until I was as cool as the river.

Dressed, I took the tin lamp and an aluminum laundry basin outside onto a concrete slab by the creek. The cicadas in the water palms seemed to amplify their songs in response to the sloshing sounds my clothes made in the basin. My laundry done, I felt my way back through darkness toward the house and the light that, coming through slits in the siding, lay like a bamboo ladder on the rainwater urns under the eaves. I could hear Second Harvest and Autumn laughing on the other side of the wall as I passed, but I slipped by the side addition to the house and entered the main room.

The old man was standing in front of a cabinet, his back to me, his height reaching to my shoulders. Varnish on the cabinet's curved door mirrored his body, making him seem more diminutive but widening his wiry frame. Holding a tiny oil lamp, he sorted through keys tied to a cord around the waist of his black-pajama trousers. Finally he opened the cabinet, then turned, a bottle of kerosene clasped against his T-shirt.

"And your father?" he asked in Vietnamese. He ran all his words together in a rural twang.

His question startled me. No one had introduced us; I wasn't even sure this man was my host.

"My father is well, Senior Uncle," I said, addressing him as *"Bac."* The Vietnamese have some twenty words used both as forms of address and as pronouns. *Bac*—"father's older brother"—is the same honorific Vietnamese give Ho Chi Minh, the father of their country. "My dad is almost ninety," I added. "He paddles his own canoe and chops his own firewood. He sends greetings."

"Then I'm his younger brother, almost eighty," Senior Uncle said as he sat by me on the board bed that, varnished like the cabinet, shone in the lamp light. As he filled and lit a stately lantern, the oily smell of kerosene saturated the air. He set a stool on top of a nearby table and, climbing atop it, hung the lantern from the rafters with the sure gestures of a man at home.

"And your brothers?" Senior Uncle asked, turning up the wick.

The room opened with light that reached to the far bed, where I would sleep. The yellow light fell across a nearby post on which hung a 1940s photograph of a young man. It illuminated the family's ancestral altar, with its small oval basket and two yellowed photographs, one of another young man, the other of a young woman.

"What a pity you've lost your mother," the old man continued. I was surprised to hear him say this. For a moment I thought of my mother, a writer and community organizer who had died from Lou Gehrig's disease eight years before. How did the old man know about her? How did he know so much about me? He returned to sit on the bed. "I have a daughter," he said. "Her mother is gone, too."

He paused, picking up the bottle of kerosene, which he turned in his hands. Compared with the rest of him, Senior Uncle's hands were huge. "My daughter came home one day when she was twenty to find the puppet soldiers had arrested her mother. 'Puppets,' that's what we called the Vietnamese who sided with the French and the Americans." He looked directly into my face. "Can you hear me in time, Child? The French and their Vietnamese puppet soldiers had left my daughter's three-year-old sister crying in a corner, can you catch my words? The French soldiers . . ."

The old man leaned forward, so close our noses nearly touched. His breath smelled like cooked rice. Wrinkles on his face intertwined like the webbing in a jute hammock. The blue mist of age edged his eyes.

"When she was ten," he continued, "my daughter came home from working for the rich landlord to find her maternal grandfather shot dead by French soldiers. Right here." He set down the kerosene and covered his eyes with his massive hands. "She found him lying on the floor, bullet holes through his hands, bullet holes through his eyes, do you understand me, Child? So yes, my daughter grew up to work for the Revolution, can you catch my words in time? She . . ."

I wasn't catching his words. They rushed at me, tumbling over each other. I nodded, yes, yes, but my attention had swerved like a boat swaying with the tide. I was also listening to Second Harvest, who chatted with Autumn in the next room. I could tell by the way Autumn's voice rose and fell that she was swinging in the hammock.

"*Troi oi*—Good heavens!" I heard Autumn say. Clearly Second Harvest had said something surprising.

The hammock stopped. There was a *slap-slap* as Autumn's bare feet hit the floor, then the padding of footsteps across tiles. Suddenly Autumn stood before me and Senior Uncle in the main room. She was tiny compared to Second Harvest, who stood there beside her. Autumn peered over her scratched glasses, which had slid to the tip of her nose. Her short hair curled in wisps, creating an aura of impishness.

"Do you know who Senior Uncle is?" Autumn asked me. She pushed her glasses up onto her nose.

"No," I said. It has always frustrated me that my Vietnamese friends skimp on introductions just as they do on explanations.

Autumn said, "I was asking Second Harvest about Senior Uncle's family and then why his children didn't visit him."

Second Harvest touched the old man's shoulder. "I said, 'Well, I'm visiting tonight!' "

I gaped. "Senior Uncle is your father?"

Now I understood why the old man had gone on so about his daughter and how he had known to ask after my father. But I was still puzzled. I stared at Second Harvest. "Last year, didn't you show me the road to your father's ancestral home? We were in another village, where the roads run on land instead of on water."

"Yes," Second Harvest said. "That's our ancestral home. We came to Ban Long in 1940, when we fled the French."

Now Autumn looked perplexed. "But why didn't you say you were taking us to your father's house?"

Second Harvest looked at Autumn and me. A teasing smile lit her face. "For the same reason I 'arrested' Last Child at nightfall." Then she turned to me, and her voice sobered. "The American GIs invaded Ban Long. Now you're the first returning American. It's best to start quietly." Her voice turned perky again. "So what do you think, Last Child?" she said. "Do I look like my father?"

I rotated my wrists, flicking my fingers in the southern peasants' gesture No.

"That's because I look like my mother."

"That's her picture, then?" Autumn nodded toward the yellowing photograph on the altar.

"No. That's my mother's younger sister and my adopted brother. We have no picture of my mother. This is all we have for her altar." Second Harvest lifted the oval basket from atop the cabinet and handed it to Autumn.

Senior Uncle reached over and caressed the woven strands of red, blue, yellow, and green nylon. "My wife's friends wove the basket to commemorate her release from prison," he said.

"They made it for her to carry betel nut," Second Harvest added, replacing the heirloom on the altar. She traced a circle around a gaping hole in her father's T-shirt. "You should wear your good shirt for company, Father."

"But you said the American wanted to live like us," he said.

"Will our home do, Last Child?" Second Harvest asked.

"Only if Senior Uncle lets me stay forever," I said.

Wandering Souls

Pity them, the souls of those lost thousands.
They must set forth for unknown shores.
They are the ones for whom no incense burns.
Desolate, they wander night after night.

FROM "Call to Wandering Souls"
NGUYEN DU
1765–1820

$\mathcal{A}$s I have mentioned, my first visit to Ban Long had been two years before, in early 1987. In December 1986, the Sixth Congress of the Vietnamese Communist Party promulgated its policy of *doi moi* (literally "new change," or Renovation). Akin to the Soviet Union's perestroika and glasnost, Renovation permitted a privatized economy and openness to the West. This openness included permission for me, with Autumn as companion, to be the first foreigner to live among villagers since the end of the war.

However, permission was one thing, reality another. My wish to work with peasants and, at night, sleep on a reed mat under a thatch roof clashed with the Confucian ideal of Right Relationship. For Vietnamese peasants, I, their first American visitor, could only be a precious guest.

During my first visit to the Mekong Delta in early 1987, the Women's Union of Tien Giang province treated me to sumptuous splendor at the Province Guest House, a new three-story hotel where Autumn and I were the only occupants. Armed guards at the gate separated us from ordinary life. My hosts meant well, but they transformed me from a farmer and school bus driver into a visiting diplomat. I felt as if I were under house arrest; I was desperately unhappy and ferociously homesick for the hills of Ohio.

I tried to be gracious at the welcoming banquet held in the former French governor's palace, but I felt awkward sitting in a chair inlaid with mother-of-pearl scenes of an emperor surrounded by mandarins. Once again my ways countered the customs attending Right Relationship. All the dishes were meat, yet I'm a vegetarian. Vietnamese won't let a guest's bowl stand empty, yet I'd been raised to finish everything I was served. That evening I ate more meat than I'd consumed in twenty years.

During the sleepless night that followed, I made my peace with reduced goals: I would content myself with gathering stories and act cheerful about being confined to the Guest House. Although I didn't know it then, I would soon be all too grateful for that hotel room.

The next morning Fourth Flower, president of the province Women's Union, took me to the home of Second Blossom, since I had asked to meet someone whose husband was missing in action. At sixty, Second Blossom was a tall woman whose shoulders drooped much like the branches of the fruit trees she raised. Her gaunt face was offset by tiny jade and gold earrings.

As we sat at a wooden table in her house, Second Blossom told a story I would hear from other women in a hundred versions. Like many in her generation, she had married just before her husband went to the North for "Regrouping" after the 1954 Geneva Accords divided Viet Nam at the end of the French War. As an American growing up in the 1950s, I'd been raised on tales of Catholics fleeing to the South in 1954. However, I'd never known and perhaps was never taught that between 130,000 and 150,000 soldiers from the Viet Minh—the Vietnamese who had fought against the French—went to the North in accordance with the Geneva agreement.

Like other couples, Second Blossom and her husband assumed he

would return home after the elections mandated by the Geneva Accords
for July 1956. But the U.S.-backed Diem government refused to allow the
elections. In 1960, Second Blossom's husband returned south as part of a
North Vietnamese Army unit composed of former Viet Minh. Subsequently she crossed over from the Sai Gon–controlled area to visit him
three times near Bien Hoa. Once she took along their daughter, who'd
been conceived during the couple's few weeks together.

Second Blossom paused in her narrative. She toyed with one of her
jade earrings. It was round and green like a wreath. The clock over the
family altar struck ten; then the house settled back into repose punctuated
by the clock's ticking. Second Blossom lifted a strand of hair from the hollow of her cheek and tucked it behind her ear.

"*Mat tich*," she whispered. "Missing."

She leaned forward. "If I knew the location of my husband's grave," she
said, "I would visit it before Tet and invite his spirit to join us. I'd offer
food and fruit to nourish his spirit. But where do I go?" She paused, examining her fingers. "And if I knew the day he died, I would invite neighbors
and family to honor my husband's spirit on the anniversary of his death.
But what day should I choose?" She ran her hand across her face, a common Vietnamese gesture. "All that's left," she said, "is the Fifteenth Day of
the Seventh Lunar Month."

Vietnamese tend an ancestor's grave on the anniversary of the person's
death. The Fifteenth Day of the Seventh Lunar Month is reserved for those
souls whose graves and death days are unknown. Since these souls cannot
be properly tended, they wander, forever restless. For years I'd been hearing about the twenty-four hundred missing Americans; now I began to
consider the one hundred thousand to three hundred thousand Vietnamese who are missing. They are Viet Nam's wandering souls.

" 'Pity . . . the souls of those lost thousands,' " Autumn said, quoting
the famous epic poet Nguyen Du. " 'They are the ones for whom no incense burns.' "

"In 1975," Second Blossom continued, her voice a whisper, "I waited
for my husband to return. The other brothers came back, but there was no
sign of my husband. I asked the men who'd fought with him, but nobody
could remember where he was buried. My heart was feverish. I went to
Eleventh Sister, who'd helped me visit my husband those three times.
'Please,' I said, 'can you help me find his grave?' I wanted to find the Stream
of Golden Stones where my husband was buried. 'I don't know the place,'

Eleventh Sister said. She was crying. I went to see Mr. Thong, the district commander. 'Please,' I said, 'can you help me find my husband's grave?' 'You must not seek anymore, Sister,' he said. 'None of us can find the spot where he sacrificed himself.' "

Second Blossom cracked her knuckles, one by one, each crack like a rifle shot.

"*Mat tich*," she murmured. "Missing."

Before I left, Second Blossom removed a long bamboo pole hanging under the eaves. I followed her into the orchard, where she harvested pomelos, a sweet and pungent cousin of the grapefruit.

"Oooh, that's plenty," I said, surprised when she caught the stem of a third fruit in the metal fingers at the end of the pole. By turning the pole, she twisted the branch, pulling the pomelo free.

"No, no, many more!" Second Blossom insisted. "You must take these pomelos as a present to the American women whose husbands are wandering souls."

That day the stories I gathered—some from scheduled interviews, others from impromptu chats—all carried the same theme: *Mat tich*. I heard the phrase again and again, "*mat tich*," "*mat tich*," "missing," "missing." And I kept hearing another word, "*hy sinh*." I could tell it meant "dead," but soon I saw the word's deeper significance: "sacrificed."

As we moved from house to house, I began to reel from too many stories and too many rich snacks. Our last stop was the house of Third Mother. At eighty-four, she had thinning hair, as white as the new *ao ba ba* blouse she wore to meet her first American. As soon as we sat down, Third Mother offered me more pomelo. "Eat! Eat!!" she said. Her invitation was close to a command. She pressed a glass of hand-crushed lemonade on me, and then cookies. "Eat and drink," she insisted. "For your health!"

Then Third Mother grasped both my hands, her gaze holding me as she described her eight children. Again I heard those words "*mat tich*" and "*hy sinh*" following one upon the other like mortar rounds. "*Hy sinh*," "*mat tich*"—the words made my head spin, my ears ring. The cloying smell of kerosene from the tiny lamps by the altar photographs added to my queasiness. All I could think about was how much I longed to stretch out on the reed mat spread over the nearby bamboo bed. Third Mother was telling me about her only surviving child when I bolted from the room, sick to my stomach.

Kids materialized from everywhere. They kept up a running commentary. "Look!" one said, "the American vomits just like we do."

"Not true!" another countered. "When did you see so much puke?!"

Of the half-dozen women in the room, Third Mother arrived first at my side. She held my shoulders while I retched again. Then from her pocket she removed a tiny tin of tiger balm, a paste made with aromatic herbs, which she dabbed onto my upper lip. The tiger balm burned my skin; its pungency seared my nostrils. As I straightened, she reached up with a handkerchief and wiped my lips. Taking my hand, Third Mother led me to the bamboo bed.

The women surrounded me, dabbing my temples, upper lip, and chest with stinging oil; they scoured my wrists, belly, and ankles. When I could sit up again, I nodded toward the mess I'd made of Third Mother's resplendent hibiscus flowers.

"My apologies, *Ma*," I said.

"It's nothing," Third Mother said as she uncoiled my hair, which I'd wound into a knot. "Look how thick!" she announced to the others, stroking my curls.

"Where did you get all that tiger balm?" I asked the women sitting around me. They all held tiny red tins with a gold star in the middle of the top. From these they dabbed their own temples and upper lips.

"Right here!" Fourth Flower tucked her hand into the pocket in her overblouse. Like the other women, she wore her black hair tied into a knot at the nape of her neck. A gold tooth distinguished her face. "During the war, we always carried medicine."

That morning Fourth Flower and Autumn would have whisked me off to the province hospital, but I insisted on remaining in the Guest House. I knew I would be fine. I needed time. And yes, under these circumstances, I was glad for a hotel room with a bathroom.

I was delirious. All afternoon and all night the words "*mat tich*" and "*hy sinh*" darted like bullets through my brain, like shrapnel ricocheting inside my skull. By morning I lay back, soaked in sweat, exhausted.

Autumn turned out to be a gracious nurse. We had first met four years before in 1983 during what I call the "Period of Silence," the twelve years from the end of the war in 1975 until Renovation began to be implemented in early 1987. During that time, few Americans visited Viet Nam. The United States, even more conservative, allowed no Vietnamese visitors. The unavoidable exceptions were the Vietnamese delegates to the United Nations, but the U.S. State Department restricted their travel to within a twenty-five-mile radius of the UN.

In Viet Nam, the Period of Silence was also a time of rhetoric, where every question seemed to bring a reply prefaced with "Report to you" and followed by an answer that felt predictable and rehearsed. But Autumn was different. She had accompanied me for part of my 1983 trip. In the early 1980s, most Ha Noi women pulled their hair straight back into a knot; Autumn wore her long hair like others then, but her glasses had their own wonderfully undisciplined way of sliding down to the tip of her nose. For me, Autumn was a delight because, at a time when other Vietnamese recited rhetoric, Autumn spoke in stories.

One day in 1983, we were driving east of Ha Noi to Con Son, home of the famous fifteenth-century mandarin poet Nguyen Trai. Traffic slowed at the entrance to the pontoon replacement for a bombed-out bridge. Autumn looked out the window at the people waiting by their bicycles.

"My husband pedaled out here during the U.S. bombing." She spoke quietly, as if thinking out loud.

"Way out here?" I asked. We were already an hour by car from Ha Noi.

"During the bombing, my husband stayed in Ha Noi when the school where I taught was evacuated to the countryside. I took our daughter with me." Autumn wiped the window glass and peered out at two boys lounging atop their water buffalo. One boy was barefoot; the other had hung a blue flip-flop on each of his buffalo's horns. "Every month Vigilance came to see us. He would travel all Saturday night by train and then by bicycle, spend Sunday with us, and then return that night in time for work on Monday."

"Stay up two nights for one day's visit?" I asked.

"We all did. You never saw such traffic! Far worse than today. The worst traffic was at Phu Luong Bridge on the way to Hai Phong. That bridge was always being bombed—so dangerous! It was constantly under repair. I went by another way." She pressed her face to the window. "See those buffalo boys? There were manhole bomb shelters all along that bank where those boys are, each shelter big enough for one person. The streets of Ha Noi were the same, a manhole every two or three meters.

"One Sunday Vigilance was about to cross this bridge when the American bombers came, *rmmmm, rmmmmmm, rmmmmmmmm.* He jumped into a manhole. *Boom, BOOM!* When it was quiet, he crawled out. After a repairman fixed his damaged bicycle, he pedaled as fast as he could, but when he reached us, it was time to return!"

Our car nosed down the slope and lurched over the pontoons. Autumn watched a man pushing his bike. With one hand, the man steadied a toddler riding sidesaddle in a bamboo seat over the rear wheel. "From one trip to the next," Autumn said, "I never knew if I would see Vigilance again."

Autumn's recollection told me more about wartime Viet Nam than weeks of rhetoric. I thought of this in 1985 as I wrote to Ha Noi yet again for permission to live in a village. I suggested that Autumn accompany me, thinking this might calm any Vietnamese security concerns that I, with my Boat People connections, might be CIA.

As I look back, I realize I could not have made a better decision. Just as the form of the sonnet can lead a poet to deeper meaning, so having Autumn as a companion drew me into unexpected depths. Autumn opened the way. We were a good balance, she outgoing and fun-loving, I quiet and serious. Before long, our work transformed into a shared effort that led Autumn on her own journey into a part of Viet Nam she had never known.

But Autumn and I hardly knew each other at the outset of our trip together in 1987, when we were confined to the Province Guest House and I was in the ignoble position of relying on her to serve as nurse. The day after I was sick, Autumn sat on the bed next to mine, reading a newspaper article about Japan's dominance of the world economy.

"History takes such strange turns," she said.

"How's that?" I asked. Although I was too weak to walk, I was well enough to enjoy Autumn's stories.

"I was thinking about my great-grandfather on my mother's side," she began. "He was a mandarin at the court of Emperor Tu Duc in 1869, when Japan opened to the West." She folded the newspaper, then continued. "The king and his court mandarins, who had never traveled, were conservatives, who followed only the teachings of Confucius. They believed the material side of life should be despised, that Western technology was an evil, mischievous trick.

"At that time, Great-Grandfather was ambassador to China. When he returned from Beijing in 1870, he suggested to Emperor Tu Duc that Viet Nam invite experts from Western nations to help us modernize and that we send students to every country—to America, England, Germany, France. That way one Western nation wouldn't have a controlling influence over Viet Nam. But Emperor Tu Duc wouldn't hear of it. My great-grandfather was disgraced."

I sat up straight. "Why?"

"Because he offered advice that wasn't received. So he returned to his ancestral land to teach."

"What about the other side of your family?"

"My great-grandfather on my father's side also was a mandarin. That's how my father was able to study pharmacy in France, but Father had to return home early when his father died. Then my father caught tuberculosis. I was two when he died."

I knew Autumn had studied at the Sorbonne, and I also knew in olden times a family had difficulty surviving without a man's income. "Then how could your family live?" I asked. "How were you able to study?"

She laughed. "It was my grandmother who had the money. My grandfather was so poor that he couldn't buy oil for a lamp to study by. He caught fireflies and set them inside an egg shell to make a lamp. But then he married my grandmother, who supported him in his mandarin studies. After my father died, we stayed on at my grandmother's house. Oh, Grandmother was hard to please! She wouldn't let my mother go anywhere, and she thrashed us kids when we were noisy. But my father had set aside money for our schooling. He told my mother that when we were grown, he wanted all of us to study in France. My mother insisted that I have a profession, that I not be stuck in the kitchen the way she had been."

Autumn looked out the window at the palace of the former French governor. I watched, too, as on one side of the majestic entrance, workmen hung bamboo scaffolding; on the other, they patched holes in the stucco. I thought about Second Blossom and her missing husband and the pomelos she wanted me to take back to the States. I kept thinking about how different all our lives might have been if Emperor Tu Duc had listened to Autumn's great-grandfather when the Far East first opened to the West.

That first visit during the dry season of 1987 I did get permission to make a day trip to Ban Long Village. I felt exuberant, like a prisoner on parole as I

CHÂU THÀNH DISTRICT

TIÊN GIANG PROVINCE
FORMERLY MỸ THO PROVINCE

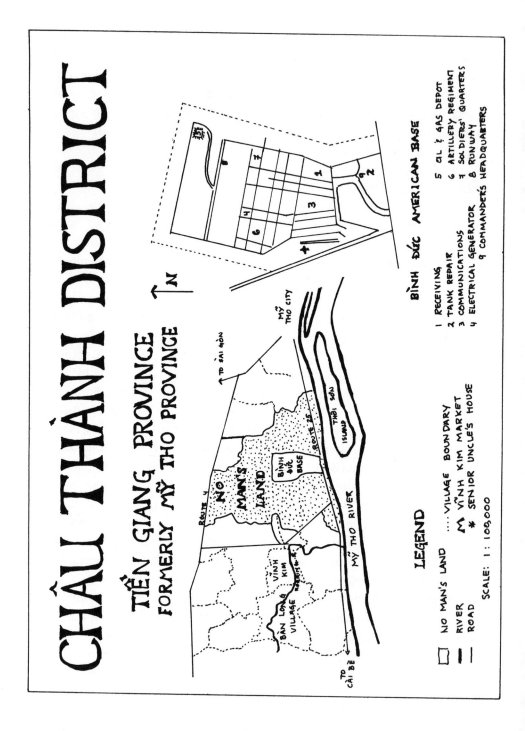

↑N

TO SÀI GÒN

NO MAN'S LAND

ROUTE 4

BÌNH ĐỨC BASE

VĨNH KIM VILLAGE

ROUTE 22

THỜI SƠN ISLAND

MỸ THO CITY

MỸ THO RIVER

TO CÁI BÈ

BĂN LONG VILLAGE

BÌNH ĐỨC AMERICAN BASE

1 RECEIVING
2 TANK REPAIR
3 COMMUNICATIONS
4 ELECTRICAL GENERATOR
5 OIL & GAS DEPOT
6 ARTILLERY REGIMENT
7 SOLDIERS' QUARTERS
8 RUNWAY
9 COMMANDER'S HEADQUARTERS

LEGEND

▢ NO MAN'S LAND   ···· VILLAGE BOUNDARY
▬ RIVER   ⋈ VĨNH KIM MARKET
— ROAD   ＊ SENIOR UNCLE'S HOUSE

SCALE: 1 : 100,000

sat in the palm-leaf cabin of a sampan plying Roaring River. Roaring River is a tributary of the My Tho River, which flows into the Tien Giang, one of the nine river mouths that form the Mekong Delta and give the Mekong its Vietnamese name, *Cuu Long,* which means "Nine Dragons."

Our sampan's wooden hull vibrated with the *put-a-put* of the engine. Water from the bilge splashed my toes; I shifted my feet atop the cargo of bricks and leaned back against the hull. Resting my arm along the gunwale, I trailed my fingers in the river. Water sprinkled the back of my hand, each drop a cheerful surprise.

"See that flat-bottomed canoe?" Second Harvest said. She was sitting across from me in the narrow cabin. I had met Second Harvest at the banquet in my honor, and we had visited several villages together, but this was our first chance to talk. Her face was broad and peaceful like the river, the wisps of hair fringing her face as delicate as bamboo lining the bank.

She nodded toward a woman paddling a canoe laden with pomelos. The boat's gunwales grazed the water. The pilot cut the throttle, and our sampan slowed, its wake diminishing to a gentle slope that lifted the laden canoe.

"I paddled a canoe like that during the war," Second Harvest said. "I loaded it with vats of *nuoc mam.*" *Nuoc mam,* a sauce made from fermented fish, is a staple of the Vietnamese diet. "Underneath the vats of fish sauce," Second Harvest continued, "I hid rifles and grenades. Then I slipped by American patrol boats the way that canoe glides past us. The American sailors never stopped me." Second Harvest paused, covering her mouth as if embarrassed. "You see, we knew the smell of *nuoc mam* made you Americans vomit."

Suddenly I remembered my first day in Quang Ngai in early 1969. Determined to impress my new colleagues on the Quaker Service team, I had arrived promptly for supper but soon fled, overcome by nausea at the stench of *nuoc mam.* Indeed, *nuoc mam* is the one Vietnamese phrase my veteran friends all remember. They, like me, would have retreated from the rank cargo Second Harvest had used to camouflage her contraband.

Our sampan nosed toward a stucco arch spanning a small concrete dock. A small boy with a fishing net shaped like a kite lounged against one pillar. The pilot cut the sampan's engine, and for a moment there was only the gentle *lap, lap* of the river against the hull. Then the boy spotted me.

"Soviet," he muttered. He dashed toward the mud and thatch houses, his fish net billowing. "SOVIET!!"

Children tore from the houses. They raced down the paths, sprinting toward our sampan. Jostling, they crowded the bank. A boy of seven lifted a younger child onto his shoulders. A larger boy with wavy hair shoved him aside. One little girl with buckteeth lost her footing and slipped toward the water.

"Watch out!" a boy with a nick over his right eye said to the girl, "you'll miss the Soviet."

"Funny Soviet who speaks with an American accent," I murmured. The boy stared, his eyes so wide that the nick disappeared into a wrinkle. Then he bolted toward the houses, yelling "*BA MY! BA MY!!*—AMERICAN WOMAN! AMERICAN WOMAN!!*" As more children came running, I stepped through the gate and into Ban Long Village.

Xa meaning "village" or "commune"—not to be confused with "Communism"—is a Vietnamese translation of the French term for the smallest governmental administrative unit. In contrast, the Vietnamese socialist economic unit is the *hop tac xa*, or "cooperative." In Viet Nam, a village is similar to a rural township in the States, while a hamlet is similar to a section. Ban Long's eight thousand residents lived in six hamlets. Ban Long "belonged" to Chau Thanh district, administratively comparable to a U.S. county. In turn, Chau Thanh belonged to Tien Giang province (called My Tho province during the war), roughly equivalent to a state.

The Vietnamese distill several thousand years of their written history into the saying: "The king's rule stops at the village gate." Once I stepped through Ban Long's gate, I "belonged" to Ban Long.

"An AMERICAN!" a boy in a straw hat yelled to kids racing toward us. "Hurry, hurry! Tell the others!"

I was the circus come to town. It had been twelve years since the war and fourteen years since the last U.S. combat troops had left Viet Nam. Although Ban Long's children had grown up in bomb rubble and defoliant debris, they had never seen an American.

"A giant!" said a boy wearing faded blue shorts. He nudged another boy's shoulder.

"Look at her hair," whispered his friend, who had a pert cowlick. He wore blue shorts and a faded blue shirt and carried a stained pith helmet. The boy inspected me from my conical hat, down my Vietnamese blouse and black peasant trousers, and then up again to the curly tendrils of my long, russet hair.

"That hair is like dead vines," the first boy muttered.

Second Harvest led Autumn and me to the village hall; the children followed, as near as gnats. The moment I stepped inside the stucco building, the kids jammed the doorway. They ran around to the windows and clung to the wooden bars, staring, their eyes like those of startled deer.

"She sits like the elephant in that magazine with circus pictures," a girl at the window said.

The girl was right. I'm slim by American standards, but I'm a head taller than Vietnamese, even the men, and I'm beamier. Engulfing a tiny stool, I was like a circus elephant beset by trainers.

"Have some tea," said the woman on my left.

"Eat some coconut candy," said the woman on my right.

"Try this milk fruit," said the woman across from me. Her name was Fifth Harmony. In her early sixties, Fifth Harmony had a slight overbite and ears that stood out as if attentive to every nuance. She used the phrase *vu sua*—"breast milk"— for the fruit's name. The milk fruit resembled a Granny Smith apple with a pinkish hue. Fifth Harmony lifted the top off the fruit as if taking a lid from a serving dish. She handed me a tiny spoon. The fruit's milky pulp was thick and sweet.

"This is our first milk fruit since Agent Orange," Fifth Harmony added. "You help us celebrate its return."

When I finished the milk fruit, Second Harvest led Autumn and me down a path behind the village hall. The children followed, stepping on the heels of my flip-flops. One boy in blue shorts scampered ahead of me over a monkey bridge. With his fingers, he covered his giggles as I teetered across.

"She's timid as a toddler," he said.

The path turned, and for a moment a thicket blocked my view of the children, absorbing their voices. Dense foliage cut off the sun, imprisoning the moisture; even at midday, the light was spooky. The breeze carried the odor of rotting vegetation, and the air hummed with the weird sounds of mysterious insects. For an instant, I felt alone, yet I could feel a thousand eyes gauging my every move.

I kept thinking of the terror that must have stalked American GIs probing for an elusive enemy in this shadowy maze of streams and sluices, footpaths and monkey bridges. For GIs, the thrumming of cicadas must have resonated with foreboding, the eerie smell of humus foreshadowing death. Their American eyes, like mine, would have been blind to the secret tunnels and to the guerrillas who, hiding under the water, breathed through bamboo straws.

Second Harvest pointed to cavities in the palm trees. "Rocket wounds," she said. She turned another corner. As we dropped off the raised path and stepped through a hedge, she nodded toward a small, round pond framed by hibiscus. Reflected in the water, the red trumpet blooms and the overhanging palm trees turned the pond into a painting. But then I noticed that this pond, like others I'd passed, was too round.

"It's a bomb crater," Second Harvest said as if reading my thoughts. I sucked in my breath. I had been born just after Pearl Harbor; I'd never known war on American soil.

A young woman washing rice bowls squatted on the pond's bamboo dock. With chopsticks, a toddler next to her tapped rhythms on an overturned bowl. Gathering up the child, the woman invited us into her home made of woven water-palm leaves. The children and neighbors followed, packing the one-room house.

"When I was carrying messages for the Viet Cong, I often hid in this house," Second Harvest said after we had sat at a rough wood table. She pointed to the corner studs, which were live coconut trees. The trees' foliage created a second roof. "Now you see why the Americans sprayed Agent Orange. Otherwise, how could the helicopters find us?"

"The palm leaves have returned," said a grandmother with sunken cheeks, "but the coconuts are useless." She giggled. "They're as shriveled as old men!"

"How old is the American?" the young woman asked Autumn as she set tiny glasses of tea before us.

"I'm forty-five in Viet Nam," I said, "forty-four in America. You add the year at Tet, but we wait until our birthday."

"Forty-five!" "Forty-four!" News of my age jumped from person to person as quickly as flames leaping between thatch roofs.

"Do you grow milk fruit in Ohio?" Fifth Harmony asked. She trimmed the lid off another milk fruit and offered it to me.

"Look!" said a girl with a minnow basket. "The American is eating."

Another girl with a rice-bowl haircut reached out and touched my arm. "The American is furry," she announced. "Like a kitten!"

"How many children does she have?" an old man with a white goatee asked Autumn.

The kids pressed closer. I could feel their breath, could smell their sweat and the fishy odor of their minnow baskets.

"Three teenagers 'to nourish,'" I said, using the Vietnamese phrase for raising a friend's children as one's own.

"Do you have a water buffalo on your farm?" Fifth Harmony asked.

"If you don't raise rice, how do you eat?" a man said. One of his eyes was white and barren.

"Do you paddle your canoe to market?" the grandmother asked.

Second Harvest poured me more tea. "Last Child was surprised to hear how we disguised our canoes," she teased.

"Ah!" Fifth Harmony said. Her eyes were the warm brown of tea.

"But didn't you worry about helicopter spotlights?" I asked.

"We hid!" Fifth Harmony said.

"But where?"

"We'll show you," Second Harvest said.

The grandmother with the sunken cheeks fetched black peasant overblouses for Second Harvest and Fifth Harmony. Two other women already dressed in traditional black led me and my entourage of curious children back to Roaring River. There, the four women cut bamboo branches and tucked the leaves into the reed rims of their conical hats.

"This is the way we used to ferry soldiers and ammunition across the river," Second Harvest said.

She and Fifth Harmony slid two flat-bottomed canoes into Roaring River. They loaded the canoes with imaginary rifles and covered their cache with the fronds of water palms. The water palm, a relative of the coconut, grows in the shallow fresh water that is inland of the Delta's brackish mangrove zone. The trunk of the water palm is submerged; its fronds, which rise directly from the water, are prized for thatch and baskets and, when dried, for fuel.

Once the women had perfected their camouflage, they climbed into the canoes and took up their paddles. Kids crowding the bank cheered as the women sped across Roaring River.

"Helicopter!" yelled the man with the barren eye.

The women spun their canoes and, diving for shore, tucked them against the bank. Their camouflaged hats and black peasant pajamas blended with the water palms, which sheltered them like protective fingers.

This time, with glee, these former Viet Cong women hid within sight of an American.

That evening, after we returned from Ban Long, several women gathered in the gracious confines of my room at the Province Guest House. A breeze from a café by the My Tho River carried the plaintive voice of a soprano singing about her lover lost in battle. The conversation quieted. Except for Second Harvest and Autumn, all the women had lost their husbands in the war.

Second Harvest peeled one of the pomelos Second Blossom had given us. "Have we given you enough to eat?" she asked.

"Last Child complains we force-feed her," Fourth Flower teased, alluding to the days I was sick. Fourth Flower always spoke fast. She smiled, and I caught a glimpse of her gold tooth. Her voice turned serious. "We worry about you."

"Why?" I asked.

She gestured to the others. "We're afraid that when you return to America, the CIA will arrest you because you've been here with us."

I laughed. "No, I'll be all right."

"Last Child looks like a Vietnamese in her *ao ba ba,*" Ninth Rose said of the collarless Vietnamese overblouse the women had given me. Ninth Rose's curly hair and flowered shirt with its pointed collar made her seem Western. "A white *ao ba ba,*" she added, emphasizing "white" as she touched my sleeve and turned to the others. "Maybe Last Child is a spy."

The women all laughed.

"I don't get the joke," I said.

"During the war," Second Harvest explained, "the Americans thought anyone who wore a black *ao ba ba* was Viet Cong."

"So then . . ." I was puzzled. A black *ao ba ba* and black trousers—called "black pajamas" by GIs—are standard peasant dress. After planting or weeding arm-deep in paddy mud, a farmer can rinse her black sleeves in a sluice and emerge looking clean.

Fourth Flower chuckled. "Your GIs thought anyone who wore a white *ao ba ba* supported the Americans."

Second Harvest touched my sleeve. "What did we do when we wanted to sneak past Americans?" she said. "We put on a white *ao ba ba!*"

"You just changed your blouse?"

"Not quite," Fourth Flower said. "We each had only the black *ao ba ba* we wore every day." Fourth Flower nodded toward Ninth Rose. "Ninth

Rose used many costumes because she lived in town. Some days she pretended to be a schoolteacher and wore a long, flowing *ao dai*. Other days
she dressed in the rags of a vegetable vendor. But we in the countryside
were poor. We had to share our one white *ao ba ba*."

What a simple trick, I thought. And how like us Americans to polarize
Vietnamese peasants into white blouses and black, as if the Vietnamese
were extras—good guys and bad—in a Hollywood Western.

"Have we told you enough stories?" Second Harvest asked.

My head was full of stories. In addition to interviews, I'd been reading
Nu Chien si Rung Dua—Woman Fighter of the Coconut Forests, a biography
in Vietnamese of Nguyen thi Dinh, a famous Viet Cong general. The book
made me wish I had talked with some women soldiers.

"I know time is short," I said, "but could I meet with some *chien si?*"

"*Chien si!*" Second Harvest said, laughing. The other women were
laughing, too.

I felt mortified.

Vietnamese is a tonal language. It sounds almost sung, rather than spoken. A given sequence of letters has only one pronunciation; however, that
pronunciation can be sung with six different tones, each defining a different word. For example, "*binh*" with a falling tone means "peace," but with
no tone means "soldier." "*Ban*" with a low, hard tone means "friend," but
said with a rising tone becomes "sell."

Maybe, I thought, I've used the wrong tone. Maybe I said something
ridiculous. Or worse yet, obscene.

Fourth Flower leaned forward. "Last Child," she said, "haven't you been
listening?"

"What do you think we were doing?" Ninth Rose added, fingering her
pointed Western collar, then tossing her curls. "I told you how I rode in an
American jeep into the headquarters of the U.S. Ninth Infantry Division.
Don't you see? That ride was a mission into the belly of the enemy!"

"We did everything!" Second Harvest said. "We climbed mountains, we
hid under rivers. We captured prisoners. We carried ammunition. We
trained ourselves to use weapons. We guided the soldiers when they wanted
to attack the American base at Binh Duc. We were the guides, *we* were the
spies. Don't you see? Ours was a citizens' war. *We* were the woman fighters."

Second Harvest glanced at Fourth Flower, who had settled back in her
chair. "For example, Fourth Flower," Second Harvest said. "She did everything. When you were sick, you saw yourself that she's a nurse."

But I was hearing other voices, as if a movie from some twenty years before were playing in my mind.

I was in my late twenties again, in wartime Quang Ngai, walking by myself on a village path. Two boys spotted me. They'd been shooting rubber bands at American C-ration cans in front of a mud and thatch house. The boys raced after me, dust billowing from their bare feet.

"*Ba My! Ba My!*—American woman! American woman!" they taunted, stepping on the heels of my flip-flops.

Another boy sprinted from a mud house across the path. "You, you, Number Ten!" he jeered, using GI slang meaning "the worst." Other children followed him, shouting obscenities.

I turned and, hunkering, engaged the boys in chitchat. I asked my usual questions: "How old are you?" "Are you in school?" "How many brothers and sisters do you have?"

Soon, a woman my age stopped. She was barefoot, her hair pulled back into the traditional nape knot. On her shoulder she carried a long bundle of sugarcane, which crinkled her blouse. The blouse was white, which struck me as unusual.

"How old are you?" the woman asked.

The woman was starting in on the "twenty questions" strangers always asked me. "How many children do you have?" "You're twenty-eight and don't have a husband yet?" "Where do you work?" "How much money do you make?" This last question was a favorite for, compared to Vietnamese, Americans in Viet Nam earned outrageously inflated salaries.

"I don't make any money," I said, "but Quaker Service provides for my needs—food and housing, these clothes. So I'm rich already."

The woman shifted her load. "We are grateful to you Americans for saving us from the cruelly vicious, wicked, imperialist Viet Cong."

I assumed as I always did when I heard overblown gratitude that the woman sympathized with the Viet Cong. "The Quaker Service Rehab Center treats any civilian amputee," I said. "We don't take sides."

"Is it true," the woman asked, tilting her head against the sugarcane, "about Americans demonstrating against the war?"

"It's true."

"Lots of them?"

"Lots of them."

⇘

I shook off my reverie and returned to the present of 1987. "You probably met lots of us," Second Harvest was saying. She peeled another of Second Blossom's pomelos and offered me a piece. "We built tunnels, and we dug trenches. We were the scouts, we were the supply route. We carried messages and maps. We formed the communications system. We were the liaison. I told you how we hid rifles under vats of fish sauce and carried them in sugarcane. We probably met you lots of times. We would have asked you lots of questions. We would have decided you were all right."

Fourth Flower laughed. Her gold tooth shone. "Carry rifles into the belly of the enemy," she said. Her tone was merry. "Along the way, meet an American who speaks Vietnamese. Stop. Ask her lots of questions. Maybe arrest her!"

I blanched, startled by my own naïveté. During the war, I'd walked everywhere, a woman alone and unarmed, chatting with anyone. I had often joked that I could talk my way out of capture by Viet Cong. Now, years later, I saw how often I had done just that.

I also saw my own blindness: Like the GIs, I had stereotyped Viet Cong as men. Now, I imagined American officers, their cheeks burning when they figured out how many of their fiercest opponents were women. But I saw, too, how hard it would be to understand our former enemy: Even years after the war, these former Viet Cong women still camouflaged their feats with modesty.

"So, Last Child," Second Harvest said, "what do you think of us now?" She touched the back of my hand. Her gesture carried with it the gentleness of water lapping against a grassy riverbank.

"We have a famous poet-general, Nguyen Trai," Ninth Rose said. Her voice, smoother than the others', reflected her education at a French lycée. "He fought off the Minh Chinese in the 1400s. 'After war,' Nguyen Trai wrote, 'the people you meet differ so from former times.'"

III

A House by the River

The veranda is beautiful with flowers
in the lingering light.
A cool breeze, sweet with the scent of lotus,
comes through the window.
After a rain, the garden wears a mantle of green.
The cicadas' yearning trembles in the evening.

"Summer Evening"
KING TRAN THANH TONG
1240–1290

A rooster crowed, waking me that first morning two years later in early 1989, when I was first allowed to stay at Senior Uncle's house in Ban Long. Somewhere in the distance, a water buffalo snorted. I peered out through the mosquito net to see Autumn reading by a tiny kerosene lamp at the table. Behind her, there was a flick of light and, with it, the phosphorous smell of a match. Second Harvest was lighting three joss sticks and placing them in a brass incense urn. Cupping her palms like a lotus bud, she bowed before the two altar photographs and her mother's basket.

I rose and stepped outside into the soft dawn just as Senior Uncle released the rooster from a slat pen. The rooster shook his comb and, preening his fluorescent green tail feathers, crowed again as if to announce his release. He strutted off, leading a hen and five biddies.

In the tentative daylight, I could see that Senior Uncle's house lay between a sluice and a stream. Barefoot, Senior Uncle made his way around the two ponds in front of the house, picking up each leaf that had fallen from the jackfruit trees. He stacked the leaves as neatly as pages in a book, then set them next to firewood piled in a shed.

"Did you sleep sweetly, Child?" he asked. Senior Uncle's face was as brown and lined as the leaves he had gathered.

"Sweetly, Senior Uncle." I dipped water from an earthen crock under the eaves and headed to the stream to brush my teeth.

"Always drink rainwater!" Senior Uncle called after me. "Do you hear me, Child, never drink from the river."

Golden light spread over the stream, dappling it with the shadows of water palms. Since the tide had turned, the river rushed in whirlpools by the narrow dock, carrying with it a coconut husk that floated like a tiny boat. I stepped out onto the dock planks and, stooping, scooped water to wash my face. The water smelled like the woods at home after a heavy summer's rain.

I heard crashing in the weeds on the other side of the stream and looked up to see a man leading a water buffalo and her calf to the edge of the creek. He scrambled onto the buffalo's back; then with a great rustling of water palms, buffalo and rider descended the bank. As the water rose up the buffalo's flanks, the man stood up on her back so that soon, with the buffalo submerged, he looked as if he walked on water.

"You came to visit, did you?" he asked.

"Yes, Older Brother. I came with Second Harvest."

"Ah! Second Harvest is home. Good news!"

Down the river the man went, standing atop his water buffalo while the buffalo's calf swam alongside.

Soon there was more splashing behind me. Second Harvest was dipping water from the stream with a basket attached to a bamboo pole. With this, she filled the earthenware crocks on the concrete washing slab outside the bathhouse. She added half a handful of alum, then stirred the water so the alum would precipitate the silt.

A canoe rounded the upstream bend. "Second Harvest!" the woman in

SENIOR UNCLE'S HOUSE

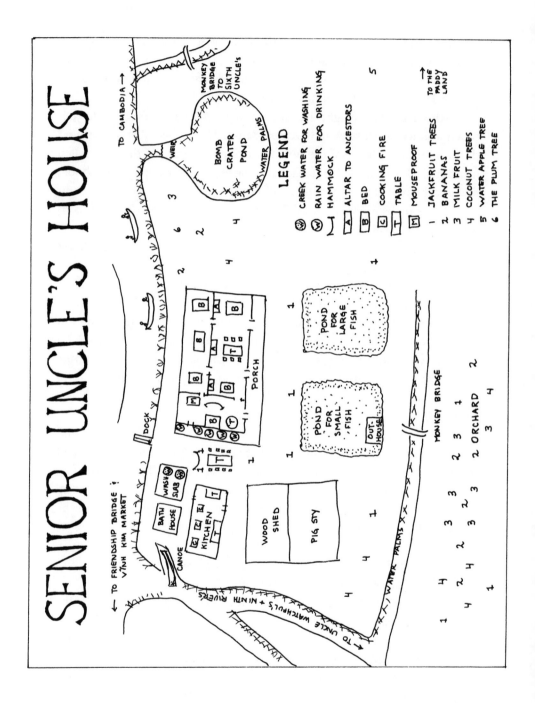

TO CAMBODIA →

← TO FRIENDSHIP BRIDGE
VINH KIM MARKET

TO UNCLE WATCHFUL'S + NINTH RIVERS →

MONKEY BRIDGE TO SIXTH UNCLE'S

BOMB CRATER POND

WATER PALMS

DOCK

CANOE

BATH HOUSE

WASH SLAB

KITCHEN

WOOD SHED

PIG STY

PORCH

POND FOR SMALL FISH

POND FOR LARGE FISH

OUT-HOUSE

MONKEY BRIDGE

ORCHARD

WATER PALMS

TO THE PADDY LAND →

LEGEND

Ⓦ CREEK WATER FOR WASHING
Ⓥ RAIN WATER FOR DRINKING
◡ HAMMOCK
Ⓐ ALTAR TO ANCESTORS
Ⓑ BED
Ⓒ COOKING FIRE
Ⓣ TABLE
Ⓜ MOUSEPROOF

1 JACKFRUIT TREES
2 BANANAS
3 MILK FRUIT
4 COCONUT TREES
5 WATER APPLE TREE
6 THE PLUM TREE

the bow called as she set her paddle across her knees. The canoe, loaded with knobby jackfruit, hung low in the water.

"Going to market, are you?" Second Harvest answered.

"You have a friend visiting," the woman in the bow observed.

"Stop by to see us," the woman in the stern invited. She gave a quick stroke, and the canoe swung around the next bend.

"By now the whole village knows you're here," Second Harvest said as we walked up the bank. "With the water high, everyone's on the river."

I put away my toothbrush and then mustered my courage to negotiate the outhouse. Soon I set about picking up jackfruit leaves from the ground, which was soft and mossy under my bare feet. Senior Uncle, his great hands filled with stacked leaves, came toward me down the path between the two fishponds. A puppy and a small orange cat with a truncated tail followed him.

Senior Uncle spotted the leaves in my hand. "Oh no!" he said. "No, no, you mustn't pick up leaves, no, no, you must rest, you're my precious guest."

"But Father," Second Harvest called from the porch, "this is my younger sister."

"Then put down your leaves," Senior Uncle said to me, setting his alongside mine. "I'll show you around my garden."

Autumn joined us, and we followed Senior Uncle and Second Harvest and the cat and puppy among the fruit trees—banana, coconut, jackfruit, lemon, water apple, breast milk, rambutan, plum, and even durian, which is a prized fruit with a smell so pungent that some people hold their noses to eat it.

Senior Uncle patted a banana leaf as if it were the head of a beloved child. "At the end of the war," he said, "I planted bananas first. I figured by the time they grew old and died, the milk fruit would have grown. If the land was still good, we might have fruit in three years or five."

"Did the Americans spray Agent Orange here?" Autumn asked.

"It came like rain," Senior Uncle said. "First we knew, our legs itched, but we didn't know why, and then the bananas bloated, and then all the leaves dropped away and our rice died and our pigs died."

"But why did they spray here, Senior Uncle?" I asked.

"Because we paddled our canoes upstream where the Americans' big boats couldn't follow, that's why they sprayed, so we couldn't hide." Senior Uncle caught a durian branch and pruned a dead twig. "I would send some

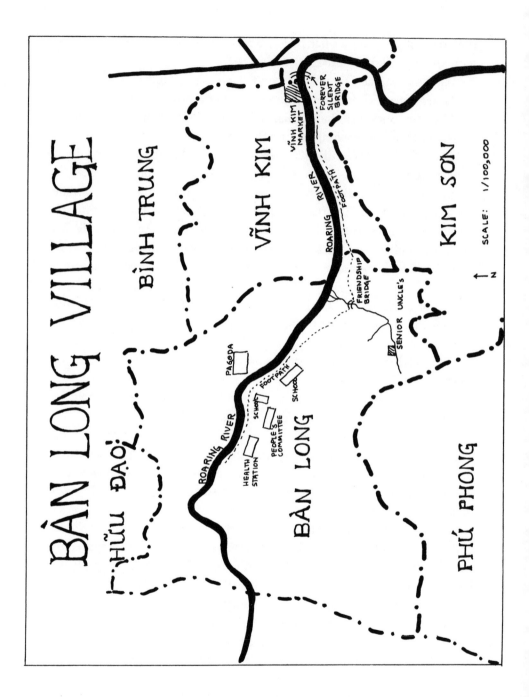

durian with you for your father, but it's the end of the season. There used to be huge trees here, but they all died, everything died. These durian seedlings came from Singapore, the breast milk also."

"But how could seedlings survive the poison?" Autumn asked.

"The rains," Second Harvest said. "And the tides."

I didn't comprehend what Second Harvest meant until I had lived at Senior Uncle's for some time. Once I fell into the rhythm of the river and the rains, I saw how at the tide's crest, water eased over the entire orchard. The house on its raised dirt foundation became an island, and then the tide receded, carrying with it the effluent from the midday rain. Ban Long's Agent Orange had long since washed into the South China Sea, known in Viet Nam as the Eastern Sea, where it joined the ebb and flow of global waters, eventually lapping at our own American shores.

"There's one of our weapons," Second Harvest said, pointing to the explosive opening in a hornets' nest. "We used to set those in our traps."

"Watch out!" Senior Uncle pulled my sleeve.

A jackfruit as large as a watermelon crashed to the ground. Its nubby rind split, filling the air with a subtle, waxy fragrance.

"And they bombed here too?" Autumn asked.

"Oh yes." Second Harvest led us to another grove of banana trees. "Before, our house was here. But by 1968, we had no house."

Senior Uncle pointed to a crater next to the stream. "That's from a five-hundred-kilo bomb," he said. "See here? I'm digging the crater out to reach the stream so that at high tide I can string a weir and catch fish."

Second Harvest paused under a plum tree that stood off alone as if keeping watch over the entire orchard. She lifted one of its branches, stroking the leaves. "In 1955, my mother and I planted a plum here. A bomb destroyed the tree, but then it sprouted again. This is all we have left from my mother: the basket on the altar, this plum tree, and my mother's grave in the cemetery for war martyrs."

Later that morning, while the water was still high, Second Harvest took Autumn and me on a tour of the village. Like my township in Appalachian Ohio, Ban Long had twisting roads that would baffle any stranger, but with this any similarity ended, for in Ban Long roads were waterways and vehicles were boats.

Vigor, Second Harvest's adopted son, removed an outboard motor with an eight-foot propeller shaft from under the bed in the side room of Senior Uncle's house. In his late teens, Vigor was tall with wavy hair, a dashing posture, and a reputation as a playboy. His father, a Viet Cong soldier, had been killed when Vigor was two. Vigor's mother then married a Sai Gon soldier, who refused to accept his wife's child. Second Harvest took Vigor in and adopted him.

Vigor bolted the outboard to the *xuong* tied in its slip like a car parked in a garage. The *xuong* was the length of an American canoe, but with a flat bottom and flared sides without thwarts. The long propeller shaft made the *xuong* look like a dragon with a lazy tail. When the shaft was nearly horizontal, the propeller drew only six inches, making the outboard perfect for the shallow stream in front of Senior Uncle's house.

"Did you fill the gas tank?" Senior Uncle called from the dock. The orange cat and the brown puppy tumbled at his feet.

Fifth Harmony, the president of the village Women's Union, joined us. I recognized her immediately by her slight overbite, sunken cheeks, and attentive ears as the woman who had offered me so many milk fruit during my first visit. Sixth Rice Field also came along. In his late sixties, he had white hair that rose from his cowlick like a patch of unharvested rice.

"The word is out," he teased Second Harvest. "I heard from three different *xuong* that you were here."

Second Harvest, Fifth Harmony, Sixth Rice Field, Autumn, and I climbed into the canoe, sitting in a row on the bottom. I sat forward of Vigor, who squatted on the tiny stern deck. As soon as we had pushed off, he yanked the rip cord; the motor caught, *rat-tat-tat.*

"Sounds like a helicopter," Sixth Rice Field said as we glided downstream. Sixth Rice Field lifted a water-palm branch so it wouldn't brush Autumn's hat. "In the North," he said to her, "you didn't learn about helicopters, did you?"

"No, but we learned about planes."

"*Wrrr,*" Fifth Harmony said. She sat in front of me. Her conical hat bobbed as she spoke. "The helicopters came so close, your hair shook. *Rat-tat-tat,* one American with a spyglass hunting you, one shooting you. They were so near, we might have shaken hands instead!"

"If a gunner saw anyone," Sixth Rice Field added, "even a woman or a small child or a water buffalo, he blew them apart. Once there was a woman in Cai Lay district. They shot off her arm so it dangled. Her husband had to cut off the rest. She had children. They might as well have killed her."

"Sometimes, Autumn," Second Harvest called back from the bow, "the helicopters hovered like dragonflies. When the helicopters dropped soldiers, they looked like dragonflies laying eggs."

"But the bombers were the worst," Fifth Harmony said.

Autumn shifted her floppy brown hat to block the sun. "We gave the American airplanes nicknames," she said. " 'F-4 Phantom Ghost.' 'F-105 Genie of Thunder.' When the bombers came, everyone jumped into a manhole bunker. There was no one left on the streets. Only the oxen harnessed to their carts were killed. One friend of mine couldn't get to a manhole in time. She hid under an ox. The ox was killed. Fifteen days later, my friend was still sick from the thought of all that blood and bits of carcass."

"*U, u, u, u.*" Fifth Harmony made a soft rumbling noise as she passed me a sliver of fresh coconut. "If you ever hear a sound like a foot-pedaled threshing machine, you run! Do you understand, Last Child? Don't wait, because by the time you hear a bomber roar, the plane has already dropped its bombs."

We rounded another curve and came upon a woman crouching on a log dock as she washed her hair in the river. "Is Senior Uncle all right that you've come home?" she asked Second Harvest.

"He's fine," Second Harvest answered. "We have friends visiting."

"When can you stop by?" asked a man standing up to his knees in water. With a machete, he hacked a dead water-palm branch.

As we rounded another bend, Second Harvest pointed to a makeshift bridge of logs lashed to concrete posts tilting at a rakish angle. "There's what's left from an American bomb," she said, pointing first to the right, then to the left. "This is the road to Ben Tre province, that one to Dong Thap Muoi."

"This?" I stared in disbelief. A preteen boy and a three-year-old came single file down the road, which was nothing more than a footpath. As our *xuong* slipped under the palm-trunk bridge, I looked up at the two boys peering down at me. How absurd, I thought: bombing a footbridge.

"The Sai Gon Air Force never could hit it," Second Harvest said, "but the Americans had better aim. We'll use the money you brought from your friends in the States to rebuild the bridge in concrete."

"There's my niece's house!" Fifth Harmony said as we eased into a canal. The house was among many we'd passed. Hidden amidst fruit trees, it was made of wood, with a thatch roof. Two boys shooting marbles in the swept yard waved to Fifth Harmony, then turned back to their game. With a whoop, the smaller boy gathered up the booty he'd won.

Suddenly Vigor cut the motor; he swung the propeller shaft until it rested alongside the hull. Sixth Rice Field, who was seated toward the bow, untangled a vine from the blades. "We heard your bombing was fierce," he said to Autumn as Vigor swung the propeller back into the water.

"It was the worst along the coast and around Hai Phong," Autumn said. "In Ha Noi everyone had a loudspeaker connected by phone wire." She made her voice crackle. " 'Attention, fellow countrymen! Airplane sixty kilometers away. Attention! Fifty kilometers. Forty kilometers!' " Then she let her voice ease. "At least we had artillery. We could shoot back."

"But here in the South we couldn't shoot back," Second Harvest said. "We didn't have any radio to warn us. No air siren. A mother with lots of little ones, how could she gather them into the bunker in time?"

With a cross-bow draw, Second Harvest pulled the *xuong* into a narrow sluice. "Vigor!" she called. "Let's take this shortcut." Vigor cut the motor and again swung the propeller shaft alongside the gunwale.

"But why couldn't you shoot back in the South?" I asked, shifting so Vigor could retrieve his paddle.

"You can't shoot a B-52 with a rifle!" Second Harvest said, paddling. Her emphatic stroke told me I'd asked a silly question. "You might shoot at a helicopter, but that would be crazy because then the Americans and their puppets would know where you were."

"Here in the South," Fifth Harmony added, "we had to hunker down and bear it. We never slept aboveground. Sometimes a bomb would blow up a whole family." Her voice lowered, as if she were talking to herself. "When a whole family dies, who will tend the graves?"

The water-palm fronds made a rattling sound against my conical hat. Grabbing branches, Sixth Rice Field pulled the canoe along. All about, insects twittered in the deep shade created by coconut and water palms hanging over the narrow sluice. "When the helicopters came," Sixth Rice Field said, "I might be slipping through this sluice. I'd jump overboard and sink my canoe." He turned toward me, holding one hand over his cowlick, the other over his nose. "I could stay underwater forever if I had a bamboo tube to use as a straw to draw in air."

Fifth Harmony also turned, pointing to her nose. "If you don't have bamboo, Little One, always keep these two holes above water."

We had reached the end of the sluice. Vigor shook the water off his paddle and swung the propeller back into the creek. He yanked the cord, and once again the *rat-tat-tat* of the motor drowned out the *whir* of insects.

"We'll show you our new pagoda," Sixth Rice Field said as the canoe crossed Roaring River. "A bomb destroyed the old pagoda. We built this one in 1988."

We climbed out of the canoe and walked along the river, crossing two monkey bridges before we came upon the pagoda, a square structure made of tightly woven water-palm leaves. All around, the fragrance of frangipani hung like a sweet cloud. As we entered, the caretaker struck a brass gong, which resonated with a great thrumming. Incense burning on the altar seared my nostrils.

The caretaker stepped outside, but through the back door I could see him squatting by a too-round pond. Although not a monk, he wore his hair cropped as close as the fiber on a coconut's inner shell. With a machete, he whacked the top off the green outer shell of a coconut and poured its milk into glasses. Soon he set the glasses before us.

"When you were here two years ago," Second Harvest said, "we wanted to offer you coconut milk, but the coconut fruit still hadn't returned. After the war, everyone had to work hard to bring back the green." She lifted her glass in a toast. "There's so much labor behind a glass of coconut milk."

"We'd had our pagoda for three hundred years," the caretaker said.

"Was there nothing left, Senior Uncle?" I sipped the sweet milk.

Second Harvest pointed to the door. "That pillar. And parts of two Buddhas."

"The world should weep," Autumn said.

Later, I came upon the two statues. Seeing them, I thought of two Buddhas I'd come upon when biking through Cambodia's Angkor Wat in 1969, before the United States toppled Prince Sihanouk's government, spreading the American War to Cambodia. The smiles on the Khmer Buddhas had seemed tranquil. Now, I contemplated two similar Buddhas propping each other up like wounded brothers. Their smiles seemed weary.

"What a labor to clear the bombs," Autumn was saying to Fifth Harmony. The two women walked under the frangipani tree bedecked with fragrant gold and white trumpets.

"There was so much to rebuild," Fifth Harmony said. "And after the Agent Orange, not a single tree or water palm to rebuild with. We harvested bombs. I didn't help at the pagoda, but at my house, we found seven unexploded artillery, who knows how many M-79 grenades, and we had seven craters from five-hundred-kilo bombs."

"Mercy!" Autumn said. "For how big an area?"

"Six *cong*."

Six *cong*, I thought: Fifth Harmony had filled seven craters—each a small pond—in an area the size of my acre-plus yard at home. "How did you get the dirt?" I asked. We had reached the canoe; I scrambled toward the stern.

"Dirt?" Second Harvest said.

"To fill the craters." I knew a bomb, like a hammer blow, compacts the earth.

Fifth Harmony laughed, covering her overbite with one hand. She was as lean as a bamboo shoulder yoke. "Baskets! My mother and I had to move the earth."

Yes, of course, I thought. I remembered how during my wartime visit to Ha Noi I'd watched women carrying dirt, basket by basket, moving in determined lines to fill bomb craters near Dragon Bridge, then the sole road link between Ha Noi and Beijing.

"But the M-79 grenades were the worst," Second Harvest said, pushing us off from the bank and alighting in the bow. "They explode into a thousand fragments, each like a snip of barbed wire. Impossible to remove."

"Never pick up an M-79, Little One," Fifth Harmony added. "You never know when you've found an M-79 whether it's just a casing or a grenade about to explode. We have special cadre to defuse them. Oh my! We wore those brothers out." Fifth Harmony's tone turned playful in imitation. " 'Come to Sister's!' 'Hurry!! Come to Brother's!' "

Sixth Rice Field touched Autumn's shoulder. "In the North," he asked, "do you still have *bom bi?*"

Terrible are the words like *bom* and *na pan* (the spelling reflects the Vietnamese pronunciation of a final *n* as our *m* sound) that the Vietnamese have adapted for use in their own language from the French and English spoken around them. The Vietnamese describe *bom bi* as a "mother bomb," which detonates in midair, spawning six hundred "baby bombs" that look like falling fruit. On impact, each baby bomb explodes into three hundred ricocheting pellets, or *bi*, each the size of a bicycle ball bearing. A baby bomb will not kill the victim unless she's hit directly; the pellets, however, create havoc from multiple wounds.

"We still find *bom bi* when we plow," Sixth Rice Field said. He shook his head, his cowlick quavering. "What kind of person would make those bombs? And then paint them orange to make them pretty!"

Fifth Harmony nodded toward four little boys traipsing across a monkey bridge. The two eldest held the hands of a three-year-old. "The children think *bom bi* are toys," she said.

"Can't you teach them?!" I asked, appalled.

"Oh we do!" Sixth Rice Field said. "But kids are so curious." His voice dropped in volume. "How long do you suppose *bom bi* hold their power?" he asked no one in particular. He trailed his hand in the creek. Each finger left its wake.

Second Harvest glanced back at me. "Do you know where you are, Last Child?"

"I couldn't escape if I wanted to," I teased.

We had ducked up one sluice and down another, turning this way and that through a labyrinth of rivers and streams, oxbows and sluices. I was lost, but I could tell that to Second Harvest, Sixth Rice Field, and Fifth Harmony, these waterways were familiar highways and byways, shortcuts and escape routes.

"Well," Second Harvest said as we rounded yet another bend, "here's the bridge we'll rebuild together. What do you suggest? We thought we should call it Friendship Bridge."

"Friendship Bridge it is," I said.

Vigor lowered the throttle; the motor's *rat-tat-tat* relaxed to a purr. Then he cut the power. By the time the *xuong* eased into its slip, Senior Uncle stood on the bank, toying with the string of keys around his waist, his puppy and the orange cat tussling with his toes.

IV

Sparks of Gold

The poor are fireflies
dazzling bright.
Roaring River will flash
a thousand generations.

NGUYEN HUE
1753–1792

*D*uring evenings at Senior Uncle's house, I read by a "baby lamp" that, no taller than the spread of my hand, tilted on a lopsided base of hand-blown glass, emitting light as fragile as a firefly's. For several generations, people in Ha Noi had called the baby lamp an "American lamp," perhaps because the first kerosene had come from the United States.

But Second Harvest said the southerners used the phrase "American lamp" because they had relied on the tiny lights to signal guerrillas about the movement of GIs camped nearby. Her version resonated with the way American revolutionaries had alerted their comrades to the advance of British colonial troops in the time of Paul Revere.

As I bent over the American lamp, Senior Uncle would invariably appear. In the darkness, his black *ao ba ba* pajama suit made his face and huge hands seem disembodied. Senior Uncle's assignment with the Viet Cong had been to assist in organizing Ban Long's literacy program. Now, years later, he welcomed me as a lost student whom war had kept him from teaching. Like any good teacher, Senior Uncle valued repetition. He would lean over me, so close I could smell the biting fragrance of his tiger balm.

"It all began with Nguyen Hue," he said one evening in 1989. He jabbed the air with his forefinger. "A century before the French invaded, the traitor Nguyen Anh invited the King of Siam (Thailand) to send fifty thousand men to help put down the Tay Son peasants' rebellion led by Nguyen Hue. Nguyen Hue sent gold and precious gifts to the Siamese and proposed a separate peace, he let the traitor and the Siamese think his will had slackened! But Nguyen Hue had hid his junks up Roaring River and up Mango River, too. He waited."

With his fingertip Senior Uncle drew a map on the table, showing the two tributaries feeding the Tien Giang River. "You know how easy it is to hide among our water palms, Child," he said, his finger defining the seven-kilometer stretch between the two tributaries. "Nguyen Hue hid his artillery along the riverbank, then as soon as the traitors' ships passed Mango River, our junks sailed out, blocking their retreat.

"Our ships sailed out of Roaring River as well, blocking their advance and ambushing the traitors, can you catch my words, Child? The French should have read about our great peasant general Nguyen Hue and how he defeated the Thais. Then the French would have known better than to invade Roaring River. The Americans should have read about him, too. Do you know why? Because Nguyen Hue taught us we could fight for a thousand generations."

Back in 1987, without letting me know she was doing so, Second Harvest had led me to Ban Long because it was her home. While confined to the Province Guest House, I made day trips to several other villages. From them I chose Ban Long because it felt more typical and because my visit there had seemed less constrained. Now, with hindsight, I realize that the exuberance I'd felt in Ban Long during that first day trip came about because, unbeknownst to me, Second Harvest had taken me to visit her closest friends.

I was utterly naïve when choosing Ban Long. Only after five years of visits did I begin to put the pieces of stories together and figure out where I'd landed. In 1989, I learned from Senior Uncle that I'd chosen the region of Nguyen Hue's famous battle. Then progressively during visits in 1990 and 1991 I began to realize I had been living at a site of the famous demonstrations in 1930, of *the* 1940 Southern Uprising against the French with the very people who then organized *the* 1960 Uprising against the American-backed Diem government.

These uprisings are the Vietnamese equivalent to the American Revolution's Boston Tea Party. In my naïveté, I had wandered down the dragon's throat. Now that I was here and welcome, maybe I could find out about these uprisings and how my hosts had participated in them over the years.

One evening in the rainy season of 1990 I was reading a Party history of Chau Thanh district. The tropics are not kind to books. Although this volume was only two years old, worms had nibbled its musty pages.

"What about Phan Boi Chau, Senior Uncle?" I asked, looking up. I knew that Phan Boi Chau, the great nationalist of the early 1900s, had been a friend of Ho Chi Minh's father. Ho Chi Minh had grown up listening to the two men recite patriotic poetry. "It says here that word of Phan Boi Chau's effort to train and organize youth reached Chau Thanh district. Had you heard of Phan Boi Chau when you were a young man in the 1920s?"

"Oh yes!" As Senior Uncle leaned closer, I could see that the lines on his cheeks cut as deep as furrows. He jabbed his finger with each point. "Phan Boi Chau taught us to organize. We had a Revolutionary Youth Association in Vinh Kim by the 1920s, and then when the Vietnamese Communist Party organized, a representative traveled from the mountains way up north on the Chinese border to choose three bases in the south. Vinh Kim was one."

"Vinh Kim, the market?" I asked, checking.

"Never underestimate a market, Little One," Senior Uncle said, shooing his small dog out for the night. He closed the accordion door.

"In 1930, in the Year of the Horse," he resumed, "we demonstrated at Vinh Kim Market, slogans and banners in May and again in June against Landlord Huong Quan Thieu, but the French arrested us. Beat us! For every eleven bundles of harvested rice, we could keep only one. And only one harvest a year! One bundle of rice! How could we feed our children?"

Senior Uncle cut off his teaching to continue his evening rounds, his black *ao ba ba* melting into the darkness, his presence traceable by the whisper of his bare feet against the floor tiles and by the creak of hinges as, one by one, he closed the wooden shutters against the night.

Other "classes" came at the end of meals. "Last Child . . . ," Senior Uncle would say as he stacked the rice bowls. He always spoke slowly when giving advice. "Never cook all your rice. Always keep some back for tomorrow. Do you understand, My Child? You never know when you'll have more rice."

One visit during the dry season of 1990, we were finishing lunch at the picnic table outside. Autumn and Fifth Harmony had moved to the hammock strung between Senior Uncle's jackfruit trees. A hen and her biddies chirped underfoot, nipping grains of fallen rice.

"Senior Uncle," I asked, "why did you leave your ancestral home for Ban Long?" I knew a Vietnamese peasant's *que huong*—the site of his ancestors' graves—is the wellspring of life. Given the choice, Senior Uncle would have stayed to tend those graves and draw guidance from his ancestors' spirits.

"I had to flee," he said. "The French were going to arrest me!"

"But why you, Senior Uncle?"

"Father, what are you talking about?" Second Harvest asked. She brought a plate of water apples from the kitchen, a separate building made of tar paper and water-palm thatch. She waved to two women paddling a canoe up the creek. "Coming back from market, are you?" she asked them.

"We're talking about the French," Senior Uncle said to Second Harvest. Then he turned to me. "We fled after the 1940 Uprising. The French were arresting us to fight the Germans, they raised our taxes for their war, I couldn't feed my children, don't you understand? We were starving! People died because of French taxes!"

"Were you a sharecropper, Senior Uncle?" I asked.

"No, no, not sharecropping." Second Harvest divided a water apple between her father and me. The fruit, the size of a crab apple, was pink and hollow, its translucent meat crisp and coarse.

"When I was small," Senior Uncle said, "my family had enough money to send me to school. But in 1940 I refused to be a soldier for the French in their war against the Germans. I fled, and then the French burned my house and all my rice." He held out his hands. "I only had these two hands left. I had to work like a serf."

"Like France in the 1300s," Autumn said, taking half a water apple.

"We were all serfs," Fifth Harmony said. "For one thousand square meters of land, we paid twenty kilos of unhusked rice, but sometimes we didn't even harvest that much. We had no land of our own, no way to eat."

Senior Uncle cupped his hands into an empty bowl. "When insects ate most of your harvest, the landlord took whatever was left, and then the landlord took back his land, and he would take your house, and if you had a pretty daughter, he took her. If you still couldn't pay, he beat you! Do you hear me, Child, the landlord beat my grandfather to death!"

I had been rubbing the belly of Senior Uncle's small dog with my foot. I stopped. Small Dog nipped my toes, her teeth like nails.

"We were slaves!" Senior Uncle said.

"These were French landlords?" I asked.

"The Vietnamese landlords paid the French," Second Harvest said. "We were starving. That's why my parents joined the Uprising."

Autumn peered at me over the glasses perched at the end of her nose. "The French didn't want peasants to organize. That's why they kept them illiterate, so they couldn't communicate."

"Like me," Second Harvest said. "I didn't learn to read until I was ten, and then I finished only the third grade."

Autumn turned to Second Harvest. "I got to go to school, but you know what the French taught me? King Louis this, King Louis that! Can you imagine? On their maps of Viet Nam, they wrote 'France Overseas'! And when I went to Paris, the only thing the French students I met knew about Viet Nam was that we had rubber and coal. They knew nothing about our culture, but only about what the French took from us back to France." She looked at me. "Why, Viet Nam didn't even have a name. 'Indochina' they called it! That's India and China, two giants. Where were we?"

Second Harvest split another water apple. "Maybe most of us didn't learn to read until we were grown," she said, "but we knew our history, and we sang our poems to give us determination."

"We had to rise up," Senior Uncle said. "For our children."

"Where was this uprising in 1940?" I asked.

"At Vinh Kim Market," Second Harvest said. "Where we bought fish this morning."

"We only had banners and signs, just like in 1930," Senior Uncle said. "No weapons. Still, the French burned our houses and rice. I escaped to

Ban Long, but it was worse for the others." He tapped his temples. "With my own eyes, I saw the French soldiers drive nails through my neighbors' hands, can you picture this? The French roped my neighbors together and dragged them into the river until the water filled their mouths and choked their cries."

"The bridge at Vinh Kim," Fifth Harmony said, pushing her foot to make the hammock swing, "the one where we tied up our *xuong* this morning. The landlords would bind the hands and feet of those who couldn't pay their taxes and shove them off the bridge. That's why we call it 'Forever Silent Bridge.' "

"One piece of land, so much blood," Second Harvest said. She looked out toward the stream, her face as calm as the water with the tide about to turn. "A span of bridge, so many splinters of bone."

"*Nam Ky Khoi Nghia*." Autumn spoke the phrase for "the Southern Uprising" as if in prayer.

We settled into silence broken only by the biddies chirping beneath the table and the slow creak of the hammock.

Histories of Viet Nam written by Americans rarely mention the 1940 Southern Uprising, yet it is memorialized by *Nam Ky Khoi Nghia*, the name of the majestic boulevard running behind former South Viet Nam President Nguyen Van Thieu's palace. However, "Southern" in the "Southern Uprising" is a misnomer, for the demonstration scarcely reached beyond Chau Thanh district.

Only by chance did I happen on the district's crucial role. The first clue came when Second Harvest took Autumn and me by the home of Mrs. Nguyen thi Thap in Sai Gon. A peasant from Chau Thanh district, Mrs. Thap had risen to become the first president of the national Women's Union. Formed in 1930, the same year as the Vietnamese Communist Party, the Women's Union is a mass organization whose effect reaches from its central headquarters down through the provinces, districts, and communes. During the French and American wars, the Union mobilized women for the revolutionary cause.

Now eighty-one, Mrs. Thap sat on a couch in an old French villa, waiting to meet an American. A stroke had left her limbs partially paralyzed and her speech impaired; her mind, however, was sharp.

"I'm the American, *Ma*," I said, taking Mrs. Thap's hand. From among the some twenty Vietnamese pronouns that define a relationship, I chose "mother" for "you" and "child" for "I." "I bring you warm wishes from your sisters and daughters in America," I said.

I couldn't decipher Mrs. Thap's reply. Her hand wavered toward the teapot; I poured us each tea, and when she lifted her hand, I lifted a teacup to her lips. She drank, and I drank. Then she settled her hand on mine and looked expectant.

As shy as I am, it was clear I must carry this conversation. I described how I hoped, through stories, to introduce Americans to the ordinary Vietnamese they had fought against. Mrs. Thap gestured toward an oil painting of soldiers raising Viet Nam's flag. The red flag with its gold star dominated the painting. Again she spoke. This time I caught one muffled word: *"co"*—"flag."

"Yes, flag," I said. I felt a keening sadness. Mrs. Thap, who had once led several million women, sat imprisoned in a body that would not follow her simplest command. Time had finally brought her close to an American, but age had stolen her ability to speak.

Some weeks later, as I was leaving the Delta, Fourth Flower gave me a book, *Tu Dat Tien Giang—From the Land of Tien Giang*, which I tucked into my suitcase. Two years after that, at home on my Ohio farm, I chanced to pull the book from my shelves. Opening it, I stared in surprise at a frontispiece photograph of Mrs. Thap taken years before, when her hair was thick and dark. Much to my surprise, I realized I was holding Mrs. Thap's autobiography. As I read, I soon came upon *"Nam Ky Khoi Nghia"* and "Vinh Kim" linked again and again.

That's when I began to see that, by following Second Harvest to Ban Long, I had thrust myself into the dragon's throat. Still, the stories I'd heard didn't fit together. If the 1940 Southern Uprising was so important, why did it seem so local? How did it relate to the rest of Viet Nam? What had Mrs. Thap tried to tell me?

Second Harvest, Fifth Harmony, and Sixth Rice Field would be no help. They were too young. Senior Uncle could remember the Uprising, but he had been peripherally involved. Then I remembered Last Gust. During the American War, Last Gust headed the Communist Party for My Tho province. I decided that the next time I returned to the Mekong Delta I would ask Last Gust about the 1940 Southern Uprising.

That happened in the fall of 1992. Last Gust met Autumn and me at his home near Forever Silent Bridge. He reached out from the steel-strip dock made from a helicopter landing pad to hold our *xuong*'s bow. His craggy face and sharp nose made him look French; however, his striped pajamas were typical Vietnamese garb for a professional man at home.

"You can't stay away," he teased, referring to our last talk six months before. Although heart distress had left Last Gust frail, his voice projected ebullience. At sixty-six, Last Gust had retired to tend his orchids and write his memoirs of thirty-five years as a revolutionary. He led Autumn and me through the garden fence he had made from recycled barbed wire. The horizontal strands were taut; he'd shaped the verticals into flowers.

"Do you know Mariana?!" Last Gust asked as we entered his stucco house.

By 1992, Renovation had radically changed Viet Nam. Now, every evening at 9 P.M., all busyness throughout the country ceased. Everyone gathered around televisions to watch "Mariana," the informal name Vietnamese gave to a Mexican soap opera, which had been dubbed into Russian, then sent from Moscow to Viet Nam, where it aired with a Vietnamese voice-over.

"Just think!" Last Gust said, offering us glasses of bright orange soda. "A brand-new play every night! I said to the station manager in Sai Gon, 'Change the title!' They'd called it *Tears of the Rich*. 'No, no,' I said, 'change the name to *The Rich Also Weep*.' Ah, Mariana! Every night I visit her living room." He lifted his glass as if in toast. "I've even entered her bedroom!"

Amazing, I thought: Soap opera conquers a revolutionary.

Last Gust nodded toward his TV covered by an embroidered cloth until programming resumed at 6 P.M. "I see now. Mariana's family may be rich, but her family is like all families. Ah, but Last Child, you didn't come to hear me talk about Mariana."

Last Gust loved to reminisce. "I was so excited," he would often say, "when I first heard about the Party! I was only eight, but I knew we would be free!! Of course that was 1930, and I was young and naïve. Freedom took a long time coming."

"Senior Uncle," I asked, leaning forward, "can you remember *Nam Ky Khoi Nghia*?"

"As clear as Mariana last night!" Last Gust stared at the bubbles rising through his orange soda. "I was in high school in My Tho in 1940. My job was to organize the youth in Vinh Kim. I knew about the planning for the

Uprising, not because I was a leader—I was too young—but because I knew how to write. I was useful as a secretary.

"I was eighteen. In 1940 the Party was weak. Then the Germans invaded France. Imagine! France became a colony! Just like us! But then the French became even more vicious masters. They increased our taxes to pay for their war against Germany, they drafted us to be their soldiers against Hitler. We couldn't stand any more!

"The Resistance center was Long Hung, only three kilometers from Forever Silent Bridge. Long Hung was the brain, but Vinh Kim was the mouth. We spread the word, from Long Hung through the Market Mouth to Binh Trung, Phu Phong, Song Thuan, Dong Hoa, and on and on."

From the river came the hum of approaching motors and of voices rippling back and forth.

"You spread the word over the south?" I asked.

"No! Not at all. *Nam Ky Khoi Nghia* happened right here. The Uprising was planned to be all over southern Viet Nam, but then one of the cadre in Sai Gon was arrested and tortured and gave names. The French then arrested our leaders in Sai Gon, all our top leaders! Nguyen thi Minh Khai, the famous revolutionary, do you know about her?"

I shook my wrists and fingers, No.

"Oh! She was one of Uncle Ho's most famous students. Minh Khai came from the center of Viet Nam, from Nghe An, Uncle Ho's home. Her father was in the administrative class serving the French. She and her younger sister went to French schools. Her sister married our famous general, Vo Nguyen Giap, and died in prison. Minh Khai's husband died in prison, too, but I'm getting ahead of myself.

"In 1929, a group of youth left Nghe An by boat for China to study revolutionary strategy with Uncle Ho. Minh Khai was nineteen and the only woman to go. She went on to Russia and was the first Vietnamese woman revolutionary to study there as well.

"It was hard to organize in the north and center of Viet Nam because the French were so vigilant. Sai Gon was more fertile ground, particularly with the port and the ships coming in and out. The laborers on the ships and the stevedores on shore linked us to the worldwide Communist movement. Minh Khai traveled from Russia through France, Germany, and Italy and returned to Viet Nam to organize in Sai Gon."

Uncle Last Gust paused, lacing his fingers together across his chest. His voice dropped to a murmur as he went on. "Minh Khai was one of our key organizers among factory workers in Sai Gon from 1936 until 1940. Oh, it was a sad day when the French took our leaders out onto the Cu Chi Road and executed them."

Uncle Last Gust rubbed his chest. "It makes my heart stop to think of Minh Khai. The French never let the prisoners have anything they could use to communicate—no pen or paper, no bit of metal to scratch the walls." He stuck his forefinger into his mouth as if to bite it and then drew in the air. "Minh Khai used her own blood as ink, her fingertip as a pen. She wrote a poem on the prison wall for those she left behind." Uncle Last Gust's voice had a gravelly sound as he recited:

> *Remain resolute whether in public outcry*
> *or quiet liaison.*
> *Both pliers and pincers serve their purpose.*
> *Sacrifice yourself! Strive to serve our cause!*
> *The only withdrawal comes with death's release.*

A breeze rustled the leaves of cucumber vines growing over the arbor in front of the house. Uncle Last Gust leaned forward. "When our Sai Gon leaders were arrested," he continued, "Central Headquarters decided the Party was too weak for *Nam Ky Khoi Nghia* to succeed. If we didn't succeed, the French would obliterate us! Central Headquarters sent messengers to tell us to wait until our Movement was stronger, but the French arrested the messengers who'd been sent to warn us. The word never arrived."

"So you were the only ones?" I said.

"A few other localities rose up, some villages in Ben Tre, but Ben Tre province was a younger sister to My Tho. You've lived here, Little One. You know the sounds of nighttime, only the cicadas singing, the bamboo whispering, maybe an owl. But oh, that night, what a ruckus!! The word went out, 'Hurry! Hurry to Vinh Kim!' "

I pictured the scene: hundreds of canoes hurtling along the dark, mysterious sluices that fed Roaring River.

"Once we'd gathered at Vinh Kim, we moved up National Highway 4—we call it National Highway 1 now—to the house of Landlord Nguyen Thanh Long. We were starving, but he had storehouses full of rice. We divided his rice among the poor, and we divided his rice fields, too! Oh, I've never seen such celebrating!

"The flag!" Last Gust pointed to the tiny flag atop his TV. "For the first time in anyone's memory, we had a country, and our country had a flag! Glorious red with a vibrant gold star in the middle!"

I leaned forward. "Mrs. Thap mentioned a flag when I met her."

"Indeed she might!" Last Gust tapped the table with his fingertip. "Mrs. Thap and her husband were among the chief organizers. She was a seamstress, she sewed the flags. Our very own Nguyen thi Thap was the first person to raise the national flag of Viet Nam!"

So that's what Mrs. Thap had tried to tell me. However, she had written her autobiography with such humility that I missed a crucial fact: I'd met the Betsy Ross of Viet Nam.

Last Gust looked out the doorway at his orchids, which were sparks of color trailing from their planters. His angular features turned somber, and his voice took on a rough edge like the sound of a grave-digger's shovel slicing the earth.

"The French retaliated the next morning. In 1940, northern Viet Nam wasn't much of a threat to the French. That's how the French could concentrate their power here. You know how busy Vinh Kim Market is at seven-thirty if the tide is up. Besides, everyone had gathered to celebrate! That's when the French bombed. The wails, the wounded. In my thirty-five years with the Revolution, I never heard such terror. Thirty or forty killed, one hundred twenty wounded. Then the French sent in the Foreign Legion. Do you know about the Legion?"

"A little," I said. I remembered the day I'd been so sick and how Third Mother had told me she'd spread pig dung on her face to frighten off Foreign Legion soldiers so they wouldn't rape her.

Last Gust wove his fingers together. "There were two types of Foreign Legion soldiers. The first were white people, but they were orphans and prisoners, the people the French didn't want. They were terribly cruel. The second were soldiers drafted from the other French colonies, but we didn't have them until 1945. The white Foreign Legion burned Vinh Kim and Long Hung. They burned any village that had taken part in the Uprising. Houses and rice, burned! Whatever they wanted, stolen. Anyone they found, raped, then shot! Oh, it was terrible.

"Everyone fled. People so feared the French Foreign Legion, they didn't gather the dead. Ninety percent of our leaders, killed on the spot. Or taken for torture, a mass migration to Con Dao Prison Island. The remaining ten percent were youth like myself. I escaped to Ben Tre.

"I was a student, and so when the older Party members sent me back to Vinh Kim several days later to care for the dead, I wore my student's uniform as a guise and spoke to the soldiers in French. The Foreign Legion had dumped the bodies or what was left of them into a bunker. Oh my God, the heat and the flies swarming, never ever has there been such a smell."

Last Gust coughed, and I was aware of the strain that remembering placed on his heart. "After two months," he continued, "we had nothing left of our new independence. Nothing. I was just a student, but I could tell the French had snuffed out our flame. What could we do? How could we have a revolution with an uprising in only one place? What we had learned here must flow to the rest of the country. We had to teach others.

"We had determination, and we had the Party. The Party was crucial. If we'd had many political parties, our push for independence would have failed. But Uncle Ho united us behind one party. Oh my, when Uncle Ho died in 1969, the bombing in the South was ferocious. As if the Americans thought bombs could break our will!"

Autumn folded the stems of her glasses in on each other. "When Uncle Ho died," she said, "Ha Noi wept tears. In the South, the sky wept bombs."

From the river came the receding *put-put* of a *xuong* and then the sound of its wake lapping against the shore. Last Gust gazed at his soda, its bubbles rising. "Thirty-five years from *Nam Ky Khoi Nghia* until peace. In 1975, we who survived came home with tears in our eyes. Our joy faced sorrow when we learned the fate of friends we'd lost. None of us who survived can ever live free of memory."

"Whenever anyone talks about prison," Autumn said later that night as she climbed under our mosquito net, "my blood runs as fast as the outgoing tide." She tucked the net beneath the reed mat, then stretched out next to me. The net's ribbing cast a shadow like welts across Autumn's chest. She shuddered.

"You were in prison?" I turned onto my side and propped my cheek on my elbow. I could hear Vigor singing from his bed in the back room. The song was a ballad about a Resistance fighter in the Truong Son Mountains, the Vietnamese name for the Ho Chi Minh Trail.

"I was imprisoned when I was eighteen," Autumn said.

"But I thought you went to the Sorbonne." I was confused. During the period of French colonialism, only Vietnamese having the best connections went on to study in Paris. I'd seen photographs of Autumn and her Ha Noi high school friends in their white *ao dais,* the traditional flowing dress worn by the affluent.

"In the early 1950s," Autumn said, "I was in the lycée in Ha Noi. I joined a group of students in the Resistance against the French."

Now I was more perplexed. "Your mother and grandmother were in the Resistance?!"

"Oh no! Our group met in secret. Our lycée had been named for the Trung sisters, who had liberated Viet Nam from the Chinese in A.D. 43. We girls followed their example. I wrote a letter from our group to one of our students with the medical corps in the mountains. The police intercepted my letter."

"You'd signed your name??"

Autumn looked over at me and laughed. "I wasn't that naïve! I only used the name 'Trung Sisters Student.' I signed in the name of our school. It took the police two months to find me."

Autumn ran her fingers over the netting. "I'd moved on to the second baccalaureate. There were only five girls in the second baccalaureate. Since forty students were needed to make a class, we girls were transferred to the boys' lycée, which was named for Nguyen Trai, the great poet-statesman. The police checked my handwriting on the letter against the exam papers in the Trung Sisters lycée and then followed me to Nguyen Trai. I was in class when they arrested me."

Autumn sighed. "They beat me for three days, they used electricity, but I refused to name others in our group. They went to my mother's house, caught my mother by surprise. She hadn't known about my activities! I was in prison a month with buyers and sellers, peasant women who'd been arrested in the market. We were like a club, reciting poetry, singing, trading stories and experience.

"Then my mother bought my way out. I'd been expelled from school and had to study for the baccalaureate exam at home alone. I was lucky to have French books from France, good books that were better than the teacher! As soon as I passed the second baccalaureate, my mother sent me to the Sorbonne to separate me from my friends and to carry out my father's wishes."

"But how could you travel to Paris," I asked, "if you'd resisted the French?"

"An uncle in Sai Gon arranged a visa. The French and Vietnamese authorities in Ha Noi had to accept it." She paused. "I'd never been on an airplane. I was the only woman and the only Vietnamese. There I was, surrounded by French officers—the ordinary troops went by ship in those days—and my heart with my friends in the Resistance! I remember looking out the window as we took off." She glanced up at a mosquito droning over our net. "The peasants underneath were fleeing their rice paddies. Like me, they thought all planes were bombers. I was at the Sorbonne when we won the battle against the French at Dien Bien Phu. By the time I returned to Ha Noi in 1956, North Viet Nam was its own country."

"And Vigilance?" I said, asking about Autumn's husband.

"He also returned to Ha Noi from Paris, although his family was in the South. We married in Ha Noi. I'd been married seventeen years before peace came and I could travel south and meet my mother-in-law. She didn't meet her grandchildren until they were nearly grown."

By now, Senior Uncle's large lantern hanging from the rafters had dimmed to a spark of gold. "Just think," Autumn said into the darkness. "Now I've turned fifty-five and retired. I have a new grandson to raise! Do you see, Little One? Being able to raise our grandchildren—that's what 'peace' means."

I lay back on the reed mat. Its tiny ribs pressed against my forearms. In the next room, the heavy sounds of Senior Uncle's breathing had replaced Vigor's singing. Outside, an owl called, *cu cu, cu cu,* as the house by the river gave itself over to the peaceful sounds of slumber.

V

Brushfire

In a sparse season, fire jumps field to field.
A wind rises; the flames roar.
The mountain forests ignite on all sides.
Flames paint the horizon red.

FROM SENIOR UNCLE'S
Guerrilla Manual, 1942

"*Coo. Coo!*" Senior Uncle called, tossing leftover rice onto a bare spot between the wood shed and the side sluice. Squawking, his chickens dove for the scattered grain. It was a morning in the rainy season of 1989, and Senior Uncle had already picked up the fallen jackfruit leaves. Now he reached down and, with both hands, caught a brown hen, which he popped into a cracked water urn. He set an old basket on top.

"Goose morning!" Second Harvest's younger son called in English to Autumn and me as we shook out our mosquito net. At thirteen, Third Ability was already as tall as his mother.

"Not 'goose,' Nephew!" Autumn answered. She laughed and made a honking noise. " 'Goose' is a *con ngong.* You mean 'Goo*d*,' with a *d.*"

"GooD morning then!" Third Ability said as he joined his grandfather, who squatted by one of the ponds in front of the house. Unlike the round bomb-crater pond, these two were hand-dug and rectangular. Senior Uncle had used the earth to build a raised foundation so his house would stand above the tide.

"Do you follow Uncle Ho's teachings on your farm, Child?" Senior Uncle asked when I sat on my heels next to him. He clapped his hands, calling *"Ohoooo, Ohoooo."*

I pictured my unkempt pond overgrown with cattails. "Not as well as you, Senior Uncle."

"To live, you need two things, Child, you need rice and clean water." He nodded toward the pond, which was covered with floating brush. "But if you want to live well, you need three more—a garden, a pigsty, and a fishpond." He clapped once more, his massive hands like cymbals. Suddenly huge fish jumped and dove, mouths gaping, tails slapping as they gulped the rice husks Senior Uncle scattered. "We have an expression," Senior Uncle continued, rocking back on his heels. "Back of the house, the garden; front of the house, the fishpond."

"But why the brush, Senior Uncle?" I asked, tossing rice husks.

"Watch this!" Third Ability said. He dumped a handful of husks. Suddenly the fish jumped to that spot, gulping and thrashing. Waves slapped the bank, studding my face with spray that smelled like moss. Then, just as suddenly, frightened by their own turmoil, the fish dove for the bottom. There was silence broken only by ripples lapping at the bank.

"See how the branches calm the water?" Senior Uncle said. "These fish are like people in Sai Gon, living so close that they can't grow their own food, so close that they scare themselves." He pointed to the second rectangular pond with the outhouse perched over it. "Now those fish over there are independent."

It was true that I had never seen Senior Uncle tend the smaller fish. However, I was aware of their feeding habits, for a single plop from the outhouse brought them racing.

The hen in the cracked water urn cackled. "Ah ha!" Senior Uncle said, hurrying to the urn. He removed the basket, the chicken, and a fresh egg.

"Come eat!" Second Harvest called from the kitchen. She set out bowls of glutinous rice, which—because it is heavier and sweeter than ordinary rice—is used for treats, for special cakes, and for distilling into rice whiskey. As we took our places at the picnic table under the jackfruit trees, Second Harvest added shredded coconut to make a dish like hot cereal.

"If you want to grow old, Last Child," Senior Uncle said, his chopsticks punctuating his point, "drink only warm water, never cold. Don't drink rice whiskey or tea. Myself, I don't want to grow old. That's why I don't grow a beard." He took another bite, cupping his bowl close to his mouth, then tapped his chopsticks against the porcelain.

"And if ever you don't have enough to eat, My Child," he said, "then chew slowly."

Talk of food fueled Ban Long. Farmer talk—how the rice crop fared and which fruit was ripe—made me homesick for our talk of hay and gardens in Ohio. But in Ban Long, as throughout Viet Nam, there was always an undercurrent we don't live with to the same extent in the United States: the memory of hunger. This memory pervades the consciousness of Vietnamese over the age of ten. It surfaces in the constant discussion of food at mealtime; sometimes it erupts in a rush, as happened one morning when we went to Vinh Kim Market to pick up Second Harvest's husband, Fifth Virtue. He was returning from My Tho with Sixth Rice Field.

Vinh Kim Market was a square with the river wharf at one end and a dirt road connecting with National Highway 4 and My Tho at the other. A half-dozen stucco buildings with shops selling hardware, grains, and traditional medicine lined each side of the market. Inside the square, tarps covered wooden stalls, turning the market into a tent city. After Second Harvest had bought fish sauce, MSG, and kerosene, we stopped in at the pharmacy at the head of the wharf. Fifth Virtue and Sixth Rice Field were waiting for us at a table in the center of the shop. This pharmacy, which was one of the most prosperous shops, had patterned floor tiles; however, in the still-lean times of 1989, only a few Western medicines dotted the shelves.

"Here's where we used to pick up our medicine during the American War," Second Harvest said as the owner served us fresh-squeezed lemonade in matching glasses. "We would send our list with Third Pear or one of the other women coming to market. Tenth Treasure here filled our request at no charge."

"But how could you do that?" I asked Tenth Treasure. "Wasn't there an American compound with GIs and South Vietnamese troops in Vinh Kim?"

Tenth Treasure nodded toward the door. In her sixties, she had a high forehead as smooth as unlined paper. Everything about her from her soft hands with their painted nails to the prim way she sat indicated distance from the rice paddies. "There were more than two hundred American and puppet troops here," she said. "They provided security for the big American base at Binh Duc three kilometers away. But our store is close to the river. It was easy for Third Pear to slip in, slip away!"

"You were a merchant then, too?" I asked.

"Lots of merchants helped us!" Second Harvest said. "Remember the fruit sellers I introduced you to in the My Tho Market? They were part of our network."

"The Market Mouth!" Autumn said.

"The Americans always thought about roads on land," Second Harvest's husband, Fifth Virtue, added. When serious, Fifth Virtue's square face and missing teeth made him look tough. He had gone to the North in 1954 for Regrouping in compliance with the Geneva Accords. When the first two battalions of U.S. Marines landed in Da Nang on March 8, 1965, former Viet Minh southerners still in the North for Regrouping beseeched Ho Chi Minh to let them return home, to the American War in the South.

In 1965, Fifth Virtue hiked for three months down the Truong Son Range Trail. By the mid-1960s, a route once used to supply the Resistance against the French had become a complex web of roads and footpaths, makeshift bridges, underground supply depots, and camp hospitals that American journalists named the "Ho Chi Minh Trail." When Fifth Virtue arrived in the South, he was assigned to a training unit in the Cambodian jungle near the Vietnamese border. He met Second Harvest there in 1970, when he was teaching cadre and she was a student.

"You've lived here with us, Little One," Fifth Virtue said. "You understand what your soldiers didn't. Our roads in Ban Long run on water." He offered his tobacco pouch to Sixth Rice Field but not to us women because very few women in Viet Nam smoke.

The two men rolled their cigarettes. Sixth Rice Field struck a match and lit Fifth Virtue's cigarette, then his own. The tobacco flared, then settled into embers. "That's how we could organize the 1940 Uprising, by relying on the women traveling to market in their *xuong*," Sixth Rice Field said. "But afterwards, when the puppets retaliated, we had to flee to Ban Long and even into Cambodia."

"Such a cruel time!" Fifth Virtue said, exhaling smoke through the gap in his teeth.

"Like my family," Second Harvest said. "When Father fled, the puppets threw my mother into prison. I was thrown into prison with her. I was two, so I don't remember this, but Mother often told me what a comfort I was."

"Can you imagine, Little One?" Fifth Virtue added. "In 1940 everyone bombed us! First, after the Uprising, the French. Then the Japanese invaded us. Then the Americans bombed us because of the Japanese. The Americans were the worst. They bombed everywhere."

"World War II," I said, nodding.

"Yes!" Tenth Treasure said.

"We had nothing!" Second Harvest pulled at the sleeve of her *ao ba ba*. "No cloth. No matches. No lamp oil."

"It was embarrassing to have no cloth," Sixth Rice Field added, covering his mouth. "Imagine! We made clothes out of leaves and stitched them with banana thread! A husband and wife might own a single pair of shorts. When the wife wore the shorts outside the house, the husband hid inside."

"How could we kids study?" Second Harvest said. "I didn't have clothes to wear to school. I had only one pair of shorts. No shirt! We didn't have paper. I learned to write my letters on the back of banana leaves, their veins for lines, a sliver of bamboo for a pen."

"If was different for the British colonies," Autumn said, turning to me. Her accent—the crisp sound of a Ha Noi intellectual—was always easier for me to understand than the rural southern accent used in Ban Long. "In India, the British built factories, but the French took our raw materials to France and brought back the finished goods for us to buy. There was one Vietnamese match factory in the north, and the textile mills were in the north, too. That's why we in the south had nothing." She turned to the others. "But at least people here didn't starve."

"No more than usual," Sixth Rice Field muttered.

"The French took our land, Little One," Second Harvest said. "Without land and water, how could we eat? We had no industry here, like they had in the north. Have you seen any machines? Our hands and our feet, deep in the mud—that's what makes rice grow, rice we can put in our mouths." She cupped her left hand like a bowl close to her lips, the two forefingers of her right like chopsticks, her mouth open.

"That's why Uncle Ho formed the Viet Minh," Sixth Rice Field said.

"Did you know about Communism in 1940 or hear about the Viet

Minh in 1941?" I asked Sixth Rice Field. I knew that during the late 1930s, Vietnamese Communist Party members who favored an international Communist revolution had disagreed with Ho Chi Minh's wish to include merchants and small landlords in his nationalist emphasis. But by 1941, with both the French and Japanese occupying Viet Nam, the Party acceded to Ho's wish to widen the nationalist movement. Independence, the Party agreed, must come first; Communism's social revolution would become a part of the independence struggle. And so in May 1941, Ho Chi Minh announced the formation of the Viet Minh—*Viet Nam Doc Lap Dong Minh Hoi*, or "Alliance for an Independent Viet Nam."

Sixth Rice Field drew his fingertips along the table as if they were harrow tines. "Most of us here had never heard of Communism or the Viet Minh in 1941! We were hungry. We wanted rice."

"The hunger was even worse in the north," Autumn added. "The Japanese forced the peasants to grow jute to make rope for their war industry. By early 1945, there was no rice. Our rice was growing—you could see the bursts of gold, but by May the peasants were as thin as rice stalks. They wandered, searching for food. They died on the road."

Autumn looked out the door at a boy buying an ice-cream stick for the child on his hip, then continued. "No one knew the names of the dead. Then when the harvest came, more people died because they ate too much! And after that, cholera, and still more died. In all, two million people died during the first six months of 1945. One person out of six."

Fifth Virtue spread another pinch of tobacco on a rolling paper. All the while, he clicked his tongue against his teeth.

Autumn's voice turned grey. "The corpse cart made a *re re re* sound as it came. Terrible. A cart with bodies stacked like sticks of firewood. I was ten. I would hide whenever I heard the *re re re, re re re*. Once I saw a dead woman leaning against my neighbor's door. It was early morning, with mist all around. The woman's *ao ba ba* was open. The baby at her breast was still alive, sucking at the corpse. That's when I understood the meaning of 'dead.' "

"I'll tell you, Last Child," Second Harvest said, "about the time I first learned about 'dead.' My maternal grandfather—he was my great-uncle, but since he'd raised my mother, I called him 'Maternal Grandfather'— and his best friend had just celebrated Tet when the French Foreign Legion entered Ban Long. The women had fled because they were afraid of rape. The French would have asked my grandfather whether he was Viet Minh."

Second Harvest held her hands up and rotated her wrists in the southern gesture No. "That's what Grandfather would have said, 'No.'

"I came back from working for the rich landlord to find the two elders lying on the earthen floor." She lifted her hands over her eyes. "Grandfather had bullet holes through his hands, bullet holes through his eyes. That was 1948. I was ten. From that moment on, I knew I would resist the French."

That same night, when the stately lantern hanging from the rafters in Senior Uncle's house had burned down to a glow and we had climbed under our mosquito net, Autumn continued her story.

"After Uncle Ho declared independence in 1945," she said, tucking in the net, "we thought the fighting would end." Autumn set our pillows in place on the board bed. "But in 1946 the French returned to Ha Noi, and the Viet Minh retreated to the mountains. Some of our French neighbors said our family was Viet Minh. They called in the Foreign Legion.

"By the time my father died, he had accumulated two large cases of books, half in French and half French literature translated into Vietnamese for my mother to read. Whenever it rained and I felt sad, I would read Victor Hugo. Father loved pictures. He'd collected postcards from all the ports his ship had stopped in on the way to Paris—from India, Sri Lanka, Port Said, the Red Sea, and from Paris itself. And he had albums of photographs he'd taken of our family. But the Foreign Legion destroyed everything! All my father's books and his picture albums, too.

"My father loved France so much," she continued as we arranged the cotton sheet over us and lay down side by side. "I knew all about Paris before I went there to study. I'd seen so many pictures and had read so many books. But I never wanted to hear another word of French after the Foreign Legion broke our mirror, smashed every rice bowl, and burned everything that reminded me of my father. The French were about to burn our house," she went on. "They would have, except the French neighbors objected because they didn't want their houses to catch fire. I was eleven. I hated French soldiers. That's why I joined the Resistance."

The mosquitoes on the other side of our net droned. Vigor sang from his bamboo slat bed next to Senior Uncle's in the back room. That night he hummed a ditty about children riding atop their family water buffalo. Then he began a ballad about a fisherman lost at sea. Autumn and I settled onto the reed mat with its salt-marsh fragrance, the mosquito net hanging all around us like mist.

One evening in the dry season of 1990 Autumn and I were sitting with Second Harvest's son, Third Ability, at the round table in the corner of the side room at Senior Uncle's. In those days, before Ban Long had electricity, we spent our evenings talking. Second Harvest dozed in the hammock. The baby lamp on the table cast a gold light on her feet with their toes spread from gripping monkey bridges. Senior Uncle was in the other room, listening to his radio. It carried news of the Vietnamese Communist Party's sixtieth anniversary celebration.

Autumn touched Third Ability's wrist. "There may have been a big crowd in Sai Gon today," she said, "but there's never been such a crowd as Independence Day in Ha Noi after the Viet Minh defeated the French and Japanese in 1945."

"You heard Uncle Ho?!" Second Harvest asked. She climbed out of the hammock and joined us.

"Oh! So many went to hear him!" Autumn said.

"Could you see Ho Chi Minh?" I passed the peanuts we'd been nibbling to Second Harvest.

"Oh, yes." Autumn laughed. "But he was tiny. There were people from here to forever."

"What else?" Second Harvest asked. She rubbed tiger balm on the back of her hands to ease the stiffness from poor circulation. The balm's pungent scent penetrated the oily smell of burning kerosene.

"My mother gave us money for ice-cream sticks!" Autumn said.

I chuckled. In those days, still the time of rhetoric, most Vietnamese I knew would have launched into a speech about how Ho Chi Minh had quoted the American Revolution's Declaration of Independence and the French Revolution's Declaration of the Rights of Man and Citizen. But not Autumn. She remained true to her childhood memory.

"It was midday and hot," Autumn said. "People were fainting from the heat. We'd walked all the way—several kilometers—to Ba Dinh Square. I only had one *hao* for an ice-cream stick, but I was so thirsty! I took off my conical hat and dipped water from the public fountain and drank that."

"Your mother let you?" I asked.

"Oh no. Mother stayed at home to light the incense. I'd gone with my older sister. Oh! There was such a clamor! As soon as Uncle Ho declared independence, the pagoda and church bells rang out all across the land. And then the fragrance of incense! So many of our ancestors had died for the cause. In each house someone stayed home to light the incense and bow before the family altar so our ancestors would know that at last we were free."

"We even had Children's Tet!" Autumn added.

Centuries before, Mid-Autumn Tet—the lunar solstice—was a festival to urge the sun to return in time for spring planting. However, in recent times the festival has become a children's holiday somewhat like Halloween.

"We'd only had independence for ten or twelve days," Autumn went on. "There was still famine, and floods, too. But Uncle Ho loved children. He asked the youth to organize Children's Tet. There has never been a Children's Tet as joyful as the one in 1945. Lanterns everywhere after years of curfews and blackouts!"

Autumn gazed out the door at the blackness, then at the tiny American lamp. "Uncle Ho gathered the children of Ha Noi together in front of the Government Guest House across from the French Bank of Indochina and the Metropole Hotel. There were no adults! Only Uncle Ho and us kids and the youth who had brought us. I was so far away, I couldn't see Uncle Ho, but I could hear the loudspeaker. Uncle Ho spoke to us as if we mattered."

Autumn turned to me. "You're a Westerner, Little One. You might not understand that this gesture was revolutionary. Ours was the Confucian age, where children had the lowest status. Uncle Ho kept the good in Confucianism, but he threw away the outmoded. Never before in Viet Nam had an adult spoken to children as if they were people with value like adults." Autumn passed the peanuts around. "Once I met Uncle Ho," she added almost as an afterthought.

"Father!" Second Harvest called. "Come quick."

"Why?" Senior Uncle appeared in the doorway. He ran his finger around the collarless neck of his black pajama shirt.

"Autumn met Uncle Ho!"

"Where?" Senior Uncle asked. "In a dream?" He pulled up a stool, his eyes shining.

"This was in 1964," Autumn said, "at a meeting of four hundred women from all the provinces and ethnic groups of the North. It was the first time I had seen ethnic minority people. So many different kinds of dress! And such colors in the fabric! I was there as a representative of teachers in Ha Noi. We four hundred women were to be emulated for having the Five Attributes."

"And they were . . . ?" I said.

"First, 'Unite for Production.' Second, 'Work and Study.' Third, 'Manage Well.' " Autumn popped a peanut into her mouth. "Oh dear! What was the fourth? I forget."

" 'Labor Well,' " Second Harvest said.

"No," Autumn countered. "Labor was part of 'Unite for Production.' 'Economize!' That was it. 'Economize Time, Resources, and Energy.' "

"Yes," Second Harvest said, "and the fifth was 'Raise Your Children Well.' "

Autumn turned to me. "You weren't good enough if you had the first four attributes. To be emulated, you must think about the next generation. And you had to think about how to enlarge the Confucian idea of family to include your school, neighborhood, factory, or cooperative."

"And Uncle Ho?" I asked, passing the peanuts to Autumn.

"All the important people sat at a long table up front." She passed the dish on. "You remember when we met Nguyen thi Thap in Sai Gon. She was president of the Women's Union then. She introduced Uncle Ho. He was very far away, but I could tell by his long, white goatee that he was an old man in his seventies. In his speech, Uncle Ho said the North must help the South. We must work double, once for ourselves, once for a woman in prison in the South. That's when we began *ket nghia*—the sister provinces between the North and the South."

Autumn pushed her stool back from the table. "Then when Uncle Ho finished talking, do you know what he did? I was sitting in a middle row. There was one empty seat in the hall. It was not directly in front of me, but one over. Uncle Ho left the table of honor, walked to the middle of the hall, and took that seat!"

Senior Uncle slapped the table. "To think of it! To meet Uncle Ho in real life!"

Autumn reached across Second Harvest and touched Third Ability's shoulder. "For the next hour I sat as close to Uncle Ho as I am now to you, Nephew. I could see the age lines around his eyes."

Second Harvest covered her mouth with both hands. "What did you do?"

Autumn smiled. "I didn't hear another word of the entire program. I stared at Uncle Ho, and I tried not to breathe too loudly."

I laughed. I loved being in a society so newly independent that people could remember meeting the father of their country; I relished the way that, in these anecdotes, Ho Chi Minh always foiled the Vietnamese formalities surrounding Right Relationship and Precious Guest. But I was also aware that many stories about Ho Chi Minh had shifted from history toward legend; although I believed Autumn's story, I often wondered how many others I'd heard were apocryphal.

As he often did, Senior Uncle jabbed the air with his forefinger. "Uncle Ho taught us so much, Last Child, he taught us always to be clean in our cooking, he said we shouldn't drink out of the river anymore, but should drink rainwater, that we should boil our water. When Uncle Ho was traveling and it would be time to rest, he would inspect the kitchen where he stopped, do you see? If the kitchen wasn't clean, Uncle Ho kept walking until he found a clean kitchen."

Senior Uncle leaned toward me. He was so small that, even sitting, his head came only to my shoulder. "One time Uncle Ho was supposed to visit the soldiers at seven P.M., but instead he came at six P.M. and by the back path. The leaders had made everything on the main path beautiful in honor of Uncle Ho, can you catch my words in time? The leaders were so proud of their work. They went out to meet Uncle Ho, but Uncle Ho slipped in the back path and found a dirty kitchen. He left without eating and without meeting the pompous leaders!"

"Once I met a man from Nghe An," I said, referring to Ho Chi Minh's birthplace as I traded stories. "He was young when Uncle Ho first returned to his *que huong* after thirty years away. Ho had been all around the world, in England, France, the United States, the Soviet Union, and China. Now he was returning as president of Viet Nam. The village elders built a new road especially to welcome the president, but he insisted on taking the old one. He left those elders waiting under their fancy decorations, too!"

I passed the plate of roasted peanuts to Senior Uncle, taking some for myself and savoring their crunchy texture. "Senior Uncle," I asked, "when did people begin to call Ho Chi Minh 'Uncle Ho'?"

"After the August '45 Revolution," he said. "Uncle Ho was fifty-five years old. He was gaunt, his hair was thinning, he had a long beard, and he'd lost some of his teeth, do you see? This was before he had false teeth. But before 1945, around here, we'd never heard of Ho Chi Minh or of Nguyen the Patriot or of any of the other names Uncle Ho used. Maybe people in the city had heard of Ho Chi Minh, but not us country people."

Senior Uncle leaned close. The yellow lamplight deepened the furrows in his face. "You should follow the teachings of Uncle Ho, Little One, do you catch my words in time? He taught us how to work with the people, how we should always think of three things, *cung an, cung o, cung lam*— eat with the people, live with the people, work with the people. Do you understand?"

"Yes, Senior Uncle," I said. "I understand."

The next afternoon, I was washing my clothes at the concrete slab by the bathhouse. The river was high. Senior Uncle squatted on the dock, two toothbrushes at his side. With one he brushed his teeth; with the other he scoured his feet, paying attention to each toe. When he'd finished, he stopped by the washstand, his tin cup and the toothbrushes in hand.

"You must rinse your blouse three times to get it clean, Child, do you hear?"

"Yes, Senior Uncle."

"Do you know why I have such white teeth?"

I rotated my wrists, No, my fingers foamy with soap.

"Because I tell the truth, that's why!"

Senior Uncle straightened the bristles on one of his toothbrushes. "I'll tell you this. If you eat anything that doesn't agree with you, don't ever eat it again. Fifteen years, I haven't drunk any tea. Only boiled water or rainwater, no alcohol, no pork, just a simple diet of rice and vegetables, maybe some fish. Whenever I have food to eat, I divide it into two because— Uncle Ho taught us this—you never know if the next day you're going to be strong or weak. Always divide your food in two, Last Child, and the next day you'll have something to eat."

After I'd rinsed my clothes three times, I hung my black satin trousers and *ao ba ba* over the jute rope strung on the far side of the rectangular fishponds. Just then Second Harvest came around the corner of the house. She had finished washing her hair, which hung down to the backs of her legs. It swayed as she hurried over to me.

"Oh no, no, Little One!" Second Harvest said, setting down her comb. I could tell I was about to be corrected and struggled not to snap at her. She aligned the tips of the tails of my *ao ba ba*. "Now that, Last Child," she said, "is a beautiful clothesline!"

I had to chuckle as I carried the empty basin back to the bathhouse by the river. I set about picking up jackfruit blossoms. Whereas the female blooms stay on the tree, growing into ponderous fruit, the male blooms drop off. They looked like grey field mice lying on the ground.

"No, no, Little One!" Senior Uncle insisted. He stopped dipping water from the river to fill the earthen crocks we used for bathing and washing when the tide was low.

I paused, blossoms in hand. "Didn't Uncle Ho say, 'Eat with the people, live with the people, work with the people'?"

Senior Uncle looked at me, his eyes so wide that his blue circles of age were visible all the way around each iris. Oh no, I thought, I've used the wrong tone; I've said something terrible.

"Didn't I say it right, Senior Uncle?" I asked.

Senior Uncle walked over to me. He bent and picked up a mousy blossom and added it to the pile in my hand. His eyes twinkled. "How could I know what Ho Chi Minh said?" he replied. "I never got to meet Uncle Ho."

V I

Shadows and Smoke

You were like my shadow, I like yours
Once. Why must we live apart?

FROM "Lament of a Wife Whose
Husband Has Gone to War"
DANG TRAN CON, 1710–1745
DOAN THI DIEM, 1705–1748

"Want to learn to carry a yoke?" Ninth River asked as we stood in her garden one day in February 1990 during the dry season. Ninth River was my age. She had a sturdy build and a square face with a broad forehead. Her eyes were the color of roasted coffee beans. We had just finished harvesting two bushel baskets of squash and okra. She added red peppers as a garnish.

I slipped her bamboo shoulder pole, which was about four feet long and four inches wide, under the jute strings attached to the two baskets. A notch at each end of the yoke kept the basket strings from slipping off. I stooped under the shoulder yoke and then rose; the yoke bent, the weight of its load searing my shoulder. I staggered toward the hum of voices rising from the far side of the monkey bridge at the end of the garden.

"Look!" a ten-year-old girl with a shoulder yoke of her own said. "Last Child is carrying squash!"

"Look at her wobble," said a boy with a fishing basket shaped like a vase. "She must be drunk."

"No," said an elderly woman, who picked over the girl's squash. "It's just that Last Child never learned to walk right."

I knew Vietnamese women could carry their own body weight with a shoulder pole. This was one way women had supplied soldiers fighting the French and then later the Americans. I also knew that a jiggle-walk helped the yoke's springiness absorb the weight, but I could do no more than totter with Ninth River's load. My heart pounded; my face burned.

"Your turn," I said to Ninth River when I reached the monkey bridge. Shouldering the yoke, she crossed the palm-trunk bridge as if the loaded baskets were weightless. I teetered behind.

We reached Ninth River's house to find Second Harvest, Fifth Harmony, and Autumn weaving thatch under the milk-fruit trees. Ninth River's father was perched in the branches of a water palm in a nearby sluice, his bare feet just above the water. With a machete, he hacked off a ten-foot frond and tossed it to Sixth Rice Field on the bank.

Fifth Harmony made a downward sweeping motion with her fingers in a Vietnamese gesture, Come here. "Now's your chance," she said. "Come sew thatch for a house like mine."

I'd visited Fifth Harmony's house of bamboo and thatch, its dirt floor swept in arcing strokes. But now, as wealth in Ban Long increased, villagers built houses of wood and even brick. Ninth Sister's father was making a thatch shed to protect his bricks, which were porous and would erode easily, from monsoon rains until he could build his new house and cover its brick walls with stucco.

"When I was a child," Second Harvest said, picking up a knife with a hand-carved wooden handle, "we were too poor even to have a house of sewed thatch." She sliced the pinnules off the sturdy stem of a water-palm branch. "We built our hut from banana leaves. Ours was a house you'd make for a pig!"

Fifth Harmony split a water-palm stem. She slit one piece of the stem into slivers for thread. "I remember after the 1945 August Revolution, when Uncle Ho read the Declaration of Independence. We sat quietly together like this for the first time ever. We sewed thatch to rebuild our houses. Twenty-one days of peace! That's all we had. Then the French invaded again. They were vicious, Little One," she said, turning to me. "They beat my father so hard that he died shortly thereafter in 1946. I was thirteen."

I shuddered. I knew that in October 1945 the United States transported thirteen thousand French troops to Sai Gon. The Second French War, which started with those soldiers' arrival, was also a beginning of the American War. I folded a water-palm leaf over my stem and stitched it. Had officials in Washington read Ho Chi Minh's Declaration of Independence? Didn't they have any idea of Viet Nam's history of resistance against foreign occupation?

Fifth Harmony leaned toward me. She took a palm leaf and folded it over my split stem. "Do it like this, Little One," she instructed, tacking the leaf down with palm-stem thread. "My mother," she said, continuing with her story, "was a Mother of Soldiers. All the time I was growing up, Mother hid Resistance fighters, tended their wounds, mended their clothes."

Autumn reached for a sliver of thread. "I've read that the U.S. Army had nine soldiers in the rear to support every fighter at the front."

"We women did that work!" Second Harvest said. "No one paid us."

"And you?" I asked Fifth Harmony. I folded a second pinnule over my first, overlapping half.

"After my father's death, I worked for the Resistance and fell in love with a nurse, also with the Resistance. My mother had other marriage plans for me." Fifth Harmony covered her overbite with her long, thin fingers. "Fourth Handsome and I eloped. Mother was so angry that she beat me! Two months later, Fourth Handsome left for Regrouping in the North after the Geneva Accords. This was the time of Ngo Dinh Diem in the South."

Fifth Harmony's southern pronunciation of Diem's name sounded like "No Dinh Yiem." The Vietnamese alphabet has two *D*s, one hard, the other soft. Ngo Dinh Diem's name contains both letters. "Dinh" has the hard *D*, which is written with a bar across the stem and pronounced like the English *D*. "Diem" has the soft *D*, which is pronounced like a *Y* in the south and like a *Z* in the north.

Autumn reached for another pinnule. "The Americans brought Diem here to be prime minister at the time of the Geneva Accords in 1954," she explained, using the northern *Z* pronunciation. "Diem had been in the

United States the four years before! From 1950 to 1954 in America! How could he be a Vietnamese leader?"

"I know," I said, feeling my face flush with embarrassment and rage.

I knew CIA pilots using U.S. planes had supplied the French at Dien Bien Phu and that the U.S. had paid 75 percent of the French costs at the end of the French War. But I'd only recently learned that the United States, a participant in the Geneva Conference, had refused to sign the Accords. Simultaneous with the signing of the agreement and contrary to it, Colonel Edward Lansdale, working for the CIA, had begun intensive covert actions in both North Viet Nam and South Viet Nam to subvert the Geneva Accords.

Second Harvest folded and sewed her leaves with deliberation, her fingers stiff. "In 1956," she said, "we wrote a petition to Sai Gon to ask Diem to carry out the elections required by the Geneva Accords. He refused. Then came 1957, 1958, and 1959. Diem started his five-family units, five families forced to live together like one, with a watcher! You had to report everything to the watcher. Anyone with family in the North for Regrouping had to post a sign announcing they were Viet Cong."

"We'd never heard of Viet Cong!" Ninth River said, her blunt fingers sewing quickly.

"Who were Viet Cong?" Fifth Harmony asked. "Diem made up that word. My family had a sign because my brother, brother-in-law, and husband were in the North. So many men went north. They had to! That was part of the Geneva Accords. We thought they would return in 1956 for the elections."

Second Harvest chose another leaf. "I bought a small *xuong* and set about buying and selling on the river. When one of our soldiers was wounded, I took care of him. I began to organize other women to help. We were a small group, very small, only a few of us in 1958 and 1959, but we were growing. Then came the 10/59 Law."

"10/59?" I asked.

"October 1959," Ninth River said, tapping my thatch. "After you fold the leaf over, bring your thread up just beyond the middle."

"Any citizen," Fifth Harmony said, "who didn't report a Resistance cadre had to face the *may chem*."

"This was some kind of machine?" I said, recognizing *"may."*

Autumn set her thatch aside. In the dirt, she sketched a frame with vertical slides. *"Guillotine,"* she said in French, adding a suspended blade, a yoke to support the neck, and a basket for the head to roll into.

I sat back. "Heavens," I said. "I thought beheading stopped with the French Revolution!"

"Maybe in France," Autumn muttered.

"Everyone had to watch!" Fifth Harmony said. She tied off the last leaf of her thatch. "If you shuddered when the head hit the dirt, the Diem soldiers said you were Communist. You'd be next. The beatings— You recall meeting my older brother, the one we call Fourth?"

"Yes." I remembered how Fourth had sat on the board bed in Fifth Harmony's house, his back against the wall of plaited water-palm leaves, his white goatee resting against his chest. He stared straight ahead without blinking.

"The puppets drove nails into his ears," Fifth Harmony said. Setting aside her thatch, she slapped her head on one side, then the other. "They beat Fourth Brother until blood flowed. To this day, he doesn't know anything."

"This was before the Americans," I said, checking.

"No!" Sixth Rice Field shouted. He dragged another palm branch from the sluice. "Diem belonged to the Americans! They brought him here! By 1954, we already had American advisors in Sai Gon and in My Tho, too. This was 1959!"

"The puppets arrested my mother," Second Harvest said, "and beat her until they thought she was dead, then threw her into the morgue. But the women prisoners begged to have her corpse. She was only unconscious. The women revived her. After that, my mother couldn't walk. That's how they treated people at Phu Loi."

"We heard in the North about Phu Loi Prison," Autumn said. "We demonstrated after the guards poisoned the prisoners."

"The guards poisoned six hundred people!" Second Harvest said to me. "Don't you understand? The prisons, the beatings, the 10/59 Law, that's why we organized *Dong Khoi*."

I paused, thread in hand. "You mean the 1940 and the 1960 Uprisings both happened here?"

"Both!" Ninth River said. She leaned over and looked at my work. "Small stitches to be beautiful, Last Child."

As is the case with the 1940 Southern Uprising, American histories also seldom mention *Dong Khoi*—the 1960 Uprising. However, the 1960 Uprising is so famous among Vietnamese that at the end of the American War *Dong Khoi* became the new, official name for *Tu Do*—Freedom—Street, wartime Sai Gon's notorious bar-and-brothel strip.

Second Harvest set aside a finished layer of thatch, its leaves neatly parallel, their fringe edges even. "The people in Ben Tre rose up first, in January 1960. We had our Uprising in the early spring, when the rice was ripe."

Fifth Harmony pulled her thread through the leaves. "Whenever a Diem hamlet chief beat his brass gong," she said, "we all had to show up for a meeting. If you didn't show, you were Viet Cong. One night, the hamlet chief beat his gong for the next day's meeting. We beat gongs in response! Whoever didn't have a gong, beat an old pot."

With a palm leaf, Fifth Harmony tapped the thatch blanket in her lap as if it were a drum. "We hated living five families together! It was so hard on Fourth Brother. He couldn't remember anything because of the nails they'd driven into his head. We had to drag him hither and yon, every morning, every evening. We didn't want to live communally. We didn't want to pay Diem's massive paddy rents. That's why we beat our rice pots all night long.

"The puppets brought in more soldiers," she continued. "We called the women together to present a petition to the soldiers to stop their shooting. Rows and rows of women from villages all around here gathered in Vinh Kim. We were unarmed, three thousand of us! I stood way in the back. I could see all the conical hats, like thousands of ripples in the Eastern Sea. The soldiers shot into the crowd. They ripped off our hats. They arrested women and interrogated them. They beat us. What could we do?"

"We had to rise up!" Second Harvest said. "Anyone who had family in the North faced life in prison. The Diem soldiers were arresting our women to be their prostitutes, our children to be their soldiers. They were poisoning us in prison. And the guillotine taking our leaders, head by head. Someone had to take responsibility, or we would all be killed."

Second Harvest picked up a clean palm stem and held it like a rifle. "We made fake guns out of water-palm stems. Women did! Our men were gone, in the North for *tap ket*—Regrouping. At dusk we put on masks and, taking our fake guns, circled the puppets' outposts. We set off homemade explosives. *Boom! Boom!* Smoke and light silhouetting us and our guns. We looked like real soldiers attacking!"

She set down her make-believe rifle. "The Diem soldiers were terrified. The next day they asked us citizens, 'How many Viet Minh soldiers are there?' 'Too many to count!' we said. 'They're streaming down from the North!' we added. 'With big guns!' We never let on that it was all make-believe! The next night, we set off more explosives, women with wooden guns running this way and that through the smoke. The puppets thought a Viet Minh company had surrounded their outpost. They dropped their weapons and ran. We snatched their guns. That's how we armed ourselves!"

Second Harvest nodded toward Sixth Rice Field, who sliced leaves from a stem. "People like Sixth Rice Field who knew how to use guns taught the rest of us. But our first guns were only shadows. The Viet Minh soldiers in the North didn't come south to rescue us. We women rose up! That's how we liberated Ban Long in 1960, when the rice was ripe."

Sitting on his heels, Sixth Rice Field sketched a map of Roaring River in the dust. He drew in the communes, then added arrows pointing toward Ban Long. "We were the only liberated commune in My Tho province," he said. "People came to us from Vinh Kim, Kim Son, Phu Phong, Binh Trung because we had become the Resistance base for the province."

"But who organized all this," I asked, "if your leaders were in the North or in prison?"

Second Harvest laughed as she dropped her thatch into her lap. She gestured toward Sixth Rice Field and Fifth Harmony, her hands held out, palms open and empty.

"We did," she said.

"You?" Autumn and I spoke in unison.

Second Harvest's laugh displayed her perfect teeth. "Yes. We were the core. And Uncle Last Gust in Vinh Kim."

I felt shaken. I found myself looking at Second Harvest through a tumble of complex feelings. What was right in all this? How could I reconcile my youth of affluence and freedom with hers of squalor and persecution? What would I have done in her place? Didn't pacifism become academic when speaking out brought death by guillotine? Would I have had her courage? No, I decided with a sigh. No.

I reached for another palm leaf, thinking the feel of its smooth texture in my fingers might be soothing. "So cadre came from Ben Tre to help you?" I said into the silence. Once Nguyen thi Dinh, who is renowned in Viet Nam as leader of *Dong Khoi* in Ben Tre, had recounted for me how the Ben Tre women terrified Sai Gon soldiers at dusk by slipping through the shadows with pretend wooden guns. Under Mrs. Dinh's command, the women liberated three districts. Mrs. Dinh went on to become the Viet Cong general whose forces helped capture Sai Gon in April 1975.

Second Harvest picked up another leaf and bent it around her palm stem. "People from Ben Tre didn't help us, but we heard about their Uprising through the Market Mouth. The women buying and selling, that's all we talked about—'*Dong Khoi!*' '*Dong Khoi!*'—how our men had all been sent to the North by the Geneva Accords, but now women in Ben Tre were rising up! So we here thought, Why don't we rise up, too?"

"The Americans never did understand the power of women!" Sixth Rice Field said as he added arrows crisscrossing between the villages on his map in the dust. He drew canoes and then wavy lines to show the *xuong* darting back and forth. "Women are the ones who buy and sell. They carry our news. Women were crucial in *Dong Khoi* and in the Tet Offensive, too."

Second Harvest folded a last water-palm pinnule and stitched it. "I told you how I bought and sold from a canoe while my mother was in Phu Loi. I organized at the same time." She began to tie off the end. "But our independence in Ban Long brought such revenge! Bombs, mortars, rockets." She lifted her finished layer of thatch and held it up for me to see.

"How," she said, "can a house made of thatch like this withstand American bombs?"

VII

Heartache

Like a fairy, you glide over the bamboo foot bridge.
My sister, you are the guerrilla who keeps us alive.
Our hearts vibrate with the rhythm of your steps.

LE ANH XUAN
1940–1968

*A*s with everything else I did in Ban Long, the villagers came to watch me help harvest Eighth Light's paddy during the second visit I made to Ban Long during 1989. It exhausted me to have my every move the subject of so much interest. My patience had grown thin. This particular day, as I crossed the monkey bridge and walked along the paddy dike, I was already seething at the prospect of having half the village watch.

Eighth Light was one of the women who had dressed in camouflage during my first visit to Ban Long. She called to me from a line of women harvesting in the middle of the paddy. Second Harvest, Autumn, and the villagers lined the dike, chuckling as I stepped into the field.

"Please, Last Child!" said a bent, old woman walking with a cane. "Don't take your pretty white legs into the paddy mud."

I sunk to mid-calf in muck and slogged toward the row of women. The mud sucked me off balance.

"Did she drink rice whiskey?" the old woman asked Autumn.

The harvesters cut the tall rice with sickles, then set the grasses aside on top of the stubble. They cut and set, cut and set, moving together in a long line as if choreographed. Sickle in hand, I joined them. I bent over and grabbed the rice stalks with my left hand.

"Hold the grass farther down," Second Harvest yelled from the paddy dike.

I slid my left hand down.

"No!" she called. "Five plants at once."

I sliced the grass.

"No, no," she directed. "Cut farther up."

I set the grasses aside.

"Be sure to lay the stems even!" she instructed.

I felt like a dancing bear. I'd had days of Second Harvest telling me when to wash my feet, how many bowls of rice to eat, when to shake out my grass mat, when to climb into the canoe. I was exhausted from stumbling through a foreign language. And I was tired of being a constantly tended younger sister.

I stood up in the middle of the line of women, sickle in hand, fuming. "Didn't Uncle Ho say, 'Eat with the people, live with the people, work with the people'?"

"Yes . . . ," Second Harvest said.

"When did Uncle Ho say, 'Stand on the paddy dike, give orders'?"

Second Harvest's face wilted. I was horrified. She had only been trying to teach me in the best way she knew. In response I had done the inexcusable: I had criticized her in public, causing her to lose face.

"Forgive me," I said in Vietnamese, bowing my head. "I was unbearably rude."

The people on the paddy dike stared. The midday sun beat down, turning the grains to gold. A breeze brushed the ripe rice, which made a whispering sound. A smile eased across Second Harvest's face. "Hello?" she said in English. She tried the other phrases I'd taught her. "OK?" "Thank you?"

"Hello," I answered in English, waving. "It's OK. Thank you."

She waved back, and I bent to the work at hand. Like the women around me, I cut five plants and set them aside; cut and set, cut and set.

Out of the corner of my eye I could see Second Harvest ushering the spectators down the paddy dike. Her laughter reached back across the mud and stubble and sheaves of cut rice.

Although Second Harvest looked robust, her circulation was poor, her heart weak. My requests for stories forced her to bring alive memories she preferred to forget. This always put me in great conflict. How could I understand if I didn't ask? But how could I justify asking when my questions made her remember her mother cast onto a pile of corpses in Phu Loi prison?

During that same second visit in 1989 when I harvested rice, Second Harvest had a relentless headache. Autumn and Fifth Harmony rubbed her forehead with pungent oil, pinching the skin between her eyebrows. They rubbed the nape of her neck until the skin turned red. But the headache persisted.

We were sitting at the small table in the side room when a neighbor arrived to administer the bottle cure. He wore his hair parted way over to one side, which accented his wide temples and gave his face a triangular look. As soon as Second Harvest stretched out face down on the board bed, the healer slid her blouse up to her shoulders.

Fifth Harmony moved to the hammock, taking with her the tin lamp with the shoestring wick. She opened the lid of the burning lamp and poured kerosene into one of the small jars the practitioner had removed from a cloth bag. Then she held the jar out to him. He dipped toilet paper into the kerosene and wiped two broad lines down Second Harvest's back.

"My first husband," Fifth Harmony said to me, "knew Western medicine, but he knew our traditional medicine, too."

"I didn't realize you had two husbands," I said. "How did this come about?"

I watched the traditional doctor dip a dauber into the kerosene and light it. The air grew dense with its oily odor. With the burning dauber, he skirted the inside rim of a bottle and set the hot glass on Second Harvest's left shoulder. I cringed. The skin inside the mouth of the jar rose, turning red. Then the healer slid the jar down Second Harvest's back, releasing its vacuum with a *pop*. He repeated the procedure on Second Harvest's other shoulder. Then with the dauber, he heated all four bottles and applied them to Second Harvest's back. I shuddered, shaking my own shoulders as if that gesture could somehow remove the bottles.

"The jars must sit," Fifth Harmony explained. She set the lamp on the edge of the bed and swung her legs into the hammock. The room was dark except for the glow of the tiny lamp wick. Fifth Harmony pulled on the jute string tied to the bedpost; the hammock creaked as it began to sway. Second Harvest faced her, eyes closed.

"My first husband was Fourth Handsome," Fifth Harmony began. "Before he left for Regrouping, I took fruit and paddled a *xuong* to visit him at his unit. At that time, my husband had a good friend named Third Clarity. Once during that visit Third Clarity was sitting on the riverbank when my husband and I paddled by. We took some fruit over to him. When we left, my husband said, 'Did you notice? Third Clarity is still looking at us!' After my husband died in the war, Third Clarity thanked me for the fruit. He and I married a year later."

"So you never saw Fourth Handsome again," Autumn said. She sat next to Second Harvest on the board bed. Leaning close to the lamp wick, she sewed a button on a blouse.

"Oh, but I did!" Fifth Harmony said. "I went to see him in Tay Ninh in 1961. Third Clarity was working in the My Tho underground. He introduced me to a guide leading recruits into the jungle. We had to do everything in secret. Oh my! It was necessary to pass one place we called 'the Yawn.' So dangerous! We disguised ourselves with branches in our conical hats. When we came to a paddy, we lay down and crept on our stomachs through the rice. Sometimes we crossed only one rice field in a whole day. It took us days and days to get out of the Delta. And then the jungle! I'd never been in a jungle. We met wild boars and monkeys!

"Once," she said, tugging at the hammock string, "I dozed off in my hammock and awoke to a flock of monkeys. Mother monkeys and their babies!" She waved her left hand toward the thatch roof. "All together maybe twenty-some, the mothers swinging first and then the little ones swinging after them. And tigers! You couldn't urinate in the jungle because the tigers would find you. You had to hold your urine until your belly ached."

The healer leaned over Second Harvest's bare back with its bottles like four tree stumps. "Are you dead yet?" he whispered.

"Shhhh!" she answered. "I've never heard this story. Go on, Harmony."

"Fourth Handsome wasn't at his camp when we arrived. They'd sent him off to work in the district hospital a day's walk away. The guide left to fetch him. My husband couldn't believe I would walk so many days to search him out! It had been seven years since we'd seen each other. But there I was, sitting in a hammock just like this when he returned to the camp.

"As soon as my husband saw me, he ran toward me as I ran toward him. The day before, the men in the camp had warned me not to cry when we met. They described a woman who had come to visit from Ben Tre. When husband and wife met, they held each other and wept a mountain stream.

"Now here's a funny thing." Fifth Harmony laughed. Second Harvest opened her eyes. "When Fourth Handsome was in the North for Regrouping," Fifth Harmony continued, "he had a chance to go to Ha Noi. This was the first time he had ever been to a city. He went to the market, where he saw a bra. We had never seen such a thing here!"

Second Harvest giggled; the bottles on her back jiggled. "Oh dear!" she said. "I'm supposed to be quiet."

Fifth Harmony toyed with the jute string. "Fourth Handsome was so intrigued that he bought a bra and tucked it in his knapsack to carry down the Truong Son Trail as a present for me. But one of his comrades stole the bra! Fourth Handsome was too embarrassed to complain."

Fifth Harmony pulled the hammock string; the hammock rocked. "Fourth Handsome told me how lonely he'd been in the North during Regrouping and how hard it was walking down the Trail. He would cry at night, he was so afraid I would take another husband. But after seven years we were together again. His loneliness floated away with his tears.

"I told Fourth Handsome how I'd been the first Ban Long woman arrested because my husband was in the North for Regrouping, how the Diem puppets had given me the 'Boat Soak,' pouring soapy water down my throat, then beating me until I vomited, my tongue hanging out like a dog's. They'd given me the 'Airplane Ride,' hanging me by my wrists from the rafters, two soldiers beating me back and forth so that I flew between them. But I never ratted. I never gave the puppets a single name. I wasn't about to give them satisfaction."

The traditional doctor leaned over Second Harvest. He pressed his fingertip against the skin at the edge of one of the jars, releasing the vacuum—*pop*—and leaving behind a red circle of raised, inflamed skin. I gritted my teeth as he released the other jars—*pop, pop, pop.*

With her teeth, Autumn cut the thread on her button. "Women rarely ratted under torture," she said. "The men were more likely to squeal."

"Why?" I asked.

"Who knows?" Autumn said. "I just know that's the way it was when I was in the French prison." She turned to Fifth Harmony. "Was that true in the South?"

"True," Fifth Harmony said. She spread her fingers over her abdomen. "Women give birth. We know how to withstand pain."

The traditional doctor nodded toward Fifth Harmony. Sitting up, she reached into the cloth bag and removed a needle, which she handed to the doctor. He pierced the top layers of skin in the four red circles on Second Harvest's back; I gulped with each prick. Then, using the lighted dauber, he reapplied the vacuum jars.

"Go on, Harmony," Second Harvest said, the bottles quavering as she spoke. "You were talking about your visit with Fourth Handsome."

Fifth Harmony set her hands behind her head and lay back in the hammock made from woven jute. "The days returning from Tay Ninh felt like a war with the enemy," she said, continuing her story. "I knew my husband was returning to his work, too, and I knew he was weeping in the forest as he walked to Camp 40. Seven days after I returned home, I received a letter from Fourth Handsome telling me how he had thought of me all the time I was returning home. A month later, I received news of Fourth Handsome's death."

Her voice took on a tremor. She stared at the traditional doctor's shadow on the wall. "The letter said he died on June 6, 1961. At the time Fourth Handsome's field hospital was only three hundred meters from the front. He was in the operating room when a shell hit.

"Three days after he died, I had a dream. This was before I received the news of his death. In the dream someone called, 'Fifth Harmony! Hurry! There's someone wounded!' I ran to dress the wound and saw the face was bloody. I looked again and saw the wounded man was my husband. I awoke from the dream crying. When the letter with the news of my husband's death arrived, I already had tears in my eyes."

She paused. The hammock creaked. The bottles on Second Harvest's back were barely distinguishable in the dim light. They rose and fell with each breath. Both Second Harvest and Fifth Harmony had their eyes closed. Autumn had stopped sewing. Tears eased down her cheeks and mine.

"After I had married a second time," Fifth Harmony continued, "I had another dream about Fourth Handsome. I'd just given birth to my first child, a daughter we called White Apricot Blossom. Strange to say, but that child had the face of my first husband. Everyone said so. In my dream, I saw my first husband holding the baby in his arms, kissing and embracing her as if she were his child. I said, 'But Fourth Handsome, that's not your child. That's the child of Third Clarity.' 'No,' he answered. 'This child belongs to all three of us.'"

"And Third Clarity?" Autumn asked. "What happened to him?"

"I was able to visit Third Clarity because he was stationed nearby. On one trip, I met puppet soldiers. There were people working in a nearby rice paddy. I ran into the paddy and asked the people to take me in as one of them. They did this, and the danger passed.

"Another time I received a message that Third Clarity had been wounded. I had to wait until our youngest child was a month old before I could make the trip to visit him. Then I packed up food and medicine to take him. But along the way I met American soldiers. The Americans were always dressed funny, all these bundles hanging off their bodies. We called them 'clowns.' The clowns I met were applying red and blue paint to their faces. And making such a racket! I dropped the food and medicine I was carrying for Third Clarity into a pond. That visit I arrived empty-handed."

The healer once again leaned over Second Harvest and, with his fingertip, released the vacuum jars. The sounds were explosive, like rifle fire. He wiped away the small slits of blood that had appeared and then pulled down Second Harvest's blouse.

Second Harvest stretched her shoulder muscles. "Thank you," she said. "My headache's gone."

"So was Third Clarity also killed in battle?" Autumn asked as the doctor left to wash his hands.

"No," Fifth Harmony said. "In 1974, he received permission from his unit to return home and care for his elderly parents. He'd been seriously injured—forty-six wounds!—and given up for dead. The brothers hadn't even taken him to the medical center. They kept him in a hammock, but they were able to treat his wounds. When Third Clarity returned to Ban Long, the Peasants' Association gave him five *cong* of deserted paddy land."

Fifth Harmony began to wipe one of the bottles with a soft rag. "Eighth Youth was another one of our soldiers," she continued. "He'd received permission to farm this land, but then he defected to the puppets' 'Open Arms Program.' That's how Third Clarity came to have the land. But Eighth Youth wanted the land back. He lay in wait, and when my husband and I were working the field at night—we had to because of the helicopters—Eighth

Youth came out and stood on the land. When Third Clarity went up to speak to him, Eighth Youth struck my husband in the face with a hoe."

She replaced the bottles in the cloth sack. "I screamed, 'You've killed Third Clarity!' 'Oh no,' Eighth Youth said in a jeering voice, 'your husband was injured. He just didn't make it to the first aid station in time.' Eighth Youth was arrested and sentenced." Fifth Harmony wiped the needle and added it and the dauber to the sack. "I'd been raised to think my husband and I would be together from the moment we married. But I never did live with either husband."

"There were so many women like that," Second Harvest said, sitting up. "We gave up our husbands, we gave up our children. We bent with the war."

"And we were bent by it," Fifth Harmony said, closing the drawstring on the cloth sack.

Vietnamese often package their favorite snacks in banana leaves, which they peel back layer by layer. Moving through the stories in Ban Long had the same feeling of layers unfolding. This was particularly true of the process by which I learned about "giving up children."

One day in early 1990, we went by *xuong* down Senior Uncle's creek, across Roaring River and up another creek to the village of Huu Dao, also in Chau Thanh district. There we stopped at the house of Eighth Senior Uncle, who was picking pole beans when we arrived.

"I call him 'Father,' " Second Harvest said, introducing us. "He took me in when I was a child, and then again in 1954 and then again after *Dong Khoi* in 1960. Plus so many times during the American War."

In his mid-seventies, Eighth Senior Uncle was a balding man, who wore black peasant pajamas. After we'd picked out the beans, he led us inside his stucco house. We sat at a small, round table in the corner. Sunlight slipping through an oval window lit up the fine hairs on Eighth Senior Uncle's head, creating an aura about him.

"Whenever I met hardship," Second Harvest continued, "this family gave me everything as if I were their child. After my first son was born, they fed me so I could nurse him, and then they raised my baby while I continued working."

"They raised Longevity?" I said, incredulous. Second Harvest's older son was eighteen. Tall and slim, he had perfect teeth like his mother; unlike her, he could bend his fingers back to his wrist as if he were a Cambodian dancer.

"How could I stand to raise my child?" Second Harvest said, turning to me, her brow furrowed. "Ours was no world for children! I had to change it, for my son's future." She nodded at Eighth Senior Uncle. "That's why when Longevity was three months old, I gave him to this family to raise. For three years, from 1972 until peace came in April 1975, I was never sure whether my son was alive."

I later learned that many women gave up their children to work for the Revolution. Once in Sai Gon, I talked for some hours with Nguyen thi Ngoc Dung, the Provisional Revolutionary Government's representative to the Joint Commission responsible for implementing the Paris Peace Accords in 1973. After the war, Mrs. Dung was Viet Nam's ambassador to the United Nations. Born in My Tho, she had joined the Resistance base in Ban Long after *Dong Khoi.* She'd given her son to relatives to raise in 1952, when he was two, and did not see him again for twenty-three years; by then, in April 1975, her son was himself the father of a two-year-old.

Another time I visited women who had lived in the Cu Chi tunnels, a revolutionary base twenty-five miles northeast of Sai Gon. Near a major American compound, the Cu Chi tunnels included a two-hundred-kilometer web with underground classrooms, meeting rooms, a smoke-tight kitchen vented into a nearby river, and a field hospital. In an effort to capture Cu Chi, the American military turned the area into the most bombed, defoliated, and gassed region in the history of combat.

The Cu Chi women had never before met an American. They were reticent, with the exception of Sixth Candy, who was in her mid-seventies. Sixth Candy led me through a tunnel that had been enlarged to accommodate Western visitors and then into a meeting room dug into the earth, its roof of camouflaging thatch only a foot above the ground. She invited me to sit at the table made of lashed bamboo. Opening her basket, Sixth Candy set out rice cakes, peanuts, bananas, and hard candies.

During the war, Sixth Candy had supplied the men and women defending the Cu Chi tunnels. This was among the war's most dangerous missions because she had to cross through heavily contested territory. Like other women, she smuggled rice and ammunition in her yoked baskets, but only Sixth Candy was famous for tucking sweets for the soldiers into the pocket of her white *ao ba ba.*

Now, layer by layer, Sixth Candy unfolded the steamed banana-leaf wrapping on a rice cake. As she began to tell her story, the other women leaned forward. Only Third Fragrance, a young woman who'd come with me from Sai Gon, turned away. She'd been a sunny companion, but now her expression turned dour.

"My son was only a few months old," Sixth Candy said as she offered me the rice cake, green from hours steaming inside the banana leaves. "I gave him to a cousin to raise. My breasts were so full of milk! I could stand that pain and even the pain of separation. But to think about my son in-heriting my life— That pain was unbearable."

She set before me a pile of peanuts and added a toffee candy. "I said to my cousin, 'Say I am dead! For my son's safety, don't say that I died for freedom. Just say I'm dead. My son must never miss his mother, but I will always miss him.'" As Sixth Candy spoke, a tear slid over the dark wrinkles on her cheek, but her voice remained steady. I felt my throat catch. Third Fragrance wept openly.

Later, as we were leaving, I put my arm around Third Fragrance's shoulders.

"I never understood," she said, staring at the camouflaging thatch.

"Understood . . . ?" I asked.

"During the war, my mother gave me up to cousins in Sai Gon. All through my childhood, I thought my father and mother were dead. Then when I was fourteen my cousins decided I was old enough to know about my family. They told me my parents were with the revolutionaries in the jungle. I was furious! I hated my mother for abandoning me. When peace came, I met my mother. I was sixteen. For years I was silent and sullen."

Third Fragrance rotated her watch back and forth across her wrist. She watched a butterfly flutter through trees thriving in what had been the Cu Chi wasteland. "Now," she said, "I'm a mother raising a daughter and a son. You'd think I would understand a mother's feelings. But only this af-ternoon while listening to Sixth Candy did I finally understand my mother's sacrifice."

For my Ban Long visits, I would fly with Autumn from Ha Noi to Sai Gon. Second Harvest then met us at the airport; we would drive to My Tho and, from there, to Vinh Kim, where Vigor and Sixth Rice Field would meet us in Senior Uncle's *xuong*. At the end of each visit, we reversed the process, leaving Ban Long by canoe before dawn so that I could catch the afternoon flight from Sai Gon to Bangkok and on to the States.

At the end of that second 1989 visit, we arrived in Sai Gon with extra time before the Bangkok flight and stopped off at the Women's Union office, an old French villa that had been General William Westmoreland's wartime residence. In one of the ironies of the war, Nguyen thi Dinh, the woman who had led the *Dong Khoi* uprising in Ben Tre province in 1960 and who then rose through the Viet Cong ranks to become one of the generals to capture Sai Gon, was now president of the Women's Union. When she was in Sai Gon, Mme Dinh received distinguished visitors in the drawing room that had formerly been General Westmoreland's.

But Second Harvest, Autumn, and I were ordinary visitors from the countryside. We ducked into a side building once used by General Westmoreland's servants. Second Harvest went to lie down while I chatted with Autumn. When Autumn was called away, I wrote thank-you notes until she returned to fetch me for the airport. Just then, I chanced to look out the window and saw two men loading a stretcher into a battered Volkswagen bus with a whirling blue ambulance light on top. Closing the rear door, the attendants drove out the gate, their light flashing.

Autumn placed her hand on my forearm as the blue light receded into Sai Gon traffic. "Second Harvest collapsed," she said. "She's unconscious. There was nothing you could do."

My palms went hollow. Second Harvest had a weak heart; I'd taken the Red Cross course in cardiopulmonary resuscitation. There *was* something I could have done.

"We didn't want you to worry," Autumn said.

I was furious at myself for the extra pressures I'd caused but equally angry at the Vietnamese need to take care of me, which added to the stress. I stared at my hands, at the notes I'd written, at their powerless words. Had I caused Second Harvest's collapse? Was this the price of my questions? What could I do now? My visa would run out in hours; there was no chance of extending. And even if I could extend, what use would that be? My staying would only increase the strain on Second Harvest. It was devastating to realize I could best help by leaving.

"We'd better go," Autumn said, helping me gather up my papers.

I opened my shoulder bag and let her stuff the notes inside. The U.S.

embargo was in full force. I wouldn't be able to phone. A letter with news from Autumn or Fifth Harmony would take six weeks. I closed the bag and slung it over my shoulder. I who had wanted to bridge the gulf between us with something positive had left behind confusion and pain. I could see nothing to do but retreat to my dilapidated farm in the hills of Ohio.

VIII

Demise of the Snake

Strive at the front and at the rear
All compatriots together in one will.
Production and combat are one thrust,
Our struggle will end in triumph!

FROM "Tet Message,
Year of the Horse, 1966"
HO CHI MINH
1890–1969

*F*or two months I fretted, waiting for news from Autumn. Eventually a letter came, telling me of Second Harvest's recovery from a sudden drop in blood pressure. And so with relief and caution I returned to Ban Long in late January 1990 for Tet, the Lunar New Year at the end of the Year of the Snake and the beginning of the Year of the Horse. Tet is the first day of spring in the lunar calendar; it falls between January 21 and February 19.

As we crossed the last monkey bridge to Senior Uncle's house, he came running, the tails of his black *ao ba ba* flapping, his string of keys jouncing.

Small Dog circled his feet, dancing. "Just think!" Senior Uncle said. "All my daughters here for Tet!!"

Fifth Harmony, who'd gone on ahead, swept jackfruit blossoms off the picnic table by the creek. She set out bowls and chopsticks, then a steaming pot of rice as she invited us to sit down.

A man with mud caked on his bare legs stood by the kitchen doorway. I recognized him from my first visit in 1987. His name was Third Success. "Helicopter!" Third Success had shouted then when the women in camouflage reached the middle of Roaring River. Now, he stared at me with his good eye. I felt intensely uncomfortable. He buttoned and unbuttoned his shirt; he tugged on his shirttails. He ran his muddy hands through his hair.

"Rice bowls on the table!" Third Success yelled. "Rice bowls."

"Go home and rest now, Child," Fifth Harmony said. Her soft voice was commanding; her use of "Child" to an adult asserted authority. I could sense her embarrassment, but what made me feel particularly sad was the need she had for everything to be perfect.

"No bad Third Success!" the man said, circling the table, his arms at full length as if groping through darkness. He moved the fish sauce from the center of the table to the end where I sat. "No, no. Only good Third Success!"

"Speak quietly, Child," Second Harvest said, sucking in her breath. "It's time to go home."

Third Success circled again. This time he reached over my shoulder and slid a dish of tiny shrimp close to my rice bowl; as he did so, I caught the stinging odor of rice whiskey. So, I thought, this isn't a man with brain damage; it's just that Tet toasts have already started.

Third Success circled a third time. "I'm a bomb crater!" he called into my ear. "B-52 almost killed me. Jumbled my head." He slapped his white eye. "A little farther over— Dead already!"

"Quiet now, Child." Second Harvest grasped Third Success's wrist.

He lowered his voice. "I was born in the Year of the Horse."

"So was I, Younger Brother," I said, relieved that we could at last engage each other, "but surely I was born twelve years before you. If you're a horse, yours must be a free spirit."

"The helicopter—" Third Success hit his eye with his fist. "—terrible. Shooting at me, black men and white men, faces black with soot, bodies covered with leaves like a tree, huge men like huge trees, terrible, terrible."

"Yes," I said, feeling the fear still alive in him come alive in me.

"I was twelve." Third Success looked down at Small Dog, who licked the mud caked on his ankles. "The dog knows me! See how her tail wags? That's because I come here every night to sleep with the old man."

"Then you save Senior Uncle from loneliness," I said.

"Yes." With his toes Third Success petted Small Dog. "Older Sister . . ." He looked at me, his white eye like a searchlight. "If I get a chicken—a plump chicken—and give it to you, will you raise it on your farm in America?"

The tide was out. Since it was dry season, no rains upstream in Cambodia fed the creek, which dropped once a day to a trough of mud with a trickle of water in the bottom. I squatted on the concrete slab by the bathhouse, scouring rice with my knuckles as if scrubbing clothes. I poured out the starchy rinse water with its floating bugs and husks, then reached into the earthen crock for water Second Harvest had dipped at high tide.

I heard a great slosh as Third Success, moving now with the confidence of a man possessing all his wits, plunged into the bomb crater near the weir Senior Uncle had built. At high tide the creek flowed over the weir into the crater; when the water receded, it left behind fish, shrimp, and crayfish flopping in the bottom. Knee-deep in mud, Third Success reached into the silt and caught a fish with his bare hands; he dropped his catch into a basket tied around his waist.

"Come on in!" Third Success called to Third Ability.

"I don't know . . ." Third Ability peered at Third Success from the edge of the crater. He smoothed his blue shorts, which were new for Tet, and wiggled his toes on the clean, firm earth. Then, clasping a water-palm branch, he stepped sideways down the bank until he stood alongside Third Success. Grasping another palm, he bent to touch the mud.

Third Success plunged ahead. Each step released a burbling sound and the smell of swamp gas; the mud rippled as tiny shrimp slithered away. Ability followed, one hand grasping a water palm. He stopped to watch two men walking along opposite sides of the creek bed. Each man dangled a cloth tied to the end of a long pole. The flock of ducks they tended waddled by, bills drilling the muck.

"Both hands into the mud, Son!" Second Harvest said, setting a basin of freshly washed clothes on the crater rim. She arched her palms and, spreading her fingers so that her hands looked like small cages, bent as if to touch her toes. "Like this!"

Ability watched Third Success; he glanced at the ducks. Releasing the water palm, he reached with both hands, then straightened, his grin wide.

"Look!" He held up a crayfish. Mud from his squirming catch slid down his forearm.

As always, the tide determined life. Since the tide was high at night that visit, the Tet Market at Vinh Kim was busiest late in the day, when those who traveled by canoe could shop. By the time we headed downstream toward Vinh Kim, the gold light of evening had already spread over Roaring River.

"In 1944, when I was nine," Autumn said, trailing her fingers in the river as we came in sight of Forever Silent Bridge, "the Japanese occupied Ha Noi. The Americans were bombing us, so the Tet Market had to be at night like this. I went with my mother. Then the air raid siren sounded! Everything went dark—no moon and a strange street. We didn't know which direction to turn. But this is so different! The lights, everything festive!"

Canoes so jammed the wharf that Vigor tied our *xuong* at a friend's store. Like wartime guerrillas, we slipped from the river into the house, felt our way through a lumber warehouse, and then emerged into Vinh Kim Market. I hung back as Second Harvest moved from stall to stall, buying Tet specialties. The market twinkled with tiny American lamps burning in each stall. Colored lights blinked over the doorway to a café selling sweet cakes and orange soda in old Coke bottles. A cassette recorder played Vietnamese rock music at full volume.

"Buy some bitter cucumbers!" an old woman with one tooth said to me.

"Take this delicacy off my hands!" called a man in an Adidas T-shirt. He held aloft a boar's head.

"Firecrackers! Hurry! Hurry!! Buy, buy!" shouted a youth in a green baseball cap. He twirled, and the strings of pink firecrackers he carried swirled around him.

I turned and followed a boy leading a nanny goat on a string. Three baby goats sauntered after the nanny. One of the baby goats stepped into a store that sold baskets, onions, garlic, and spices. The kid nipped an onion, then a garlic. He nosed a tier of baskets, tumbling them.

"Watch out!" an ice-cream vendor in a black fedora yelled at the owner. He jangled his bell in warning.

The basket-and-spice vendor looked up from her money bag. "*Chet roi!*—Dead already!" she muttered. Flapping her arms, she dashed after the goat, her gold bracelets jangling. The little brown kid clicked his heels and pranced deeper amidst the teetering baskets.

"*Thoi!*—Enough!" the vendor shouted.

For years I'd had goats at home in Ohio. I ducked down the far aisle, nabbed the kid by the neck, and spun his rump; together the goat and I cavorted out of the shop.

"Did you see that?!" a vendor asked the women clustered around her tub of limp fish.

I swatted the goat's rear. "Off you go," I said in Vietnamese. The kid frolicked off after his mother; I followed at a more sedate pace.

"Little One!" Second Harvest called from the crowded lane. She took my hand and led me back to our *xuong*. "I was worried! Where on earth were you?"

"Playing farmhand," I told her as I moved toward the stern. There, at Vigor's feet, in the place I normally sat, rested a duck and a string of firecrackers; near them lay the biggest firecracker I had ever seen.

The ice-cream vendor pushed his bicycle onto a junk tied near us. "There's the lady I saw herding the goat," he said, retrieving an ice-cream stick from the tin box lashed to his back bicycle fender. He handed it to a woman, who held a branch of yellow apricot flowers. The woman stared at me.

"Look at that hair," the woman said. "She must be overseas Vietnamese."

The ice-cream vendor helped himself to an ice-cream stick. "Probably returning home to eat Tet," he said.

Wherever they are, if possible, Vietnamese return for Tet to their *que huong*—their ancestral home—to tend their ancestors' graves and visit family. The Vietnamese expression *an Tet*—"eat Tet"— couldn't be more descriptive. At Senior Uncle's, we compressed into a few days the weeks that villagers usually spent preparing Tet delicacies. There were candies to make and bitter cucumbers to tend to. And there was the duck.

The morning of Tet Eve, we sat on our heels on the concrete washing slab. I felt apprehension and revulsion as I watched Autumn sharpen a cleaver on the rim of an overturned china plate. I stood ready with a pot of boiling water. Autumn held open the duck's bill while Second Harvest poured cool water from the earthenware crock down the throat so the duck's blood would run easily. With a whack, she cut the neck, which she bent, emptying the blood into a bowl. Turning my face away, I poured the boiling water over the limp duck. The air turned heavy with the odor of hot feathers.

"I remember the week before Tet in the Year of the Goat, 1967," Autumn said to Second Harvest, who was stuffing a bitter cucumber with fish paste. The vegetable, a Tet specialty, looked like an Ohio cucumber with warts. "The school where I taught had been evacuated to a town outside Ha Noi. I had a duck half finished like this one when the siren wailed. The authorities cut the electricity. Blackness! I couldn't boil any more water! And the bombs were coming!"

Autumn began to pluck. "My hands were so matted with feathers that I looked part duck! I picked up the duck and ran to the shelter. I'll never forget the stench of feathers inside that bunker."

She flicked her knife blade against the rim of the water urn; then she slit the duck's belly, pulled out the esophagus, and flung it into the river mud. She cleaned the intestines and gizzard with salt and tossed them into the soup kettle. "We squatted like this in the bunker. The Americans were so far up in the sky, what did they know about our customs? They pushed buttons and dropped bombs. Then they flew away to fancy hotels in Thailand."

Second Harvest picked up a cucumber which, stuffed, looked like a loaded bomber; with a shallot green she tied the cucumber shut. " 'Music from Thailand,' " she said. "That's what we called the Americans' bombers."

"Rooom, roooom, rooom." Autumn whacked a drumstick with her cleaver; bones shattered. "In the North, we had airplanes and missiles and artillery. Whenever I heard that *rooom roooom*, I knew our planes were chasing the Americans away."

Second Harvest set the wrapped cucumber in a pot. "But here we could only squat together and bear the bombs."

"I know," Autumn said, tossing fragments from the drumstick into the soup kettle. She paused, and the two women faced each other, their hands momentarily idle. "Not to have any defense against B-52s," Autumn said. "It's beyond my imagination."

It was one thing to make the traditional dishes—duck soup with turnips, pickled shallots, salted Chinese cabbage, pork boiled in coconut milk, fish soaked in molasses, stuffed bitter cucumbers, and the tiny shrimp Third Success and Third Ability had caught in the bomb crater. But it was quite another to prepare traditional confections. Perhaps it was the rhythm of so many hours slicing and stirring, but there was something particularly intimate about making pineapple candy.

Second Harvest set the ingredients on the picnic table. "Here's what you need, Last Child," she instructed. "Three medium pineapples to two rice bowls of sugar to two rice bowls of peanuts."

"Don't forget the orange rind," Fifth Harmony said.

Second Harvest picked up a pineapple and a cleaver. She had the blunt, powerful hands of a farmer. "First, top the pineapple. Cut off the bottom and shave the rind."

"But thinner than that, Younger Sister," Fifth Harmony said to Second Harvest. Fifth Harmony's fingers were long and thin like those of a seamstress.

Second Harvest looked at me. "You think you're the one who's bossed," she said. "See? Fifth Harmony will always be my older sister and my teacher. She taught me midwifery."

"Really?" Autumn quartered her pineapple and began to slice it into the basin between us.

"Fearless Second Harvest . . ." Fifth Harmony's voice turned playful. Rotating a pineapple in her palm, she removed the eyes in long V-shaped slivers. "I took her along when Seventh Sister's labor started. The baby was crowning. I was about to catch the child when I turned to Second Harvest. She was gone!"

"Thinner slices, Little One," Second Harvest said to me.

"You left?" I countered, not about to let Second Harvest miss her turn at being younger sister.

Second Harvest's eyes twinkled. "Not exactly!"

"She'd collapsed on the floor," Fifth Harmony said, "with her eyes rolled back into her head."

"Really?!" Autumn laughed.

"I wasn't married then," Second Harvest said. She cupped her hands as if catching a newborn. "I didn't know how babies came, I saw that baby coming. Oh! Shocking!"

"Our hero fallen," Fifth Harmony teased.

Second Harvest laughed; her cheeks took on a rosy hue like prize milk fruit. "I'll tell you another funny story, from several years later," she said, picking her pineapple up again. She finished slicing. "Sixth Peach Blossom was in labor when our scouts warned that the Americans were coming. The helicopters landed, but by then the baby had started to crown. I caught the child, cut the cord, and gave the baby to Sixth Blossom. I was about to flee. They'd posted a reward for me dead or alive!"

Second Harvest shaved the rind off another fruit. "But then I noticed Sixth Sister's belly was still huge. What should I do? There had to be a twin inside. By now I could hear the Americans shouting. I was catching the second baby's head, like this"—she cradled the wet pineapple—"when two GIs entered. The first GI was black. They always sent the black soldiers first to trigger our traps. The black man took one look at that baby coming out. His skin turned as white as yours, Little One! The white man fled first. The black man fled after him."

I laughed and popped a nubbin of pineapple into my mouth. Its sweetness startled me. "Now what's this about a reward?" I asked.

"You know Forever Silent Bridge," Fifth Harmony said. "The puppet troops were terrified to cross over from their base at Vinh Kim because Second Sense controlled the territory on the other side."

"Who's Second Sense?" Autumn asked.

Second Harvest grinned. "Me."

Senior Uncle came around the corner of the house. "She had an extra sense, like an extra set of eyes," he said, lifting the bamboo ladder off the fresh water urns and propping it against a jackfruit tree. He climbed up and scraped a wormy spot out of a young jackfruit. "She was like a mosquito inside the enemy's sleeping net, do you understand? They knew she was there, but they couldn't catch her. Not even with their huge reward!"

Fifth Harmony poured sugar into the basin. "Little One, you remember piasters from when you lived in the South." She turned to Autumn. "Five hundred thousand piasters, Autumn. It was a fortune! A teacher's salary for more than a hundred years. Enough money to marry off over a hundred brides from wealthy families. Still, no one fingered Second Harvest."

"This is true, Little One," Second Harvest said, touching my fingers. Flecks of gold pineapple freckled our hands. "Once, I was among villagers the puppet soldiers had rounded up. I was terrified! This is it, I thought. 'Where is Second Sense?' the puppets demanded. 'Take us to her, you'll win the reward!' I was standing there among the villagers when the puppet soldier said that. But no one betrayed me."

"This must have been the Phoenix Program," I said, referring to a joint effort between the South Vietnamese government and the CIA to "neutral-ize" the Viet Cong infrastructure largely through assassinations.

"I don't know what you Americans called it," Second Harvest said. "I only know there were different rewards, beginning with twenty-five thousand piasters for people they didn't care much about. The puppets offered ten thousand piasters for an old photograph of me, but to get the five hundred thousand, villagers had to bring me in alive. The people were told that if they had to shoot me, they were to wound me, but if they killed me by mistake, they were to bring back the corpse. The women in the strategic hamlets knew there was a reward for me. They lit tiny lamps, the ones we call 'American lamps,' as a signal when it was dangerous for me to enter."

"But why did they put such a price on your head?" I asked. I couldn't imagine anyone wanting Second Harvest dead.

"I carried a rifle," Second Harvest said, "and I shot that rifle, but I'll tell you the truth, Last Child. I never killed anyone." She sliced another pineapple. "I'll tell you why they posted such a reward. Because I fought with my mouth. That's what made me effective: what I had to say, the truths I told.

"Once," Second Harvest continued, "I ducked into Sixth Spring's house. This was inside the puppets' strategic hamlet. Terror! Puppet soldiers sat on the bed! Sixth Spring wasn't home. Her four-year-old son was there. I don't know how he knew to do this, but he cried out, '*Ma!*' He ran over and hugged my knees. Such a little child. How did he know to do that? No one had taught him. He saved my life."

"Another time when I was at Sixth Spring's house, the puppet soldiers were about to arrest me. Sixth Spring wasn't there that time, either. All four of her children clung to my trousers. '*Ma, Ma!*' they cried. 'Don't leave us!'

" 'Where's your father?' the puppets asked. The oldest boy was seven. 'Dead and buried under the earth,' he said. He pleaded with the puppets. 'If you arrest our mother, who will take care of us?' "

Senior Uncle leaned over the side of his ladder to examine another young jackfruit. "If any of those children had called her 'Aunt Second Sense' or 'Aunt Second Harvest,' " he said, "she'd be dead now. We never taught the children what to say. They just knew."

Fifth Harmony wiped her hands and gave the towel to Autumn. "Once the puppets thought they'd captured Second Harvest," she said. "There was this journalist named Phuong who'd come down from the Central Women's Union, from Ha Noi. She was captured and killed, her body turned in for the bounty."

"Phuong!" Autumn dropped the towel. She stared at Second Harvest. "I knew Phuong by her photo. I never thought of it until now, but you do look like her, the same round face and full lips."

"Phuong and I had spent the day working together," Second Harvest said. "We were near the American base at Binh Duc and were to work together the next day, too. I told Phuong she should cross over to Ban Long for safety, but she said, 'No, I'll sleep here,' so I went on to Ban Long. The puppets arrested Phuong that night. When she resisted arrest, they killed her, thinking she was me."

Second Harvest's face sagged and her voice took on a bitter cast. "The puppets put out the word that I was dead. Third Pear heard about my death from Tenth Treasure while she was in Vinh Kim Market picking up medicines. Third Pear paddled back to Ban Long to give my mother the news. My mother cried herself to exhaustion."

"One of the old women told me," Fifth Harmony said. "I cried and cried. Then I decided to go look at the body—the puppets had put it on display—just to be sure. I checked the teeth and knew it wasn't Second Harvest."

"I refused to believe the news," Senior Uncle said, climbing off his ladder, which he set back on the fresh water urns. "I knew the puppets couldn't catch Second Harvest."

Second Harvest wiped her hands on a cloth. Settling into the hammock strung between two jackfruit trees, she stared up at the small fruit. "I've never before told those stories," she said, speaking softly, as if to the air. "Who would want to think back on those times?"

Even at mid-morning, the inside of the tar-paper kitchen was dark as night. Fifth Harmony made fires in two earthenware pits. She twisted dried water-palm leaves and lit them with the wick of the oil lamp, then tucked the flaming leaves under the kindling. She reached for two woks.

Handing me chopsticks, she poured peanuts into the woks. The nuts crackled as, roasting, they gave off their rich aroma. Soon she added the sugared pineapple. "When that boils," she said, shaking juice from the basin, "we'll begin to stir." Stir we did. For hours we sat on our heels, side by side on the dirt floor, the flames licking our wrists and our knees, the smell of wood smoke and hot, sugary pineapple twirling in the air.

"Do you cook this way in Ohio?" Fifth Harmony asked.

I was taken aback. How could I cross over the differences? I described a gas and electric stove and explained how a refrigerator cut down trips to market.

Fifth Harmony rapped her chopsticks against the wok, then continued stirring. "It takes me two hours to paddle to Vinh Kim Market, two hours to paddle back depending on the current, so I don't go to market often. That's why we catch fish from the river and raise our own rice. Just the cooking is so much work—gather the dying palm branches, set them to dry, stack them in the wood shed, carry them to the kitchen, make the fire, tend the fire." She laughed, rubbing her sleeve against her eyes. "Wipe away smoke tears!"

Autumn entered with a live catfish. She set it on the dirt floor and, reaching for a water-palm stump, whacked the fish. She rolled it in the ashes of an unused fire pit. "Improves the cleanliness," she said, taking the fish to the dock, where she cleaned it.

The pineapple bubbled, sputtering as we stirred; the conversation turned once again to midwifery. "I've lost count of the number of young people who call me *Ma*," Fifth Harmony said, adding orange rind, a pinch of salt, and two packets of vanilla to each wok. "Long ago I began delivering my babies' babies." She looked out the doorway into the daylight at Ability, who sat high in the jackfruit branches, watching the neighbor across the creek bathe his two little boys in the creek. "Some of the babies I delivered after they sprayed Agent Orange would frighten you."

"I know," I said, feeling a soberness that is never too distant begin to close in. "In 1980, I worked in a camp hospital for Boat People. A lot of them came from Tien Giang. We had one stillborn with two heads. The carpenters had to design a special coffin."

"Once," Fifth Harmony said, "I delivered a baby as big as a calf but with a face like an owl. He took a few breaths and died. The mother wanted to hold the child, but I lied and said he was too weak. It was better later to tell her the child had died. And there was a child with extra fingers and toes and a face with only a mouth. I kept the mother away, but the husband saw the child. He was so frightened that he couldn't sleep for months."

As Fifth Harmony spoke, I remembered standing in the specimen room of the major gynecological hospital in Sai Gon. This was in 1983. The smell of formaldehyde tinged the air. In the dim light I could make out glass crocks lining each wall, floor to ceiling, wall to wall, row upon grey row. Each crock cradled a full-term baby. One infant had four arms, another a bowl in place of her cranium, a third a face on his abdomen, a fourth his navel protruding from his forehead.

All the babies had been born in the early 1980s to women from provinces that had been heavily sprayed with Agent Orange. A Vietnamese doctor opened the wooden shutters. Sunlight flowed in, transforming the crocks with their silver liquid into mirrors that shimmered, row upon row, each mirror reflecting my own image back to me. To this day I can't look in a mirror without shrinking at the memory of those bottle babies.

The pineapple spattered, stinging my wrist. I jumped back and watched as Fifth Harmony lifted a gob of thickening candy. It slid off her chopsticks. "Not ready yet," she said. She resumed stirring. "I was responsible for burying our dead," she whispered. "They brought the dead to my house, sometimes missing a hand, sometimes a leg blown off at the knee. At the beginning I was so frightened. Once some of the brothers, about twenty of them, paddled into a trap and triggered an underwater mine near Vinh Kim. By the time the dead were brought here, they were bloated and bleached and shedding their skins. Everyone fled at the sight."

Fifth Harmony added another pinch of salt. "I couldn't handle it either. We had to leave the corpses and come back at midnight, when it was too dark to see the faces. What an awful night. We were burying all night long, I and the others digging, the carpenters hammering."

"Have you ever gotten over the shock?" I asked, testing the candy's thickness.

"You go on," she said. "You teach yourself not to think about it. And you pray to your ancestors."

The fire sputtered. Fifth Harmony added dried coconut husks; the flames leapt up, illuminating the hollow in her cheek. Her voice lightened. "From when I was very small I've been afraid of ghosts," she said. "I was always skittery about passing the graveyard. After that night burying bodies without skins, I always carried a torch of dried water-palm branches at night. Whenever I neared the graveyard, I'd protect myself by lighting the torch and whispering 'Midwife! Midwife!!' "

I chuckled as I scooped a dollop of pineapple and held it over the wok. It eased back into the bubbling mass.

"Almost," Fifth Harmony said, testing hers. She slid her wok onto the dirt floor. With her chopsticks, she waved a snippet of candy in the air. "Autumn!" she called, "we're ready to test."

Soon Autumn stood in the doorway, the bright light behind her creating a halo effect. I wiped my eyes on my sleeve and set my wok next to Fifth Harmony's.

"For years none of us had this candy," Autumn said, waiting by the woks. "Not even in the North. My children didn't know about such things. The first time we made candy was Tet in the Year of the Buffalo, 1973, after the U.S. bombing ended. Everything was so expensive that I made only enough so my children would know our custom."

"Take a taste," Fifth Harmony said, offering us each a pinch. The candy was superb—the sharp sweetness of pineapple textured with peanuts and tempered with orange rind and the touch of wood smoke.

"I couldn't keep my kids from tasting," Autumn said, laughing as she took another sample. "By the time we'd finished testing the candy, it was half gone."

That evening, we filled tiny plates with delicacies we'd prepared—the duck soup, bitter cucumbers, sautéed shrimp, catfish, slivered coconut, pressed bananas, and pineapple candy. We placed the plates in layers on the three altars. By late Tet Eve, everything was ready. Ability and I sat at the table in the large room, watching Senior Uncle fix the battery pack he'd improvised for the radio he'd had since 1945. Second Harvest had stretched out on the bed. We waited for midnight, when Vigor would light the firecrackers to welcome the ancestors home.

"In the old days," Senior Uncle said, "we would wait to hear Uncle Ho read his Tet poem at midnight."

Somewhere in the distance, a firecracker exploded. Ability squirmed, restless.

"Why can't they wait?" Senior Uncle complained, fiddling with the tuner. "We would gather around the radio like this, can you understand, Child? The old men wept to hear Uncle Ho's voice because they knew they would never live to meet him."

"People even listened to Uncle Ho in the puppets' strategic hamlet," Second Harvest said. She turned onto her side and pulled a cloth bag under her ear like a pillow. "One woman would listen with her ear against the radio like this, so the puppet soldiers wouldn't know. Then she whispered the poem to the rest of us."

" 'Even more than the beauty of Spring,' " Senior Uncle recited, " 'News of triumph lightens the Land! Northerners, Southerners facing the Americans, Advance! Victory is ours!' "

"What year was that, Grandfather?" Ability asked.

"The Year of the Monkey," Second Harvest said. "1968."

From outside came a *rrrrr rrrrr* sound as Autumn passed under the thatch eaves. Instead of batteries, her flashlight had a hand pump like a flour sifter.

"Ability!" Autumn called. "Come look!"

Ability jumped off his stool; Senior Uncle, Second Harvest, and I followed. Soon we all gathered around Autumn in a clearing beyond the fishponds. The air was clear like mid-autumn at home. With the new moon not yet visible, the stars were crystalline. The Silver River, as Vietnamese call the Milky Way, poured across the sky. The night felt as if it were filled with hovering spirits.

"See that bright star?" Autumn rested one hand on Ability's shoulder and pointed with the other. "Look closely now, Nephew, and you'll see the Genie of Agriculture's conical hat. There, to the Genie's right, that's the head of a duck."

Senior Uncle pointed to one side of the sky. "Watch that star carefully, Grandson," he said. "When that star is overhead, it'll be midnight."

A string of firecrackers exploded next door; another exploded across the stream.

"Why don't they wait?" Senior Uncle complained. "The star never runs slow!"

But Vigor couldn't wait either. He hung the huge firecracker from the eaves and lit its fuse; a sputter of light crept up the string.

KA-BAMM!

The porch rafters shook; the fibro-cement roof rattled, and the thatch roof on the side room fluttered. Small Dog tore through the main room, tail tucked, claws clattering. Senior Uncle, Second Harvest, Autumn, and I dove behind the folding doors. Only youthful Vigor and Ability remained in the doorway, laughing.

"Oh!" Second Harvest held her hand over her heart. "Just like a grenade!"

Senior Uncle clapped his hands. "But nobody died!!"

"Here goes!" Vigor lit the wick on the string of firecrackers laid out in two rows, wick to wick like the pinnules on a fern.

"Here's an easy riddle, Ability." Autumn peered out from behind the door. "It has a body an inch long, yet wears a lot of clothes. It doesn't say anything from birth but shouts when it dies."

"A firecracker!" Ability said.

Tat tat, tat tat, tat. Explosions like machine-gun fire ripped apart the night; the searing smell of burnt phosphorous spread through the crystalline air.

"They all caught," Senior Uncle announced, looking through the window. "The Year of the Horse will be a good one!"

"Oh my," Autumn said. "One Tet, our firecrackers wouldn't light. All around Ha Noi the firecrackers exploded, *bang, bang,* just like now, but not a single one on our string. Two days later, we learned that my husband's mother had died at *giao thua,* the transitional hour between the old year and the new."

"Abil . . . ity," Second Harvest warned, but it was no use. Ability was already pawing through the pink papers scattered over the yard, searching for any unexploded treasures.

Debut of the Horse

Birth and old age, sickness and death
Plot their course from our earliest days.
If from one of these we could win release
Another would emerge to consume us.

DIEU NHAN
1072–1143

*T*he next morning I awoke to a computerized melody of "Happy Birth-day." The new clock bought by the family on the other side of the monkey bridge played predictably at twenty past the hour, followed by a cuckoo. I counted the cuckoo's calls; so, I thought, it's five-twenty.

Autumn bent quietly over a book, a baby lamp nearby. I put my feet on the floor, but before I could slip my head out from under the mosquito net, Small Dog was there, licking my toes. No one had remembered to put her out after the firecrackers the night before; Small Dog had slept all night under the bed Autumn and I shared.

"Goose morning," Autumn said in playful English.

Without using an alarm clock, Autumn regularly rose at three-thirty to read. Although her spoken English was hesitant, her fluency in French gave her a strong base for reading English. She looked up from *In the Combat Zone*, a book of interviews with American women who had served in Viet Nam. "It says here, 'I began to unravel . . .' What does that mean, 'unravel'?"

I shook the stiffness from my bones and sat next to Autumn at the table. Searching through sleep for the Vietnamese words for "knitting" and "thread," I drew a picture of a sweater and expanded the meaning to a psychological resonance. As Autumn and I talked, Senior Uncle opened the folding doors to let in the first light of the Year of the Horse. Small Dog dashed over to him, tumbling over his toes. Second Harvest set on the altar the small plates of food, which had been kept overnight in the mouse-proof, which was a cabinet made from wood and screening to keep out the field mice. She lit three joss sticks; the heady fragrance of burning cinnamon and sandalwood expanded throughout the room. Cupping her hands, she bowed three times.

Soon Senior Uncle stood by me, framed by two new calendars he had posted for 1990. One displayed a picture of the Louvre, the other a large color photograph of a baby. He opened a tiny tin of tiger balm and with his forefinger scoured his temples and then his upper lip. He handed me the tin. "Always start your day with tiger balm, do you understand, Child? Go ahead, go on now, begin your day."

I dabbed and rubbed even though my preference was to start the day and the year more slowly. The paste burned, its fumes searing my sinuses.

"Harder!" Senior Uncle insisted. "Always take from the side of the tin, Last Child, always run your finger around the edge of the top, never dip your finger into the middle, do you hear me? Do this and your tiger balm will last forever. Go on, now. Side of your neck, top of your throat, back of your neck, top of your spine."

My eyes watered from successive doses of tiger balm. My upper lip tingled; my head felt strangely clear, like a meditative trance. I watched Second Harvest move to the middle altar and light three more incense sticks. She moved on to the third altar and lit three joss sticks there, too. By now the air, like that in a Buddhist pagoda, was thick with the fragrance of frankincense, cinnamon, sandalwood, and myrrh.

"Senior Uncle," I said, "why do Vietnamese use three incense sticks? Why bow three times?"

Once again Senior Uncle dabbed tiger balm on his temples and between his eyebrows. This time he scoured his forehead so hard that I thought his wrinkles would disappear. "I don't know," he said. "I suppose one stick of incense for your mother, one for your father, and one for all the ancestors who went before."

He nodded at the picture I'd drawn for Autumn. "Without your mother, your father, and your ancestors, Last Child, how could you have life? Without homage to them, your life will unravel."

Much of Tet honors the ancestors, but much of it also centers on visiting. If the first visitor, who may arrive as early as midnight on the first day of Tet, is healthy, wealthy, and handsome, then the coming year will be a good one. However, if this "first foot" is deemed wanting, he may be invited to return later in the day; if an appropriate person isn't available, then a family member is chosen to leave the house and return as the first foot.

"A good year indeed!" Senior Uncle exclaimed when Uncle Watchful arrived. Senior Uncle ushered his old friend to the table in the main room. During the American War, Uncle Watchful had headed the village literacy program; Senior Uncle had been the assistant head.

Uncle Watchful's square face, thinning white hair, and white mustache reminded me of my Quaker grandfather. Like him, Uncle Watchful wrote a poem for every occasion and delighted in flowers. Bowing, his white hair slipping forward, Uncle Watchful offered me a bouquet. He did this with both hands, as is considered gracious in Viet Nam.

"This white flower," he said, pointing, "is a changeable rose, a member of the hyacinth family. Watch it and you'll see that by noon it will be pink, and by night purple. And these small red blooms are firecracker flowers, a specialty of Tet!"

As Senior Uncle poured tea, I asked after the health of Uncle Watchful's family. Generations of war had split families throughout Viet Nam. By 1990, every Vietnamese I knew—including the most committed revolutionaries—had a family member or close friend living in the West. One of Uncle Watchful's daughters had left by boat and lived in Buffalo, New York. Two other daughters lived in Sai Gon; the husband of one of them had been a colonel in the Sai Gon Air Force. He now lived in Camden, New Jersey. Uncle Watchful's overseas kin had sent back money for the first brick and stucco house in Ban Long.

"Respectfully I thank you," Uncle Watchful said in response to my inquiries about his family. He always spoke with an extra touch of gentility. Uncle Watchful was telling about his two daughters visiting from Sai Gon when Small Dog yelped, bolting out the door. Moments later Sixth Uncle, who lived in the neighboring house with the "Happy Birthday" clock, joined us. He had given Small Dog to Senior Uncle when she was a puppy. Whenever Sixth Uncle came to visit, which was several times a day, Small Dog ran out to the monkey bridge to greet him.

"Oh! Oh! What a good year!" Senior Uncle said, clapping his hands once more. "I may be poor in money, but I'm rich in friends!" He turned to me. "Whenever you have lots of meat and rice whiskey, Little One, friends will flock to see you, but listen to me, when your meat and rice whiskey are finished, those friends won't come. Don't follow such friends."

"Follow the friends who are constant!" Uncle Watchful said, placing his hand on Senior Uncle's; the gold cuff links of Uncle Watchful's white shirt rested on Senior Uncle's faded black *ao ba ba*. "Like my younger brother here," Uncle Watchful said. "He is my constant friend."

Contrary to what Senior Uncle had predicted, the Year of the Horse did not have an auspicious beginning. In some ways, life in Ban Long had been easier during the war, when people united around the common cause of fighting the Americans and the South Vietnamese Army troops. But now, with the change to a market economy, energy centered on the individual. The permission to grow wealthy encouraged personal initiative, but it also fostered greed. In both northern and southern Viet Nam, the tone quickly swung toward selfishness; with the general increase in wealth came a greater disparity of incomes and an increase in theft.

"Don't leave things around, Last Child," Senior Uncle would caution me. "Can you catch my words in time? Someone might take your notebook."

I am by nature sloppy, but I soon learned to police myself. Nothing of mine was taken. However, Senior Uncle did not fare so well. During Tet, someone—perhaps the group of youths who had stolen a Buddha from the pagoda—stole the entire crop from Senior Uncle's milk-fruit orchard. A year's work: gone.

After Vigor brought the news, Senior Uncle sat at the small table in the side room, staring toward the fishponds, his shoulders hunched. His hands rested on the table, cupped like an empty bowl. "I've known hunger," he said when I pulled up a stool and sat near him. "I've shared my fruit with you,

Last Child. I would share it with anyone. But why did we work so hard for independence and freedom only to treat each other this way?"

Another afternoon I was dozing on the board bed when I awoke to shouting. Second Harvest was off with friends; Autumn and I had stayed at home with Senior Uncle. For a few minutes I couldn't understand the words; then I realized the speaker was drunk. He was railing at Senior Uncle for allowing an American to enter Ban Long.

Had I been awake, I would have spoken with the man before Senior Uncle swung the folding doors shut and bolted the shutters, locking me inside. I might have calmed the man by allowing him to speak. But sitting on the board bed while this drunken visitor beat on the door, I knew such a step would terrify Senior Uncle. He was "responsible," and so I chose to remain inside.

When Sixth Rice Field heard about the drunken visitor, he shook his head. "We struggled so during the French and American wars!" he said. "This isn't the life we wanted for our children. Now what are we to do?" He shook his head again as he sat down at the table in the main room of Senior Uncle's house. He stared out the door at the fishpond covered with brush.

Suddenly Sixth Rice Field's face broke into ripples of laughter; he jumped up from his stool. I turned to see Fourth Honesty standing in the doorway. She was in her mid-sixties. Pure white hair, which is rare among Vietnamese, framed her face. She exuded a rare presence, like the white rose Uncle Watchful had brought.

Vietnamese men often hold hands with each other, and Vietnamese women do as well, but traditionally men and women do not show affection in public. However, the whole time we visited, Fourth Honesty and Sixth Rice Field sat side by side, holding hands. They had not seen each other in fifteen years. Both had been in the "tiger cages," generally considered the worst of the prisons used by the French-and-American-backed South Vietnamese governments. Sixth Rice Field had been imprisoned after the 1940 Southern Uprising against the French; Fourth Honesty had been held during the American War, when the tiger cages first confined women.

I had first met Fourth Honesty in early 1987, when I was still confined to the Province Guest House in My Tho. The main room of the province

Women's Union office, which was filled with women, fell silent the moment Fourth Honesty entered. No one, it turned out, had ever heard Fourth Honesty's story. Until I arrived in the province, no one had ever asked.

During every subsequent visit I made to the Mekong Delta, Fourth Honesty repeated her story for me as if doing so might help erase it from her mind. "If you ever visit Con Son Island," she would say, "you will see the sixty tiger cages." Now, sitting in Senior Uncle's main room, Fourth Honesty pointed to the rafters as she repeated her story. "A catwalk ran across the top of our cage so the guards could look down on us. Each cage was 1.2 meters wide and two meters long. Five sisters in that space! We slept two on the bottom, three on top."

"Same for the men!" Sixth Rice Field said. He wore a new white shirt for Tet.

Fourth Honesty tucked a strand of hair into her nape knot. "I had epileptic seizures from so many beatings, and then I would bleed. There was a hole in the floor with a wooden bucket inside for our excrement. For eight months I had to sit on that hole so that my blood would not mess the cage. Up above us on the catwalk, the guards kept a bucket of lime. If we sisters sang or spoke to each other, the guards would throw lime down on us. But we had to sing and ask about each other! Otherwise we would surely die."

Sixth Rice Field shook his head; his brush of white hair wavered. "So many died from starvation," he said. "One night I heard a shudder. The man lying on my right died. I heard another shudder. The man on my left died."

"We lost so many." Fourth Honesty spoke just above a whisper. "The gruel stank. It wasn't fit for rats! We organized a hunger strike. Then the guards took away our bathing privileges. Six weeks without a bath!" Fourth Honesty fingered the embroidery on the cuff of her *ao ba ba,* which was as white as her hair. "Our clothes rotted. Our hair fell out. Finally they let us wash, but in only one liter of water!"

The United States and Sai Gon governments had denied the existence of the tiger cages. But in July 1970 Tom Harkin, then a congressional aide and subsequently a senator from Iowa, and two congressmen, Augustus Hawkins and William Anderson, visited Con Son Island with Don Luce, a journalist working in Sai Gon. Released detainees had given Don a map of the prison. With Don as guide, the congressional delegation came out onto the catwalk on top of the cages.

Fourth Honesty pointed once again to the rafters. Her voice lightened. "We looked up through the catwalk—Americans! We were so surprised! They were talking in English to Tao in the next cage. They took pictures. We looked so terrible, filthy, our hair gone, we were bald—the lice. But within a week the guards moved us to a larger cell. The puppets claimed we were hardened criminals until we smuggled out a list of political prisoners."

Several years before I held that list in my hands during a visit with Tao, the woman who had spoken to the Americans in English. Tao had been eighteen and a senior at Sai Gon's prestigious Marie Curie School when she and her sister Tan, then fourteen, were arrested for taking part in a student demonstration.

When the Sai Gon and United States governments denied the prisoners' existence, Tao and Tan's mother secured a list of prisoners' names, ID numbers, parents' names and addresses. The list was written in compressed lines on a woman's underblouse worn by a released detainee when she left the prison. The fabric I held some fifteen years later was as frail as gossamer, but the inscribed names made the cloth feel as heavy as marble.

Fourth Honesty nodded toward Senior Uncle's calendar with the photograph of the Louvre. "They presented the list of our names at the Paris peace talks! The Americans and the puppets could no longer deny that we political prisoners existed. They had to release us in exchange for the American pilots."

"But why were you arrested?" I asked. I knew Fourth Honesty had been captured three times and had spent a total of sixteen years in prison.

"I was caught!"

"But three times?!"

Sixth Rice Field laughed. "You don't understand, Little One. Fourth Honesty did liaison work." He touched the sleeve of her white *ao ba ba*. "She put on the white blouse and crossed from our base here at Ban Long into puppet territory. She memorized messages, carried maps, gathered intelligence. For women like her, the chance of arrest was so great!" He ran his hand across the top of his head, ruffling his hair. For a moment he sat still, his forearm resting on top of his head.

"Good liaison work was essential," he added, "but so dangerous. Much more dangerous than combat."

Lady and Second Harvest on Friendship Bridge in 1992. *(Photo by Autumn)*

Right: In 1960, southern women under the command of Mme Nguyen thi Dinh (second from right) captured three districts in Ben Tre province. First the women spread a rumor through the Market Mouth that Viet Minh soldiers had returned from the North; then they used wooden guns and fire-crackers at dusk to deceive the Diem soldiers into think-ing the Viet Minh had indeed returned. *(Ngo Vinh Long Collection)*

With most of the Viet Minh men in the North, women became the main organizers and participants of the 1960 Uprising. *(Ha Noi Women's Museum)*

A rare photo shows Mme Nguyen thi Thap (far left) and Mme Nguyen thi Dinh (center), the two southern women who served as pres-ident of the Women's Union from its beginning in 1930 through 1990. A mass organization, the Union mobilized women during the French and American wars. *(Ha Noi Women's Museum)*

Known at one time as Nguyen Ai Quoc (Nguyen the Patriot), Ho Chi Minh, age thirty, attended the French Socialist Party Congress in December 1920, when the Communists broke away to form their own party. *(Ngo Vinh Long Collection)*

Viet Cong women guerrillas in Quang Ngai province, the central Vietnamese province where I worked during the war, prepare booby traps for enemy soldiers. *(Ha Noi Women's Museum)*

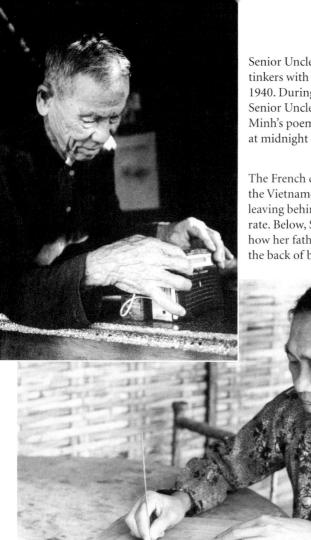

Senior Uncle, Second Harvest's father, tinkers with a radio he has used since 1940. During the American War, Senior Uncle listened to Ho Chi Minh's poems broadcast from Ha Noi at midnight on the eve of Tet.

The French colonialists educated only the Vietnamese administrative class, leaving behind a 5 percent literacy rate. Below, Second Harvest shows how her father taught her to write on the back of banana leaves.

Mme Nguyen thi Binh, now vice president of Viet Nam, was foreign minister for the Provisional Revolutionary Government of South Viet Nam, the government of the region of South Viet Nam held by the Viet Cong. *(Ngo Vinh Long Collection)*

Tending the ancestors' graves is an important part of Tet. Fifth Harmony stands by the grave of her mother, who, as a "mother of soldiers," fed and clothed guerrillas during the French and American wars.

Fifth Harmony (left) helps make rice flour cakes for Tet.

Above: Fifth Harmony demonstrates how she once hid amid the water palms along the bank of Roaring River until American and Sai Gon helicopters passed.

During the French and American wars, children as young as three and four could tell who was friend and who was foe. Once when Second Harvest slipped inside a Sai Gon–controlled strategic hamlet, a friend's four-year-old saved her from arrest by Sai Gon soldiers when he clung to her legs, crying, "Ma! Don't leave me!"

Whenever the Viet Cong women needed to work near Americans, they wore a white blouse because GIs assumed that any woman wearing white supported the Sai Gon regime whereas anyone wearing traditional "black pajamas" was Viet Cong. Fourth Honesty (bottom right) was arrested three times; she spent sixteen years in prison, including nine months in the "tiger cages," as seen at top. Guards walking on the catwalk over the cages threw lime down on prisoners if they sang or called out to each other. *(Ngo Vinh Long Collection)*

I'm with Mme Nguyen thi Thap (second from left), who helped organize the famous 1940 Uprising against the French at Vinh Kim Market. Autumn (second from right, next to Second Harvest, right), a northern intellectual, was arrested for writing a letter to a schoolmate, who had joined Ho Chi Minh in the mountains. During the American War, Third Fragrance (center) was raised by relatives inside Sai Gon–held territory while her parents worked for the Revolution.

"*You can beat* foreign invaders, Little One," Second Harvest said, "if you know how to wrap Tet cakes." She set a basin of glutinous rice on the picnic table. "I'll tell you why we wait until after Tet to prepare this dish. Do you remember how Father told you about Nguyen Hue, the peasant general who hid his junks up Roaring River, then ambushed the Thais? When he became emperor, Nguyen Hue took the name Quang Trung."

Fifth Harmony brought a basin of black beans from the kitchen. She mixed them with the sticky rice in an aluminum basin, then added the coconut milk Autumn had set on the table. "Always use an old coconut to make Tet cakes, Last Child," Fifth Harmony said. "The old coconuts are sweeter." She took a banana leaf, which had been cut into a square. "Lay the banana leaves like this." She overlapped two leaves and set a third on top. "Now spread the rice."

As Second Harvest set out her banana leaves, she continued the story of Quang Trung. "King Le Chieu Thong, the emperor Quang Trung had ousted, asked the Chinese for help."

"When was this?" I asked, arranging my banana leaves. I piled on rice and beans.

"I'm not sure," Second Harvest said.

"Seventeen eighty-nine." Autumn turned to me as she reached into the basin for rice. "Remember the two-hundred-year celebration in Ha Noi last year?"

"Quang Trung and his troops were in the center of Viet Nam," Second Harvest continued, "when two hundred thousand Chinese invaded Ha Noi. We called the city 'Flying Dragon' then." She reached for a handful of rice and beans. "But Quang Trung was wily. He recruited a huge army, nearly three hundred thousand men! This was the biggest military operation in Viet Nam until then. Quang Trung had his soldiers eat Tet ten days early. Then the troops packed up their Tet cakes."

"Now, roll the banana leaf like this, Little One," Fifth Harmony said. She had fingers as slim as chopsticks. Deftly she rolled the rice and banana leaves, then folded the ends, creasing each seam to make a tidy cylinder.

"Quang Trung's soldiers never stopped marching," Second Harvest added, rolling her cake. "Two soldiers carried a third. They kept changing places between the riders and porters. The peasants along the way gave the soldiers Tet cakes because they were enraged to have the Chinese eating Tet in Ha Noi."

"Now tie the cake this way," Fifth Harmony instructed, wrapping her cylinder with strings she'd stripped from the central spine of a banana leaf. Her motions were quick.

Second Harvest reached for a banana string. "Quang Trung was twenty kilometers from Ha Noi before the Chinese scouts noticed. By then it was the fifth day of Tet, and the Chinese were drunk. The Chinese had built a pontoon bridge across the Red River so they could invade Ha Noi, but so many drunk soldiers ran onto the bridge that it collapsed and the soldiers drowned. Quang Trung chased the rest of the Chinese back across the mountains. Then his soldiers ate Tet a second time, but in Ha Noi. That's why we wrap these Tet cakes now."

"But not that way!" Fifth Harmony scoffed at Second Harvest's cake. "Tie it this way for a beautiful Tet cake."

Second Harvest started to roll another cake. "Quang Trung's army could travel so fast because all along the way the people fed his soldiers. Otherwise the soldiers would have had to stop and cook rice. Like your American soldiers. They carried everything! Your American soldiers even carried stoves! That's why they could barely walk. All that junk banging against their bodies! But from Quang Trung we learned about *chien tranh nhan dan*," she said, meaning "people's war."

"So is that how you organized the Tet Offensive?" I asked.

"Yes!" Fifth Harmony said.

"But did you know you were part of such a big operation?" I added.

"Oh no!" Fifth Harmony spread three more banana leaves. "We knew only to prepare for an offensive. We thought it would be local. We had no idea until we listened to the radio. Not just our uprising at Vinh Kim Market, but a hundred cities and towns all across the entire country!! The whole world heard our cry!"

I had finally finished tying one package. I held up my Tet cake, which was squat and lumpy like a jackfruit. "So what do you think?" I asked. "Would Quang Trung accept this?"

Laughter rippled across Second Harvest's placid face. "Oh Little One," she said, starting another cake, "I don't think you were born under the right stars to cook for an emperor."

All the people who gathered at Senior Uncle's and whose houses I visited during the holiday had participated in the 1968 Tet Offensive, but they knew nothing of the plan for the offensive until the last minute, and even then, their knowledge was local. However, I wanted an overview so that I could understand how the Vietnamese had organized simultaneous attacks on a hundred province capitals and district towns with such secrecy the CIA never noticed.

During the American War, Last Gust had been president of the My Tho province People's Committee for the National Liberation Front ("Viet Cong"), precursor of the Provisional Revolutionary Government of South Viet Nam. At the end of 1992, Autumn and I made another trip, particularly to see him. I did not know it then, but that would be the last time I would see Uncle Last Gust. He died of heart failure shortly after Tet in 1993.

"Uncle Last Gust," I said as Autumn, Second Harvest, and I sat over tea in his house near Forever Silent Bridge, "did you know about the Tet Offensive before it happened?"

"Indeed I did!" Last Gust moved from the table to his chaise lounge made of rattan. He had a chiseled face, as craggy as the limestone karsts common in northern Viet Nam. But unlike other Viet Minh who fought against the French, Last Gust had not gone to the North in 1954 for Regrouping.

"I told you," he said, "how I went underground after I retrieved the dead from the 1940 Southern Uprising. In 1967, I was working at Central Headquarters at our Political Affairs Center in the jungle west of Sai Gon. Pham Hung was general secretary, I was deputy chief of cabinet. Our task was to prepare for the Tet Offensive."

"Political and military," Autumn said, lacing her fingers together so that her palms locked. "The two hands."

"Indeed!!" Last Gust said. "You know about our other uprisings, but this one was different. By 1967, we'd built a movement among the students in Sai Gon. We decided to try again, this time not just in one place but in many. Day and night—we didn't sleep. We prepared everything."

I had respect for the detail encompassed by Last Gust's sweeping statement. I once met a man from Sai Gon whom the Viet Cong had trained as a political organizer. For the two years of his training, he wore a cloth sack over his head even when eating, sleeping, and washing his face. He removed the sack only when changing it for a clean one. Keeping his identity anonymous would prevent any unraveling of the Viet Cong network in Sai Gon in the event of arrest and torture.

Last Gust coughed. "How could we fight in Sai Gon? I'm from Vinh Kim, from the countryside! I wouldn't know how to hide in a city. I'll tell you the secret of how we organized. Women. Some women went to the North for Regrouping, but mostly men went. The women stayed behind. The 1960 Uprising showed the power of women—women soldiers, women cadre, women guerrillas! Women like Second Harvest, our Second Sense. No matter how great our force of arms," Last Gust said, "if we hadn't had women, there would have been no victory."

"A body with blood vessels," Autumn added, "is worthless without blood."

Last Gust gestured toward Roaring River, a patch of blue beyond his garden of orchids. "When it came time for the Tet Offensive, the women notified people hither and yon. The women told the people just what to do and where to go, told them the day, the hour. Ours was a guerrilla war! We had to slip around undercover amidst the enemy.

"From 1967, we began first to organize in Sai Gon and then later in the provincial and district capitals. Those towns were the centers of the system belonging to the Americans and President Thieu. Their power was so great that we had to be fierce organizers. You must have a huge number of people to rise up."

"Ninety percent," Autumn said to me.

"That's what Khe Sanh was about! We attacked on January 21, 1968. Your General Westmoreland thought Khe Sanh was our attempt to have a victory over the Americans the way we had over the French at Dien Bien Phu. Ha! General Westmoreland was cocky. He thought his American soldiers were better than the French. He thought the Americans would win their Dien Bien Phu at Khe Sanh. But that's not what Khe Sanh was about! We didn't want that hill!!

"No, no, we just wanted to distract the Americans while we finished preparations for the Tet Offensive ten days later. We listened to the American radio! Your president was talking about Khe Sanh every day! A hundred thousand tons of bombs the United States poured on Khe Sanh. An armada of airplanes and helicopters. Plus all those American troops, and how many more supporting them behind the lines?? General Westmoreland thought he was fighting a traditional army. Ha!"

Uncle Last Gust's voice turned light. "Westmoreland and Johnson never did realize that they were fighting us, the Vietnamese people. They never understood they were fighting women!! So yes, the North Vietnamese Army distracted the Americans at Khe Sanh! Meanwhile, all over the country, women like Second Harvest and Fourth Honesty and Fifth

Harmony and Third Pear were preparing for Tet. But they didn't know they were part of a great offensive. Secrecy! The web!"

I thought about Ninth Rose, whom I had first met in early 1987. Then, she had pretended coyness as she told me about donning an *ao dai* to ride in a jeep driven by an American soldier into Binh Duc, headquarters for the U.S. Ninth Infantry Division. She described how Viet Cong working inside Sai Gon–controlled territory divided themselves into units of three people each. Only one of the three reported to one person in a superior unit. Should a woman be arrested and tortured, she could give information about only four people in the vast web—the other two in her unit, the person reporting to her from below, and the one to whom she reported.

Ninth Rose had also described the spontaneous party celebrating liberation in My Tho on the night of April 30, 1975, and how she was surprised to find so many people there whom she hadn't known were part of the Resistance. The web in My Tho, she would often remind me, had been a tight one carried out largely through the Market Mouth.

Uncle Last Gust shifted in his chair. "We couldn't write out our orders—"

"Death!" Second Harvest said.

"How's that?" I asked.

"The courier might be arrested!" Autumn said.

"Everything had to go by mouth," Last Gust said. "The Market Mouth! In Sai Gon, women in the Special Task Force worked in the hotels where the Americans stayed. They worked in the American bases. They watched and listened. They were our eyes and ears. That's how we knew what the American officers thought. The women played coy and dumb. All the while, they kept an eye on the officers' maps, and they counted the newly arrived munitions."

I found myself thinking back to wartime Quang Ngai, where one of my chores had been to pick up the Quaker Service mail at the American army compound. Since the Viet Cong controlled 90 percent of Quang Ngai province, I assumed that most Vietnamese I met, including those working inside the American base, were VC sympathizers.

I often chatted in Vietnamese with the women who cleaned the officers' quarters. They were straightforward with me since I was a woman and could talk, but with the officers they were flirtatious. I always assumed the women measured and counted as they swept and that no change in military activity escaped their notice. I used to watch with amusement as the military police searched the women's reed baskets when they left at the end of the day. It seemed never to occur to the MPs that whatever the women carried out of that American base resided inside their heads.

"Women were our spies!" Last Gust was saying. "And our guides!! Brother Kiet, now our prime minister, talks about when he went to Sai Gon, how the women took him here and there. They knew every alley, they knew which Sai Gon police they could trust, which they couldn't. In all the war, Little One, this was the most dangerous work. The women were facile. They knew the paths, they knew where the enemy was camped.

"The children as well! The kids would play with the American soldiers. They knew your soldiers' routines. Some of the children even learned English. Wonderful, the kids were. Smart. Busy with their little fishing nets, their fish baskets. All the while, their ears alert.

"We had a web of secrecy. The people like Fourth Honesty who were liaison knew only a little bit of information. To this day they can't tell you much. The chance of arrest for them was too great. This way, if they were tortured, what could they reveal? Not much because they knew only a tiny bit of the web."

"We even had secrecy in the North," Autumn said. "Nothing on paper and you wouldn't tell anyone anything, not even your husband, not even your friend."

"Just like here," Second Harvest said. "We knew only one spot of reality. We had the three 'No's.' Whenever we were questioned, we would answer, 'I didn't see,' 'I didn't hear,' 'I don't know.' "

"During the bombing," Autumn continued, "I taught in a school outside Ha Noi. Once, when my husband came to visit, he left Ha Noi at eleven at night, first by train, then by bicycle. On the train he met a colleague of his. 'Where are you going?' Vigilance asked his colleague as they left the train. They started pedaling down the same road. 'To visit my husband,' his colleague said. They kept biking and they kept making the same turns until they turned into the same gate! Only then did Vigilance realize that his colleague's husband was a colleague of mine."

"Here's the result of secrecy," Last Gust said, laughing. "Just before Tet, we read Westmoreland's speeches. He said the war was almost over. There was a light at the end of the tunnel. Ha! The Tet Offensive of 1968, the Year of the Monkey, was the light at the end of the tunnel! Uprisings in one hundred cities and towns, but did your CIA know? No! We penetrated the American embassy! Where was the CIA? They never knew a thing! Secrecy, that's what did it. Secrecy and stamina. Look, I'll show you."

Last Gust went to the cabinet with the family altar on top and removed an old photo album, which he set in my hands. Mold had eaten its binding. He opened the book to its first page. "See this picture of me? Hardly more than a schoolboy! I went underground in 1940, changed my identity. For thirty-five years, *I* didn't exist. That schoolboy you see in the photo disappeared. No one heard of him because I took on a whole new identity. That's what secrecy means."

"Uncle Last Gust . . ." Second Harvest's tone carried expectation. She leaned forward, her eyebrows drawn together; she rubbed her thumb across her forefinger as if paging through papers. "Do you by chance have a photograph of my mother?"

Last Gust rubbed his chest. "Child," he said to Second Harvest, using the intimate address, "your mother was my dear sister. How I miss her! I wish I did have a picture of her."

"You could check," I said when I noticed Second Harvest examining every face in the photos in my lap.

The album gave off the musty smell of decay. Together we turned pages, searching through eroded snapshots that had survived the French and American wars but not the humidity of the tropics. When we had finished looking, there was nothing for Second Harvest to hold on to but the soft blue-grey powder of dried mold on her fingertips.

That evening in 1992 Second Harvest and I sat outside at the picnic table, a tiny American lamp throwing a flicker of light on her placid face. A generator across the narrow sluice by the outhouse kicked on. From the side addition under the thatch roof came the laughter of teenagers—Vigor and Third Ability and neighbors. They were playing cards. Senior Uncle was folding away the red tablecloth for next Tet, the Year of the Monkey. Autumn, suffering from chronic bronchitis, had turned in early.

Second Harvest glanced at a passing *xuong* with a woman paddling in the stern. The sound of the paddle against the gunwale was but a murmur in the darkness. The woman's husband sat mid-canoe, their daughter in his lap. The girl, perhaps six, sang softly, her voice quavering.

"Our lives are like the river," Second Harvest said, watching the canoe disappear around the upstream bend. "Whenever I meet the elders who remember my mother, I come back home to this house my mother never knew, and I see her face. I remind myself that she's gone, but then I walk into another room and I see her face again. I can almost hear her voice.

"I have plenty of food now, and I live with the peaceful sounds of birds and cicadas. Still, the sadness never leaves. Can you understand, Little One?" She paused, gazing at the stream. "Our sorrow comes and goes like the river. Even at low tide, there is always a trickle."

Friendship Bridge

In the night rain, my dreams are cast
        to the trembling glimmer of the lamp.
After war, the people you meet differ so
        from former times.

> FROM "Autumn Night
> Far from the Family"
> NGUYEN TRAI
> 1380–1442

At noon on the day of the dedication of Friendship Bridge, the creek was too low for a canoe. Instead, we went by footpath and monkey bridge to the new structure that had replaced the one bombed during the American War. The new bridge was three feet wide and arched, its concrete as white as sun-bleached bone. After teetering across monkey bridges, the concrete felt wonderfully solid and predictable under my feet.

Firecrackers exploded as we crossed to the house of Eleventh Strength on the far side of the new bridge. A small man with wide-set teeth, he invited us women to sit at one of the four tables set up in his yard. Ability sat with the men at one of the other tables. Eleventh Strength had hung a Vietnamese flag from a bamboo pole under a milk-fruit tree; his wife, Fourth Spring Blossom, had arranged chrysanthemums next to a photograph of Ho Chi Minh.

"You can't imagine what it used to look like here," Second Harvest said as she pulled out a stool for me.

I surveyed the yard: The milk-fruit foliage was so thick that hardly a ray of sunlight penetrated. "Are there pictures from before?" I asked.

"Who had a camera?" Fifth Harmony said as she dropped a piece of beef into my rice bowl. "We were too busy running!"

"The bombs blanketed us," Fourth Spring Blossom said, adding another piece of beef and a slice of turnip to my bowl. She broke off a piece of French bread from a six-inch loaf and gestured with it toward the new bridge. "Our soldiers crossed there on the way to Ben Tre and Dong Thap Muoi provinces, that's why the B-52s bombed us so."

"You Americans call the B-52s 'carpet bombing,' " Autumn said to me.

"We called it 'harrow bombing,' " Second Harvest said. "After the B-52s flew off, the land was pulverized, like a field after the harrow has turned the earth over on itself. Following a B-52 raid, there was nothing left but bombs."

"People died twice," Third Pear added. She spat out the betel nut she had been chewing, then wiped her mouth on the grey-checked scarf special to revolutionary women from southern Viet Nam. During the war, Third Pear had smuggled medicines from Fourth Treasure's pharmacy in Vinh Kim Market. Once Third Pear paddled to Vinh Kim to buy cloth to sew a uniform for her oldest boy, who was leaving to join the revolutionary soldiers in the jungle; she returned from market to find a bomb had killed her son.

"First, people died from the war," Fifth Harmony said. "Then, another bomb would hit their grave and they died again."

"We all have souvenirs," Fourth Spring Blossom said, touching two scars on the back of her hand. She deposited another morsel of beef in my bowl.

"I'll show you my souvenir!" an elderly man said, joining us. He had a white goatee and long, thin hair tied into a knot at the nape of his neck, as was the custom for men many years ago. He pulled up his trousers leg to show me his knee, which was hollow like a crater. "I was in my thatch house eating rice when the Americans came." Demonstrating, the old man twisted away from me, as if I might strike him. "I was lucky enough to turn away from their grenades."

Fourth Spring Blossom dropped a potato into my rice bowl. "Two Americans held cigarette lighters against our house," she said. "You walked by the place where it used to be when you came along the paddy dike. They burned our rice, too. We had no food! But it was Agent Orange that drove us into the strategic hamlet. After Agent Orange, we had no fish, and we had nothing to drink."

"To think that now we make houses of brick!" said a woman in a pale grey *ao ba ba* and a grey-checked southern scarf. She passed around a shot glass of rice whiskey.

"And a concrete bridge from friends in America!" Second Harvest took a taste and handed me the glass. I sipped; the whiskey seared my throat.

Fifth Harmony touched my sleeve and nodded toward a table of men, who had grown rowdy. "Fourth Loyalty has drunk a quarter bottle of rice whiskey," she said. "He's getting ready to sing!"

Sing Fourth Loyalty did. He was a short man with a powerful chest that gave his voice a wide range. Small wrinkles curved like smiles around his eyes. "Oh Americans, Americans," he sang, his chest swelling. He held out his left hand and tapped his right sandal which, like those worn by guerrillas during the war, had a sole cut from a truck tire and straps made from an inner tube.

"Come meet our guerrillas!" he sang. "Oooooh, Ah! Come meet us in our jungles, come face us in our paddies! Oooooh, Ah!" Then, extending his left hand, he lifted his trigger finger to his eye and squinted for the finale: "Ready. Aim! Fire!!"

Sixth Uncle, the neighbor who had given Small Dog to Senior Uncle, joined our table as Fourth Loyalty sang a wistful song about a soldier far from his family in autumn.

"How did you set the bridge pilings?" I asked Sixth Uncle. I knew he had engineered the bridge and that the creek was fifteen feet deep at high tide. To accommodate the arch of the bridge, each of the concrete pilings must have been about twenty-five feet long.

Sixth Uncle rubbed his eyes, which were a soft brown like the color of his pajama suit. His sunken cheeks made him look older than seventy-two. "I helped build the old bridge in 1956," he said. "I may be too old to work, but I'm not too old to give directions!"

Sixth Uncle explained how the young men lashed a bamboo pole perpendicular to one of the concrete pilings, making a cross. Using ropes, they tilted the cross until it stood vertical in the river. Then two men scrambled up onto the bamboo crosspiece and, perching on either side of the piling, jumped in unison, driving the concrete post into the mud.

When the post stopped sinking, another pair of youths joined the first, one on each side. Sixth Uncle sketched the concrete-and-bamboo cross and, pair by pair, added stick figures until ten men stood on the bamboo crosspiece, on each side of the piling. His drawing looked like two facing, midair lines of the "Bunny Hop."

" 'Dancing' we called it!" he said. "You have machines in America," he added. "Here, we have only each other. But twenty strong men, each weighing fifty kilos [110 pounds], all jumping in unison, that's a metric ton driving a piling!"

Sixth Rice Field came over from the men's table. He puffed on a cigarette as he looked over Sixth Uncle's drawing. "In one day," he said, "the young men drove all sixteen pilings. Oh, it was fun to watch!"

That afternoon the songs under the milk-fruit trees in Fourth Spring Blossom's yard went on until dusk. As the neighbors dispersed, Second Harvest, Autumn, Ability, and I climbed into Fourth Spring Blossom's canoe. The last slanting light cast a glow over the fields of ripening rice. The canoe slipped past a burst of cicadas buzzing in the water palms and passed a neighbor's water buffalo lolling on the bank, her tail slapping at gnats.

" 'Friendship' means what?" Ability asked, practicing his English. He turned to look at Autumn and me. "Friends in a boat?"

"Silly goose," Autumn teased back in English.

When Fourth Spring Blossom had paddled us as far upstream as the water allowed, she let us off at the bank and, turning in her seat, paddled back downstream. We made our way along a paddy dike amidst tree frogs calling into the darkness. I held a sandal in each hand, my toes feeling for hardened footprints that told me I remained on the path. At each monkey bridge, Second Harvest stopped and offered me her hand. I teetered across, my toes spread like fingers gripping the slick bamboo trunk.

Second Harvest laughed. "When you can cross a monkey bridge alone in the dark without removing your sandals, Last Child," she said, "you will have become one of us."

"*Step back.* This one's rotten!" Ninth River called. Several years before, Ninth River had showed me how to carry yoked baskets and weave thatch. Now she stood twenty feet above me in the glossy leaves of a milk-fruit tree. Perching on a narrow branch, she looked like a distant tightrope walker, her sturdy body hidden by foliage. She opened her hand; the milk fruit she dropped landed with a *spat,* releasing a heady, sweet fragrance.

Then Ninth River curled her toes around the branch. Using both hands, she wielded an eight-foot bamboo pole, snaring the twig of another fruit between the pole's split end. With a twist of the pole, she broke the twig, then removed the fruit from the pole and dropped it. I stood waiting, a sack tied around my neck, my hands holding the bottom corners out like a fireman's net. With a *whoosh,* the soft fruit hit the cloth, rolling back and forth.

In the next tree, Ninth River's nieces and nephews jumped from branch to branch, their clothes flashing like plumage. The children chattered as they dropped fruit to their grandparents, who waited with outstretched cloths. "Careful!" Ninth River's mother called. Another fruit missed and landed, *splat,* useless but fragrant.

Once we'd harvested the trees, Ninth River set straw and then banana leaves in the bottom of a large, loosely woven basket. Although her fingers were thick and blunt, she handled each fruit as if it were a jewel. She arranged the first layer with stems on the side. Then she tucked the stems of the second layer into the open spaces between the fruit on the bottom. As Ninth River filled the basket, she discarded blemished fruit and set aside those with a rose blush. These she arranged on top.

In a good season, Ninth River's twenty milk-fruit trees might produce three thousand fruit each. In addition, she raised cherries, pineapples, oranges, lemons, pomelos, bananas, sugarcane, black pepper, and coffee. "Stay two weeks longer," she said, opening a coffee pod to show me beans that were almost ripe, "and you can help me harvest coffee!"

Ninth River's house was farther downstream than Senior Uncle's. By late afternoon there was enough water in the sluice to load the heavy baskets of milk fruit into her family's canoe. I climbed aboard. She attached her motor, keeping its long propeller tail in the *xuong* until she'd poled the canoe from the creek into Roaring River. Then she yanked the starter cord, and we joined river traffic headed to Vinh Kim Market.

Vietnamese consider milk fruit a great delicacy; since the most succulent fruit are grown in only a few villages of Chau Thanh district, fruit brokers prowled the wharf at Vinh Kim, ready to snare the best fruit from the arriving canoes. As we approached the wharf, I ducked to hide my white face; as soon as I could, I melted into the crowd, leaving Ninth River free to haggle a better price.

I paused on the riverbank upwind of the wharf, which had the acidic smell of rotting fruit. A breeze lifted the two-tailed kite trailed by a boy running across Forever Silent Bridge. Near me, two little girls dove topless into the river from a canoe moored to a junk. With squeals, the children broke through the water and scrambled back into the *xuong,* their wet pajama bottoms clinging to their thighs, their dark gold backs glistening. On the shore near them, a man washed a new red bicycle. With a toothbrush he scoured each spoke.

By the time Ninth River had finished bargaining and we'd loaded her empty baskets and bamboo yoke back into the *xuong,* the sun hung low and orange, turning the river gold. With the money from that day's harvest safely tucked into the pocket of her inner *ao ba ba,* Ninth River started the motor. It responded with a soft *put-a-put-put.* We turned west toward a fisherman who, standing in his canoe, cast his net. It spread into the sky like a butterfly taking flight. Drops of water in the net caught the last rays of sunlight.

One evening toward the end of that same visit to Ban Long in 1992, Second Harvest and I were washing dishes in the river when there was a crashing noise around the next bend. Two little boys in faded green-print shirts made from the same bolt of cloth pushed free of the water palms. Paddling, they crashed into scrub *o ro* bushes, which have leaves like a white oak but with points sharp as pins.

"Ouch!" yelled the boy in the stern. He was perhaps six. "Don't you know how to paddle?"

"Don't you?" countered the boy in the bow. He might have been five.

"My brothers and I paddled like that when we were kids," I said to Second Harvest as I scoured the rice pot with a wad of coconut hair. "We would visit my grandfather in the house my father sent your father pictures of. It's on a creek rather like this, but my father doesn't have any water palms or *o ro* bushes in New Jersey!"

I thought of the dark creek my family loves, its water stained the color of tea by the roots of cedar trees. Senior Uncle's creek tugged at me in the same mysterious way. I longed to feel the smooth wood of a paddle against my palms, to feel my back and arm muscles stretch with each stroke. I'd often hinted at my wish to explore Ban Long's creeks on my own. But I knew Second Harvest would be "responsible" should I prick myself on an *o ro* bush or bump into a water palm. Still precious, I remained grounded.

The children crashed once more. Second Harvest laughed. Her face, round like a harvest moon, relaxed. "You're always wanting to paddle the *xuong*," she said, "and now you'll leave soon. Try it if you like."

I didn't wait for Second Harvest to change her mind. Climbing into the canoe, I grabbed a paddle and pushed off.

"No, no!" she yelled. "Not yet! Not downstream! Come back!"

I spun the canoe.

"Father!" she yelled. "Come quick!"

Senior Uncle came running, his keys jangling; he arrived breathless just in time to see me slide the *xuong* alongside the dock.

"Father!" Second Harvest said. "Little One knows how to steer!"

Senior Uncle clapped both hands against his jaw. "Who would have guessed? An American who can paddle a *xuong*!"

"Ability!" Second Harvest called. "Come ride with Auntie."

As soon as Ability climbed aboard, we took off upstream. It was clear at the first bend that Ability, who'd been raised in the city of My Tho, had never learned to paddle. I showed him the cross-bow draw. Soon, we picked up an easy rhythm. We passed a paddy with two raised graves. Further upstream a buffalo and her calf grazed while a young woman with a heart-shaped face washed clothes in the river.

"Where are you going?" she asked in Vietnamese.

"For a ride!" Ability said.

"Suppose we kept going, Ability," I asked, finishing a J stroke, "where would we end up?"

"Cambodia." He drew the canoe around the next bend.

In places, water palms rose like stakes of a fishing weir stretched across the creek. Ability grabbed the branches and pulled us through; I ducked as the fronds rattled across my conical hat. *O ro* bushes scratched the side of the *xuong*, their pins grazing my forearm.

Ability and I paddled on in silence. The air smelled sweet and dense with dew. Darkness comes early to the heavily shaded creeks of Ban Long; soon the water palms seemed to turn into spirits with craggy bodies and ghostly fingers. Except for the occasional swishing of palm fronds, there was an eerie silence. The diurnal insects had ceased buzzing; the nocturnal creatures had yet to begin.

"Maybe we'd better go back," I said. "Want to paddle stern?" In a *xuong,* unlike in an American canoe, there's space behind the stern seat. When changing directions in a tight spot, paddlers simply turn in their seats.

"I don't know how to paddle stern." Ability's voice was as quiet as dusk.

"Dark as it is," I said, turning the canoe around, "we'll wait until our next trip for you to learn the J stroke."

We rounded one bend after another until Senior Uncle's house with its ladders of light came into view. Barking, Small Dog announced our arrival. Second Harvest had reached the dock by the time Ability executed his cross-bow draw, settling the *xuong* at his mother's feet.

"Where on earth did you go, *Em?*" Second Harvest asked me. The use of *"Em"*—"Little Sister" instead of "Last Child"—was enough to warn me that I'd pushed too far beyond an expected limit.

Ability looked at me, his lips partly open as if contemplating the best reply. Then we both laughed.

"Cambodia!" we said.

After that ride, Second Harvest often put me in the bow to paddle; when it came time to turn around, I spun in my seat, assuming the stern. Once it was dark of the moon; we had paddled way upstream to visit Ninth River's aunt. Ability, who sat with Autumn in the bottom of the *xuong,* pumped Autumn's Soviet flashlight. With each wheeze, the beam of light rose and fell.

"Stop your light, Son," Second Harvest teased, "the helicopters will spot us!"

In time Ability tired of the flashlight; the voices of night creatures replaced its wheezing. Blackness engulfed us. I could feel Autumn's warmth against my legs and make out her shape, but I couldn't see Ability or Second Harvest.

"So this is what it felt like to move weapons and soldiers," Autumn said. Her voice carried respect.

"When I was a child," I whispered into the darkness, "my father taught me that the bowswain must know how to steer. Is that true here?"

"True," Second Harvest whispered. "The bow leads the boat."

We bumped into *o ro* prickers. Second Harvest pushed off and drew us to the right; we hit more prickles.

"A backwater," she muttered. "Turn in your seat, Last Child."

"I can't see anything!" I protested. "How am I to steer?"

Ability shone Autumn's wheezing flashlight into the water palms, searching for the creek.

Second Harvest took a stroke. "This is why you should always take a local guide, Little One. Even I don't know this part of the river. We'll go back and fetch Eighth Apricot Flower. You met her the day you harvested rice."

Eighth Apricot Flower served us tea in her house made from woven water palms. Then she led us back to the canoe. She took the bow, I the stern. The flashlight lay silent in Ability's lap.

"Left," Eighth Apricot Flower directed, paddling now and again. "Now, hard right."

We slid through blackness. A frond grazed my face, another brushed my shoulder, but the touch of both was as gentle as a whisper. The canoe made a delicate rippling sound hardly louder than that of the current bubbling past a water palm. The night belonged to the frenzied cicadas and the giddy tree frogs and to those from the neighborhood who could slip quietly among them.

On my last evening the women I'd harvested rice with three years before came to visit. They brought milk fruit, water apples, breadfruit, and dried tamarind. Tamarind is the essential ingredient for sweet-and-sour soup, which the women knew was my favorite dish.

"Please," they said, "take our gifts to the women in America."

Middle-aged, these Vietnamese women looked like a bridal party posing for a silver anniversary photo. All wore go-for-a-visit *ao ba bas* in varying hues and the traditional loose black trousers. That night Third Pear had tied her grey-checked scarf around her head so that the ends stood up like rabbit ears. She was one of the women who had run messages to and from Vinh Kim Market during the American War and the one who had gone to buy new-recruit supplies for her son and returned to find him killed by a bomb. Third Pear mashed her betel nut in a small American shell casing as she asked about Western bridal dress.

"What?" she said in answer to my description. "No trousers?!"

The women rollicked at this immodest thought. They had never seen a Western dress. To them, a dress was an *ao dai,* which has two skirt panels that flow over loose trousers.

"Just think, the Americans wear only panties!" Third Pear spat a bright red splotch of betel nut. It arced out the door and landed in Senior Uncle's swept yard.

Ninth River joined us. She had brought newly picked milk fruit and a squash particular to Viet Nam. She shook the squash, her square face breaking into laughter when it rattled. "Plant these seeds in your garden, Last Child," she said, "but save some for your father."

After the visitors left, I sat at the table in the main room, writing by the light of the overhead bulb that, with the advent of electricity, had replaced Senior Uncle's stately lantern. With my toes, I rubbed Small Dog's back; mosquitoes stung my ankles.

I became aware of a dark form in the corner and looked up to find Senior Uncle sitting there on a stool, his black peasant pajama suit merging with the darkness.

"Senior Uncle," I asked, "will you be sad when we leave?"

He dragged his stool closer, then changed his mind and fetched an American lamp, which he lit. "So you can read better," he said, turning up the wick. "When living, Little One, you need a lamp. After death, you need music."

He disappeared into the back room and returned with a large package wrapped in plastic. "The puppets called us rats," he said, untying its blue twine. "It's true we dug secret bunkers, I dug lots of them, and we lived underground, can you catch my words in time, Child? We slept by day and prowled by night. Our toes knew the way!" He chuckled as he unwrapped another layer of plastic. "But we were different from rats. We were smarter."

Senior Uncle opened the last layer of plastic to show me his treasures: a Confucian primer, a photo book on Lenin, and a volume of Ho Chi Minh's poetry. To these he had added my father's gift, a photo book of New Jersey. He pointed to the Amish horse and buggy on the cover of my father's gift.

"A horse must go far before you can know its strength, Last Child," he said. "A heart is hard to know at first."

From an envelope that had been tucked in the Confucian primer Senior Uncle took a small, yellow photograph two inches square. He held it cradled in his huge hands. I recognized the photo as the original for the one of Senior Uncle that hung, enlarged, on the post near the family altar. The spotted, yellow original showed a studio pose of Senior Uncle in a suit jacket and tie. It had been taken before the 1940 Uprising and the French retaliation that had forced Senior Uncle to flee to Ban Long.

"This is the only picture of me young," Senior Uncle said. "Give it to your father. Tell him to come live with me in Ban Long. I am his younger brother. I will take care of him in his old age."

Later that evening, Second Harvest and I swung together in the hammock under the jackfruit trees. We nibbled hot, roasted peanuts. Second Harvest touched my temples. "In a few years, you and I will be old," she said. "The black hair of a Vietnamese and the russet of an American will both be white. Then, you and I will be the same."

We spoke about Vigor, her adopted son, who had been a handsome, wild youth when I first met him. Now Vigor, his wife, and their toddler lived with Senior Uncle. Nevertheless, Second Harvest worried about her father. Recently he'd fallen from a water-apple tree.

There was a lull in the conversation. I noticed how much the sounds of Ban Long had changed since my first trip six years before. Now, there was electricity. From downstream came the sound of a cassette tape playing Vietnamese rock music. From the side room, where Vigor had hooked up a borrowed TV, came the dubbed Russian and Vietnamese voices of Mariana in *The Rich Also Weep*.

Second Harvest took the peanuts I offered her. Their aroma mixed with the tangy fragrance of jackfruit. The hammock made a creaking sound as we swung. I looked at Second Harvest, thinking that now I would broach the question I had longed to ask. "Older Sister," I said, touching her sleeve, "are you a Communist?"

"Me?" she said, laughing. She shook her wrists, No.

"And Senior Uncle?" I asked.

Once again she shook her wrists. "No. Only Uncle Last Gust. None of us you've spent time with here in Ban Long are members of the Communist Party."

A *xuong* passed, a woman paddling bow, a man in the stern. Between them, on a reed mat on the floor of the canoe, three little boys slept curled around each other like bananas from the same stalk. The cicadas buzzed; a tree frog chortled. Somewhere in the distance, an owl called *cu cu*, sounding its name in Vietnamese.

"Don't you understand, Little One?" Second Harvest said, gesturing toward the creek and the house with its ladder of light lying on the fresh water urns under the thatch eaves. "This is all we wanted."

Book II

Khanh Phu Village
Red River Delta
Northern Viet Nam

A Boat on the River Day

The stream slips by, as calm as smooth paper.
A single star guides the sampan; the moon trails behind.

While the oar creaks, the sculler ponders a maze of dreams
That might free the rivers and mountains of an ancient land.

As the sampan draws homeward, dawn lights the sky,
Tingeing the horizon with the flush of a new day.

HO CHI MINH
1890–1969

X I

Rescued

Straw roofs hide in the village smoke.
A solitary boat stops for a moment.
Groups of children from the hamlet
Search for crabs along the river.

"At the Hoang River Landing"
THAI THUAN
Fifteenth century

*B*efore the changes in Viet Nam that would come with Renovation, the
Thais relegated the one airplane that flew each week between Bangkok and
Ha Noi to a remote spot at their domestic airport. Waves of heat shimmered over the runway as I walked toward that solitary Air Viet Nam plane
one day in February 1987. I felt as if I were crossing a beach, snorkel in
hand, ready to submerge myself in intricate, alien waters.

We flew out over the Eastern Sea and then circled in across the Red
River Delta, the seat of ancient Vietnamese culture, toward Ha Noi, which
lies some fifty miles inland. By now, most of the bomb craters I'd noticed
when I first flew into North Viet Nam during the war had been filled.

Below me now, villages spotted the plain, the houses clustered amidst flooded paddies that shimmered with the iridescent green of newly trans-planted seedlings. The panorama suited the Vietnamese word for "the State" and "country," which combine *nha* meaning "house" with *nuoc* meaning "water." Rivers and canals of red-brown water snaked through the fields and were offset by straight roads of the same red brown.

Soon I was looking down at Ha Noi, a city of treetops, tile roofs, and buildings of dusty yellow. I could see small houses under construction all around the city. Then we were flying over rice paddies once more and over houses clustered beneath bamboo and flame trees.

As we came in to land, I could see oxcarts laden with manure and women carrying baskets of seedlings slung from shoulder poles. We coasted along the short airstrip, past a boy riding atop a grazing water buf-falo. Soon I walked across the tarmac toward the airport's one small build-ing, where all the men were dressed in olive drab.

"American?" the immigration officer asked, his eyebrows raised.

"Yes," I answered.

He toyed with a scar slicing across his chin. "Hard to believe," he said, stamping my passport.

I waved to Autumn, who waited on the far side of the immigration booth. She looked far younger than when I had first met her in 1983. She'd cut her hair; curls had replaced the traditional, more severe nape knot. Tiny age lines curled like impish grins at the edge of her eyes. Autumn took my hand while two other women tugged the suitcase I'd brought full of books and medical journals.

As we climbed into a Soviet van, we were joined by two men, who turned out to be Polish citizens returning from a month's vacation in Singapore, Malaysia, and Thailand. They'd flown from Bangkok to Ha Noi to catch the weekly Aeroflot plane, which connected Viet Nam to the Soviet bloc.

"How is it with you now?" one of the Poles asked, speaking to Autumn in French. He looked out at the emerald green paddies, their seedlings bent in the breeze.

"Better," Autumn said. "But still hard."

The van's engine sputtered, then died.

"Soviet gas," the other Polish man muttered.

The driver pulled off the road, removed the gas filter, and blew into it, releasing grit and the stinging odor of gasoline. We started off again, but stopped three more times to clean the filter.

In early 1987, the rare car in Ha Noi carried foreigners or a Vietnamese minister of state. This was the time before automobiles and motorcycles, before the city had traffic lights and a functioning phone system. In those days, clothes were black, white, and grey, dark blue and olive drab. There were no private shops or sidewalk vendors and no veneer of advertisements in plastic and neon. Ha Noi was still a quiet city resonating with the soft whir of bicycles and the ripple of casual conversations between riders.

There were few hotels in Ha Noi then, and these stood empty. Autumn took me to the Thong Nhat ("Unification") Hotel, which had been an aristocratic gathering place during the French colonial era, when it was called the Metropole. History emanated from the Thong Nhat's long corridors and deep rooms with their high ceilings and tall, shuttered windows.

As I climbed the sweeping but shabby staircase to my room in the back of the top floor, I pictured French Foreign Legion officers posturing in their starched "whites" for flirtatious French women in evening dresses. I could almost hear the rapid spill of the French commands and the scurrying steps of Vietnamese servants.

I knew I must stay in Ha Noi while Autumn secured the papers then necessary to visit a province. I forced myself to be patient, but as the days passed I worried that after almost four years seeking permission to stay with a family, I had traveled halfway around the world only to be a tourist. I tried to be appreciative about trips to the Museum of the Liberation Army and to the Temple of Literature, Viet Nam's first university.

But I never fare well as a tourist. I grew depressed, watching Ha Noi from inside that Soviet van, its sealed windows cutting me off from the odor of charcoal cooking fires, the sound of voices, and the soft texture of Ha Noi humidity. I longed to be on a bike, pedaling among the commuters, who held hands as they chatted. Returning each evening to the empty Unification Hotel, I would climb its bleak staircase, growing more defeated with each step.

But Autumn persisted. Finally, permission came through for us to visit a village of four thousand people living sixty miles southeast of Ha Noi in Tam Diep district of what was then Ha Nam Ninh province but in 1992 became Ninh Binh province.

In preparation Autumn and I made a trip to the State Store. During early 1987, before the thousands of shops and informal "squatting mar-

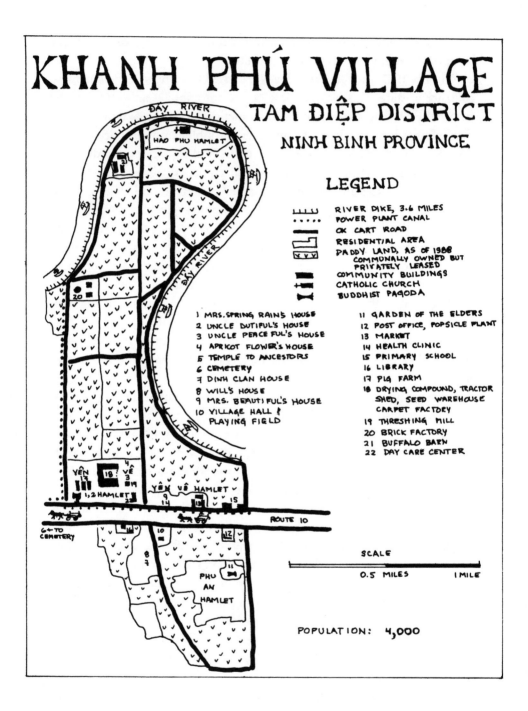

KHANH PHÚ VILLAGE

TAM ĐIỆP DISTRICT

NINH BINH PROVINCE

LEGEND

- RIVER DIKE, 3.6 MILES
- POWER PLANT CANAL
- OX CART ROAD
- RESIDENTIAL AREA
- PADDY LAND, AS OF 1988 COMMONALLY OWNED BUT PRIVATELY LEASED
- COMMUNITY BUILDINGS
- CATHOLIC CHURCH
- BUDDHIST PAGODA

1 MRS. SPRING RAIN'S HOUSE
2 UNCLE DUTIFUL'S HOUSE
3 UNCLE PEACEFUL'S HOUSE
4 APRICOT FLOWER'S HOUSE
5 TEMPLE TO ANCESTORS
6 CEMETERY
7 DINH CLAN HOUSE
8 WILL'S HOUSE
9 MRS. BEAUTIFUL'S HOUSE
10 VILLAGE HALL & PLAYING FIELD

11 GARDEN OF THE ELDERS
12 POST OFFICE, POPSICLE PLANT
13 MARKET
14 HEALTH CLINIC
15 PRIMARY SCHOOL
16 LIBRARY
17 PIG FARM
18 DRYING COMPOUND, TRACTOR SHED, SEED WAREHOUSE CARPET FACTORY
19 THRESHING MILL
20 BRICK FACTORY
21 BUFFALO BARN
22 DAY CARE CENTER

DÀY RIVER

HÀO PHÚ HAMLET

DÀY RIVER

YÊN VỀ HAMLET

1,2 HAMLET

YÊN VỀ

ROUTE 10

6 ← TO CEMETERY

PHU AN HAMLET

SCALE

0.5 MILES   1 MILE

POPULATION: 4,000

kets" that would later cram Ha Noi's streets, Vietnamese lived in a state-controlled economy of shortages and rations. People used their meager government wages to buy vegetables in one of the city's markets and to purchase rare household goods at a State Store, whose bare shelves held shoddy merchandise covered with dust. I bought two bicycles, in those days a lavish purchase. Autumn and I loaded the bikes into a Soviet jeep. Joined by a Women's Union cadre and the driver, we left for Khanh Phu.

If you want to swim in the ocean, you must first reach the beach, and then you must cross the sand; by the time you step into the water, some of that sand has stuck to your feet. In Viet Nam, particularly before the early 1990s, I had to meet (and gain the permission of) first the central level, then the province, and then the district in order to relate to a village. As the Vietnamese would say, I had to pass through many gates. Usually at least two cadre from each level joined me. I reached Khanh Phu in despair, an entourage of several jeeps and a dozen officials in tow.

Vietnamese sometimes describe their country as shaped like two large rice baskets (the two deltas) suspended from a bamboo carrying pole (the Truong Son Mountains). The Red River Delta in northern Viet Nam has an entirely different feeling from that of the Mekong Delta in the southern part of the country. The northern soil is less fertile and lacks the Mekong's web of sluices with houses hidden here and there beneath lush foliage. In the Red River Delta there are typhoons, and the population pressure is so intense that every square foot of land is used.

As a first impression, Khanh Phu looked much like other northern villages. Its rice paddies stretched toward the horizon, giving a sense of openness, but this feeling was countered by the clusters of walled compounds with squat houses and compact gardens.

To welcome me and my entourage, the head of the village People's Committee beat a gong made from an American bomb canister. Uncle Peaceful was also head of the village Communist Party. In his mid-sixties, he had a square face and close-cropped, bristly hair. His right shoulder sloped down and his grin tilted up in the opposite direction.

Uncle Peaceful led us into the People's Committee building, a stucco structure furnished with a long table and stools. The entourage settled around the table. We sipped tea, we exchanged speeches. Since I made this first trip to Khanh Phu before I visited Ban Long, I had no clue that my arrival was a sensational event. No foreigner had been allowed to stay with a family or even in a village. Furthermore, I was an American, and this was the time when no diplomatic relationship existed between the United States and Viet Nam and when the U.S. embargo was stringent.

I suspect that every one of the well-meaning listeners sitting around that table worried that he or she would be held personally responsible if a problem occurred during my visit. The easiest way for these officials to ensure that nothing went wrong was to see that nothing happened. Perhaps that's the reason everyone insisted I return to the Province Guest House, where I would be safe and utterly comfortable.

The meeting with the People's Committee lasted an hour and madly frustrated me. Afterwards, I paused at the gong hanging from a jackfruit tree and ran my fingers over the rusty bomb casing. At home in Ohio, it was calving season. With the twelve-hour time difference, it would be after midnight in our hollow. I pictured my neighbor, having finished his afternoon shift at the tire mold plant, walking through the moonlit snow to the barn to check my cows. What am I doing here? I asked myself. I should be back home tending to my own chores.

I rapped my knuckles against the bomb casing; it resonated, *thoong.* Just then someone grabbed my elbow. During the previous week in Ha Noi, people had often grabbed my elbow, leading me here, tugging me there. But this particular grip felt different: It was fierce, with a strength that comes only from hard labor.

I turned to find a woman in her sixties whom I'd noticed during the meeting. She had sat alone against the side wall. Sunken cheeks accentuated her unusually high cheekbones. The woman's eyes had narrowed when I told the People's Committee of my wish to live with a family in order to help Americans understand ordinary Vietnamese. Now, her eyes narrowed again, matching with their intensity the grip she maintained on my elbow. With her free hand, she pointed to herself and then to me.

"One, two *Ba My,*" she said in Vietnamese.

My means "beautiful" and, ironically, also "America." *Ba* means "Mrs." and also "woman." *Ba My* could mean "Mrs. Beautiful," naming the woman who grasped my elbow, or it could refer to me as an American woman.

"One, two *Ba My,*" she said, repeating her pun.

"Yes," I answered, too discouraged for jokes. "We must be alike."

Mrs. Beautiful's grip on my elbow became even more proprietary. "You are coming to my house for lunch," she said. She looked me straight in the eye. "And you are going to stay at my house with me. You are *not* going to the hotel."

I had no idea then what gave Mrs. Beautiful the power single-handedly to overturn the collective decision of the whole People's Committee. But she had done it. I could feel the passion surging through her fingertips as she propelled me across the road, down a narrow path between high stucco walls and through the gate in the wall surrounding her house.

That first day, as I ate lunch with the officials at Mrs. Beautiful's house, I caught snippets of intense whisperings about my fate. Whatever her reasons, Mrs. Beautiful seemed determined to have me remain as her guest. She insisted on taking responsibility for my health and safety with the help of Autumn and the head of the village Women's Union. After lunch, Mrs. Beautiful dispatched the national Women's Union cadre and driver back to Ha Noi. Soon, she began to usher the provincial and district officials to her gate.

Once all the officials had left, I retrieved clean clothes from my bag. I was dipping a pail of bathwater from the courtyard cistern when the head of the village Women's Union came running. In accordance with the custom of northern Viet Nam, she went by her name, New Moon, without the prefix indicating birth order as is customary in southern Viet Nam.

New Moon was about forty years old, with blunt hands and widespread eyes. Strands of hair slipping from her nape knot gave her an appearance of openness. "Oh no!" she protested, taking the bucket from me. "You must have hot water."

"No, no," I countered, "this is fine."

I continued into the brick enclosure, which had been built for people far shorter than I; before I could remove my sweaters, New Moon appeared with a blackened kettle. She insisted on mixing the bathwater lest I burn myself, and then she stood next to me, watching as, bent over in the low enclosure, I bathed. When I'd finished, she took the soap and washcloth and scoured my back.

"Oh!" she said. "You are full of muscles."

Once I was dressed, New Moon appraised me from head to foot. "You wear a white shirt and black satin *quans* like us, and sweaters like us, too. You wear your hair tied back in a nape knot." She took my hand and ran her fingertips over my knuckles. Then she tested the calluses on my palms. "You have the same hands, rough from work." Her wide gaze settled on my face. "But your eyes are different."

New Moon led me back to the house. While Autumn bathed, New Moon, Mrs. Beautiful, and I sipped tea from demitasse cups at the table in the center of the main room. Like other houses in Khanh Phu, this one had three rooms in a straight line. A recessed alcove for the family altar had been built in the center of the middle room to create spiritual harmony within the architectural symmetry. When the daylight faded, Mrs. Beautiful lit a second baby lamp from the one burning on the family altar, which sat atop a cabinet inlaid with mother-of-pearl. Her fingers were as slim as the straw she used for a taper.

"And your family?" I asked her.

She told me about her married daughters living nearby and her youngest son still at home. We talked quietly about her children until a clock in the house across the courtyard struck six. Mrs. Beautiful rose. The moment she stepped into the courtyard, there was a ruckus of squeals and snorts from the nearby pigsty.

"She's a champion pig-raiser," New Moon said, pouring more tea.

New Moon explained how Mrs. Beautiful sold her pigs to the cooperative, which in turn sold them to the central government. The cooperative paid only 180 *dong* per 100 grams (then about twenty cents per pound), but the open market brought 250 *dong* (about twenty-eight cents per pound). Each time Mrs. Beautiful sold a pig on the free market, she bought bricks and roof tiles which, particularly during inflationary times, doubled as savings account deposits. By 1986 Mrs. Beautiful had accumulated enough supplies to build a new house for her son to live in whenever he married. At the moment, the house was available for Autumn and me.

Before long, Mrs. Beautiful returned with a tray holding rice bowls, rice, an omelette, and sautéed bean curd. Although she refused to eat, she scrutinized my every mouthful. "Two bowls of rice are not enough!" she said, taking a chew of betel nut. Her gums, bright red from the betel, stood out against her teeth, which had been lacquered jet-black as was the custom of beauty in northern Viet Nam years before.

"Eat!" Mrs. Beautiful insisted. "You must finish four bowls of rice!"

"Yes!" Autumn nodded, her wisps of hair bobbing. "We must fatten you up."

Vietnamese were hungry in those days before the changes that came with Renovation. In 1987, the government still rationed rice and meat. Everyone was thin, but in Khanh Phu no one was more gaunt than Mrs. Beautiful.

Facing her sunken cheeks, I couldn't possibly eat so much rice, but neither could I refuse.

Mrs. Beautiful took her role as my guardian seriously. Late that night, I awoke to the strong smell of burning kerosene. I lay motionless, shoulders against the reed mat, eyes closed. A light glanced across my face. When it faded, I peered through the mosquito net.

Baby lamp in hand, Mrs. Beautiful bent over Autumn's bed. When she turned back toward me, I closed my eyes, except for a slit, and watched as she checked my mosquito net. Then she held the baby lamp over my face as if to examine every feature. Finally she was gone, as silently as she had come.

Mrs. Beautiful appeared twice more that night. Each time she checked my mosquito net, and each time she stared into my face. With every examination, my awareness grew: Mrs. Beautiful had rescued me from the Province Guest House for some compelling reason I didn't yet know. I began to feel as if I were living in the house of a woman haunted by some deep sorrow.

XII

Within the Wall

Many breezes make a storm;
Trees together make a forest.
Let us sharpen spears and lances.
Why be afraid to crawl like the crab,
Who sets out to conquer the ocean?

LANH CO
Dates unknown

I awoke that first morning in Khanh Phu to a slit of daylight falling across my face. I could see the gap in the shutters, the bars in the glassless windows, and the netted shape of my bed and Autumn's. It was an eerie feeling. Autumn slept on; in her breathing I heard the reedy sound of her chronic bronchitis.

I also heard squeaking and rustling in the rice storeroom on the other side of the wall at my feet. Then there was the slap of sandals in the courtyard, the scraping sound of a door opening and the yelping rush of dogs, followed by squealing. A rat raced over the wall, escaping the Siamese cat lurking in the rafters.

Slipping out from under my mosquito net, I rewrapped the Malaysian sarong I'd worn to bed. Its wild orange patterns were cheerful in the somber light. Barefoot, I opened the double wooden doors and stepped outside onto the narrow stoop. The air was grey and soft with mist that hung in droplets on the leaves of the courtyard mimosa and on a pink rose blooming in the garden. A rooster crowed. The pigs began to snort and snuffle. I headed toward the outhouse.

Three dogs approached, growling. They were brown curs, cousins to the Appalachian farm dogs used at home to terrify strangers. The middle dog closed in, teeth bared. He was missing half an ear. The others followed, snarling, the hair on their necks bristling. When I stepped back, the leader sounded that single, high-pitched yelp a hunting dog makes after cornering its prey. Suddenly the three dogs erupted into a frenzy of barks, darting at my ankles. Mrs. Beautiful raced from the rice storeroom, rat stick in hand.

"Into the house!" she yelled at me, rapping the steps to chase the dogs away. She glanced at my orange sarong. "And change into your *quans*!"

I backed into the house.

"Are you all right?" Autumn asked, her laughter a comforting sound. She folded her mosquito net up over the bed, nodding at my sarong. "Getting you here was an achievement," she teased, "but in Viet Nam even the dogs don't know what to do with that much color."

I changed into my black peasant trousers, made tea. But I still had to use the outhouse. Mustering my courage, I stepped outside onto the porch. The satin *quans* rustled. The lead dog with the mangled ear looked up from where he lay at the base of the stoop; seeing me in *quans*, he settled his chin back onto his paws. His tail swished the courtyard stones in a slow sweep like that of my dog's tail at home whenever I pass from one room to another.

Throughout that visit, Mrs. Beautiful hovered over me as if I were the last remnant of an endangered species. At meals she sat next to me, chewing her betel nut as she plied me with tofu and eggs, peanuts and rice. She ate only a bite or two.

"Eat four bowls," she'd order, tapping her chopsticks against the rice pot.

"But I'm full," I'd counter.

"Eat four!" she would insist.

I resented the martial way Mrs. Beautiful watched me eat. I tried to engage her in conversation, and gregarious Autumn tried as well. But Mrs. Beautiful would deflect our talk and serve more rice. Then she'd slip out to tend to her pigs.

Each night, I'd awaken to frail, gold light glancing across my face. I would pretend to sleep as Mrs. Beautiful stood by my bed, baby lamp in hand.

For the first week, I never left Mrs. Beautiful's walled compound. The bicycles Autumn and I had brought leaned unused against the pigsty. My hands turned soft; the calluses on my palms peeled. I struggled against the swirling depression that, for me, comes with physical inactivity.

New Moon arrived every morning. She and Autumn and I did a lot of sitting, and we drank a lot of tea. Sometimes New Moon brought her friends to visit me. Gradually the visitors began to open up, but the stories they told me often had the rehearsed sameness of preapproved rhetoric. Villagers would *noi chung*—speak in general, using the first person plural, their language peppered with "report to you . . ." When I pressed them to tell their own stories, they complied but often in a predictable litany.

"I report to you, I was born in 1946, the year after the famine," New Moon said one afternoon as she, Autumn, and I sipped tea at the table by the altar. Mrs. Beautiful sat on my bed, listening.

With her sturdy build New Moon seemed as solidly rooted to the earth as a banyan tree. "I finished fourth grade when I was fourteen," she said, "then joined the construction brigade digging the irrigation canals. I was eighteen when the American War came to us. I became a platoon leader in the women's militia." New Moon interlaced her sturdy fingers; her knuckles were ingrained with dirt. "Our village was close to the main road to the South, and we were close to the sea. Your planes came in from the ships to bomb us. They came so fast, with so little warning."

"What did you do?" I asked.

"We listened to Uncle Ho. He urged us women to make Viet Nam secure by working the paddies so our children and the soldiers could eat. When the Americans bombed by day, we plowed at night. But usually we worked the paddies by day. By night we repaired the bombed roads. We carried a rifle slung over our backs for the low-flying bombers and a rope nearby in case a pilot parachuted."

New Moon stood up and bent over, settling her hands onto the floor as if she were transplanting. "If we stood up to shoot," she added, pretending to dip rice seedlings into the mud, "the planes would bomb us. That's why we'd skitter to a trench."

"*Ruuuuuu, ruuuuu,*" Autumn said, imitating a bomber.

New Moon squatted and, like a crab, scuttled across the room to my bed. All the while she held her arms raised, imaginary rifle ready. She ducked behind Mrs. Beautiful's legs as if hiding behind a tree. "The planes would dip close to the earth to release their bombs," she said, squinting as if taking aim. "Then they would level and race upward again. When the planes leveled, we could shoot them in the belly!"

"Did you have artillery?" I asked when New Moon returned to the table.

"Oh yes." She swung the tiny teapot slowly as if it were made of heavy steel, its spout a gun barrel. "It took two women to manage the artillery. Our task was to be ready whenever an American plane flew over. We took turns." New Moon giggled, covering her mouth as she looked over at Mrs. Beautiful. "That's how my husband and I courted."

"Ah ha," I said.

Mrs. Beautiful laughed and edged closer.

"My husband was a platoon leader in the men's militia," New Moon continued. "He was also president of our section of the Youth League." She laughed, a light sound. "I became vice president. He had the watch after mine. Every evening I would chat with him as we changed shifts!"

"But what happened when the men went to the South?" I asked.

"We had to learn their work," she answered. "We had to study the theory of farming, how to gather and store the next crop's seed, how to repair machinery. We women had dug the irrigation canals, but we'd never run the pumps. We studied about the best time to open the sluice gates for irrigation and how to use the system to protect our harvest from floods." She paused, her voice dropping in pitch. "When the dike was bombed, we called everyone. 'Bring your shovels!' we yelled. 'Hurry to the dike!' We worked all night. We women had dug that irrigation system. We had to protect it!"

"In the old days," Mrs. Beautiful added, "women would transplant, weed, and harvest. But when the men left for the South, we women had to plow and harrow. Whatever it was, we had to do it."

New Moon nodded toward Mrs. Beautiful. "We had great teachers. Mrs. Beautiful! She'd been a guerrilla against the French. She taught us how to fight. I will report this to you," New Moon added. "Times have changed for women in this village. We're not beasts of burden the way we used to be before we built roads into the paddy land. Now, we carry manure in oxcarts and haul it only a short distance by shoulder yoke. After we dug the irrigation sluices, we no longer had to haul water long distances to the paddies. And now we have pedal machines for threshing and fans for winnowing! Oh my! Life is much easier than it used to be."

"Yes," Mrs. Beautiful said, touching her right shoulder as if steadying a bamboo yoke. "But the paddy road. That was the greatest development in the history of this village. An oxcart instead of women's shoulders!"

When New Moon's younger sister, Plum, came to see us, she brought with her a written speech. Plum resembled her sister, though her build and features were more delicate. As a youngster, she had corralled other children to play student while she stood before them as teacher. When she was seventeen, Plum finished middle school and began to teach first grade.

After much urging, Plum tucked her written report away in her cloth bag. She looked me in the eye and started talking. "I report to you, the year I started teaching was the year the Americans came. There was no safe place. Bombs everywhere. If the Americans bombed in the morning, we held school in the afternoon. I report to you, we never stopped school. Once, a bomb hit a bunker in a neighboring province and killed a whole class. After that, we divided our classes into groups of three and moved between the groups. Then if a bomb hit, we'd lose only three children. I was lucky. All my children survived."

"Did you have evacuees?" Autumn asked. Her daughter was six when Ha Noi's children were evacuated to the countryside.

"Yes, ours came from Nghe An and Quang Binh," Plum said. "Every family took in one or two children and raised them as their own. We gave those children extra attention. They were so young and far from their parents. They'd cry when they heard bombing in the distance because they worried their parents had been killed. Sometimes we would just hold the children." She spread her arms. "But our arms weren't long enough.

"I report to you," she continued, "when the Americans began dropping baby bombs, we made a helmet and shield out of straw for each child. A baby-bomb pellet couldn't pierce a straw helmet."

Autumn touched my shoulder. "The kids loved wearing the helmets," she said to me, "because then they looked like soldiers."

"The children stopped saying 'airplane,' " Plum added. "Instead, whenever they heard bombers, they would call out, *'Xon Son! Xon Son den!'* " Plum laughed as she imitated the children saying, "Johnson! Johnson's coming!" She continued, "Then later, they'd call, *'Nix Xon! Nix Xon den!'* In the bunkers, the kids drew pictures of Nixon."

Autumn laughed and pushed her glasses up onto her nose. "Forgive us if we tell you this, but Nixon was the most fun to draw." She sketched a likeness of the former president that could have earned her space on a newspaper editorial page. "We drew Nixon with a nose like an elephant!"

"We also built swings in the bunkers," Plum said, "and we sang."

"Can you sing one of the songs?" I asked.

Plum cleared her throat. She had an ethereal, childlike voice that wavered around each note:

> *The sun flashes through the clouds.*
> *The breeze tussles my hair.*
> *Mother, I'll bring you rice as you transplant.*
> *Eat for your health while I tend our buffalo.*

Plum paused, as if searching for words, then picked up the wavering melody. New Moon joined; her voice had a deeper resonance.

> *Mother, you try to teach me,*
> *But I'm slow to learn.*
> *Maybe tomorrow I'll wake to victory*
> *And Father's return.*

The sisters faltered. They looked at each other, laughing.

"We can't remember the rest of the song," New Moon explained.

"It was so long ago!" Plum said.

"And you?" New Moon asked of me. "Did you have special songs?"

"Of course," I said, remembering how we would sing in the bunker in Quang Ngai during mortar attacks. I began with "Where Have All the Flowers Gone?" but couldn't remember the words. I tried "If I Had a Hammer" and faded on that one, too.

"I can't remember," I said. "It's so long ago."

>

One afternoon Mrs. Dream and Mrs. Pearl came to visit. They'd heard an American was staying at Mrs. Beautiful's, and they were curious. Mrs. Dream was seventy-seven. She had the reputation for the best singing voice in Khanh Phu when she was young and still had her teeth. However, despite Autumn's numerous requests, Mrs. Dream refused to sing. She sat in silence throughout the afternoon except for one crucial sentence that freed me from what had felt like house arrest.

At sixty, Mrs. Pearl was irrepressible. She wore a green-plaid head scarf tied with the knot on top, the ends in the air. She laughed often, flashing her beautiful black teeth. Mrs. Pearl's parents had been coolies in the French coal mines. She had lived on boiled hibiscus leaves during the 1945 famine; three of her six brothers and sisters starved to death.

"I was eighteen years old during the famine," Mrs. Pearl said, retrieving the spittoon from under the altar. Dabbing an areca leaf with lime, she wrapped the leaf around a betel nut and popped the tiny green package into her mouth. She chewed, the betel saliva slurring her words. "During the famine," she said, "we had both the French and the Japanese as masters. I saw the dead. They were everywhere! In 1946, when the French invaded again, I asked my father if I could join the Viet Minh."

"Father said, 'As long as our country survives, our family will survive, but if we lose our new country, our family will die.' " Mrs. Pearl spat, a perfect shot. " 'You may work with the women,' Father said, 'but you may not run with the men. You may not return with a bursting belly!' "

"Oooh!" Mrs. Dream giggled, covering her toothless grin.

"So," Mrs. Pearl continued, "I joined the Resistance. I led a unit of thirty-two women until I was arrested.

"I worked as a secret agent for Unit 66," Mrs. Pearl said. "I was eating a rice cake in the market on March 3, 1950. I had two maps in my pocket to pass along to a contact. Someone must have pointed me out to the Vietnamese puppet troops. The puppets arrested me, they beat me. 'What were you doing in the market?' the puppets asked.

" 'Chewing a rice cake!' I said.

"Oh! The puppets beat me harder, they slashed canes across my face, up one side, down the other. When I fainted, they waited until I revived, and then they beat me again. They poured a solution made from red peppers into my eyes. They poured fish sauce down my throat, and then they beat me again. They tried electricity.

"While I was in prison," Mrs. Pearl went on, "there were skirmishes between our guerrillas and the French. A Frenchman was killed. The French prison guards blindfolded me, dragged me out on parade in front of all the people, then to a hole waiting in the earth. They were about to shoot me in a public execution. But Good Fortune smiled on me. Just then a jeep arrived with orders from the French garrison to throw me in prison. I was in Kim Son for a year. That wasn't too bad, though they beat me from time to time. But the French confiscated everything in my family's house. They took the house itself. I was horrified to return from prison and see my parents living in a hovel with no roof.

"I asked my father, 'What should I do?'

"He said, 'If we lose our new country, we lose our family. Continue your work, Child.'

"That's when I became a regular soldier fighting hand-to-hand combat. When peace came in 1954, I joined the movement to divide the rice land among the people." Mrs. Pearl wrapped another betel nut. Her fingers were creased with dirt. "For years now, since we've had the cooperative, we've had a better life than under the French." She nodded at Mrs. Dream. "Now that we're retired, we no longer work on a labor brigade. We can be part of the Garden of the Elders."

"Garden of the Elders?" I said. "Is this a real place?"

"Real!" she and Mrs. Dream chorused.

"I'd like to see that garden," I said under my breath.

"Then come!" Mrs. Pearl said.

I glanced at Autumn and New Moon, who looked at each other. Mrs. Beautiful appeared out of nowhere, hovering. The clock struck five. The dog with the bedraggled ear rose, circled, and settled into the same spot.

"We invite you!" Mrs. Dream said in the "we" of *noi chung*—to speak in general. That one sentence, an invitation from a revered elder reputed to have once had the best singing voice in the village, was all I needed to step outside the walled confines of Mrs. Beautiful's compound.

"Will you sing for me in the Garden of the Elders?" I asked Mrs. Dream.

"I will sing," she said, speaking for herself.

Over the subsequent years, I often stopped by the Garden of the Elders, but no time was more special than that first visit. The irrepressible Mrs. Pearl led me out Mrs. Beautiful's gate and across the road, passing two women who stood by their bicycles, chatting.

"Greetings, Soviet," one of the women said. She wore black *quans* and a grey sweater and carried a bundle of greens in her conical hat.

I nodded and smiled. "Greetings," I answered, "but I'm American."

"Heavens!" the other woman said as we passed.

I could still hear their excited voices as Mrs. Pearl and I turned down a lane between newly transplanted rice paddies. Soon we reached the temple honoring ancestor Ly Quoc Su, who had driven out Chinese invaders and founded Khanh Phu several centuries before. As patron saint, Ly Quoc Su guarded over the village. The temple, made of grey, typhoon-seasoned wood, might have seemed earth-bound except that the eaves of its tile roof lifted gently toward the heavens.

Several dozen elders were working in the gardens surrounding the temple. A man in his nineties trimmed a courtyard bonsai, taking care not to catch his long, white beard in the wake of his knife. Nearby, two women wearing plaid head scarves hoed around lettuce plants. On the far side of a low brick wall a number of elders were planting fruit trees in a small orchard.

Picking up a shovel, Mrs. Pearl looked among saplings ready for planting and chose a jujube. The jujube, a member of the buckthorn family, has tiny apples that are so sour, they pucker the mouth. I followed Mrs. Pearl to the orchard, where we planted the tree, crumbling dirt around its roots.

"Uncle Ho taught us we should plant trees," Mrs. Pearl said, pressing her bare foot against the mounded soil. " 'Plant a tree every Tet,' Uncle Ho said. 'Then every day thereafter the earth will give you Spring.' "

At mid-morning, the elders stopped for a break. The men shared a long bamboo pipe, smoking *thuoc lao,* a hallucinogenic tobacco. We women sat under the jackfruit trees. Mrs. Pearl poured green tea, which had a clear, fresh taste. "Uncle Ho said the elders must be a model if the youth are to be brave," she told me.

"Did any of you ever meet Uncle Ho?" I asked, looking around the circle of women, their heads wrapped in scarves.

"Only in our dreams," Mrs. Pearl said with the impishness of a child. "Sing, Older Sister," she said to Mrs. Dream. "You have the best voice."

"Not without teeth I don't!" Mrs. Dream protested.

"Who cares?" Mrs. Pearl said, flashing her red gums and magnificent black teeth.

Mrs. Dream chose the song Vietnamese children often learn first. Her voice cracked as she sang:

> *Last night I dreamed I met Uncle Ho*
> *I sat up, though still I dreamed,*
> *So happy near Uncle Ho, I sang and danced.*

The other women joined in, their voices wavering; the men set aside their bamboo pipe and joined, too:

> *I sang the song, "Long live Ho Chi Minh!"*
> *I danced the dance, "Long live Ho Chi Minh!!"*

XIII

Soundings

These hills, high or low, are measured by clouds.
These trees, supple or straight, are tested by wind.
. . . .
Everything is known—
Only the human heart remains unfathomed.

"Improvisation"
NGUYEN TRAI
1380–1442

$\mathcal{T}$he next day, Mrs. Water came to visit. Her wet hair hung down below her waist. The sweet fragrance of the *bo ket* beans she had boiled for shampoo lightened the air. Mrs. Beautiful poured tea, then sat on the bench across from Mrs. Water and me.

Mrs. Water was fifty. She told me her father had been killed by French artillery in 1945 after Ho Chi Minh's Declaration of Independence. When Mrs. Water was eighteen, her mother arranged her marriage. Mrs. Water had been married eight years and had three children when the American bombing began in 1965. Her husband volunteered for the army.

"Report to you," Mrs. Water began.

I struggled not to roll my eyes.

"Report to you," she repeated, "if our children were to have rice, then we had to learn to plow and harrow beneath bombs. We never knew one day to the next whether we would live or die. Once when I was plowing, an old man in a nearby field was hit by a baby bomb. It was awful, seeing the buffalo and the old man collapse together into the paddy mud."

Mrs. Water paused. Mrs. Beautiful drew her knees up to her chin.

"After three months of basic training," Mrs. Water continued, "my husband left for the South. He sent us a letter. 'The Truong Son Trail exhausts us,' he wrote. 'We've had to climb so many mountains! Children,' he said, 'listen to your mother! Study hard so your father can be at peace during the Struggle.' That's the only letter I received from my husband. He died in 1969."

She paused again, wiping her eyes with her sleeve. I settled my arm across the back of the bench and lifted the heavy hair from Mrs. Water's shoulders. "In 1971," she whispered, "I received a package my husband had sent with a friend returning to the North. This was two years after my husband died. In the package were three book satchels for our three children. If there was another letter, it was lost."

From the other side of the walled garden came the heavy tread of water buffalo and the lilting sound of children's voices. "So, I raised our children alone," Mrs. Water added. "I work now as the cooperative's veterinarian. I'm away on my bicycle much of the day, vaccinating animals. And if a buffalo or sow has trouble delivering, why then I'm away at night, too."

Her voice lightened. "My children are grown now. They keep saying, 'You're up in years, Mother. You don't need to work so hard.' But I can't forget my husband's death. If I work, I think less about him. Then at night, I can sleep."

That night I awoke once again to the delicate spot of light from Mrs. Beautiful's baby lamp on the other side of my mosquito net. This time I stirred, shifting toward her. She padded away. I rose and sat in darkness at the table. Shortly she returned and set the baby lamp before me.

She poured hot water from a thermos into the tiny teapot. Then she sat next to me. We sipped green tea. We didn't speak. All around us there were thick walls: regulations forbidding individual conversations with foreigners, the U.S. embargo, bombs, death. Between us there was green tea and silence.

The next afternoon, Uncle Beautiful appeared, riding through the gate on his bicycle, along with Uncle Peaceful. I was washing out my *quans* near the cistern. I stood up, shaking soap from my fingers to greet the two village leaders.

"Why haven't you come to visit me at the buffalo barn?" Uncle Beautiful teased, leaning his bike against the cistern.

"When will you invite me?" I said, unwilling to let his small opening slip by.

"You know how to ride a bicycle?"

"Of course."

"Then come tomorrow afternoon."

After hanging out my clothes, I sat with Autumn and the two uncles over tea. Both men were in their late sixties. They both had bristly, close-cropped hair and flat, square faces that looked straight out at the world as if to take it on their own terms. But Uncle Peaceful had a chunkier build and a sloping right shoulder as if his dual role as head of the cooperative and the Party were two loads hanging from a bamboo yoke. He rapped the table with his fingertip the way he might if calling a meeting of the People's Committee to order.

"The taxes, the debts!" Uncle Peaceful said, recalling the years when the two men fought the French. "If you couldn't pay your paddy rent, you had to pay interest. If by the third harvest, you still couldn't pay, the landlord took your land and your house, and you had to sell a child. That was the worst. We had a phrase for it, *tat den*—'snuff out the light.'"

"I remember one old man," Uncle Peaceful continued. "He had worked all year but didn't have enough to pay back his loan. He cried, '*Hu, Hu,*' because he couldn't keep on living. By 1945, after the Japanese made us grow jute instead of rice, we had nothing to eat. There were dozens of people dead over every kilometer of the road. No one had the strength to dig them separate graves."

Uncle Peaceful stared at the Siamese cat sitting on a rafter, its tiny body overshadowed by huge eyes. Autumn refilled his teacup.

"In 1945," Uncle Beautiful added, "this village had three thousand people. Some five hundred left, searching for food. No one heard of them

again. I could read a newspaper. That's how I knew Uncle Ho had declared independence. I read about the Youth League and joined so that I
could become a guerrilla. I was overjoyed to see the red flag with the gold
star. That gold star made of cloth was worth more than one made from
real gold!"

Uncle Peaceful leaned forward. "We'd had guerrillas as long as there
was memory," he said. "There were resistance movements, guerrilla bases,
guerrillas attacking here, guerrillas attacking there, but there was no organization, no concerted effort. When Uncle Ho declared independence, he
opened a single road for us to follow. Then the French invaded a year later,
and we were drawn once again like oxen under the French yoke. But we'd
seen the starvation the colonists brought us! We knew it was better to die
fighting than to starve slowly."

Mrs. Beautiful brought in her tray of betel nut. Autumn and I scooted
over, making room for her to sit next to us and across from her husband.

"So," I said, taking a chance, "tell us how you two met."

"Yes!" Autumn said. "Was your marriage arranged?"

"In 1952," Uncle Beautiful began, "we guerrillas won independence
from the French in this region. The French retaliated. Their artillery killed
my first wife, her mother, and my own mother. My three-year-old daughter was wounded."

Mrs. Beautiful looked up, her hands busy with the betel nut. "My
mother and I lived in another village three kilometers away," she said.
"We fed guerrillas, and I guided them around our traps. Mr. Beautiful
had his daughter with him. Whenever the child would cry, the guerrillas
would sing. It was touching, Mr. Beautiful so lonely, with a child to raise,
his wife dead."

Mrs. Beautiful popped a betel nut into her mouth. Her words thickened with the chew. "My mother had already arranged my marriage to
someone from another hamlet. I said, 'I will walk three meters in front
of that man or three meters behind, but I will not walk with him because I do not love him.' I couldn't stand to marry that man, but my
mother had already received his family's betel nut. I said, 'Well, give it
back!'" Mrs. Beautiful leaned over, spitting into the spittoon. Then she
sat up again, grinning, her gums a triumphant red. "So, my mother gave
back the betel nut!"

Uncle Peaceful sipped his tea. "Report to you," he said, "Uncle Ho
taught us how to make our new society better than the old for women as

well as for men. He said we should all fight three enemies—famine, illiteracy, and foreign occupation. After we won independence in 1954, we engaged in 'paddy land to the plower.' We formed a small cooperative and then made it into a larger cooperative, where we kept part of our produce and turned part over to the government. Uncle Ho showed us how to feed ourselves and our nation's soldiers, too."

"Did you ever see Uncle Ho?" I asked.

"Twice!" Uncle Peaceful's infectious grin tilted in the opposite direction from his shoulders. "Once in Ha Noi and once in a neighboring village. Uncle Ho told us we must study tirelessly, from books, from each other. He said that as soon as we conquered one accomplishment, we must press on to the next if we were to maintain our independence.

"Uncle Ho didn't just meet the leaders," Uncle Peaceful said. "He wandered among the people, asked them questions. There was a drought on then. He stood on a paddy dike and dipped water. He taught us how to cooperate on large projects like the irrigation system, the cooperative barns for buffalos and pigs, the brick kiln, the road through the paddy land."

"Tomorrow," Uncle Beautiful said, "we invite you to pedal down the paddy road to the buffalo barn. You'll see all this for yourself."

The next afternoon, Autumn, New Moon, and I left by bicycle for the buffalo barn two kilometers away. I had never thought riding a bike would take such concentration. Autumn and New Moon escorted me, one on each side, riding so close that our handlebars almost touched. To make matters worse, they pedaled so slowly that I could barely keep my balance.

On both sides of the road, paddies stretched out in collectivized expanses of twinkling green shoots. Since the women of the collective had finished transplanting the week before, the paddies were empty. In the whole expanse of green there were only our reflections wobbling in the paddy water.

The buffalo barn, a huge stucco structure, stood at the far end of the paddy. Dairy buffalo were rare in Viet Nam; the Khanh Phu buffalo, a special experimental breed that had been flown in from India, were so precious that Uncle Beautiful lived in a small room next to the barn so that he could tend them day and night. We sat in his room at a table made of rough lumber. He invited me to drink a glass of warm, raw milk dipped from the drum taken each day to the cooperative's ice-cream factory.

"You've heard about the straw helmets we wore against the baby bombs," he said. "Have you ever seen one?"

"No," I answered. "I'd like to." I sipped the warm buffalo milk, which tasted thick and sweet.

"I think we have the only one left," Uncle Beautiful said. He went into the storeroom and returned with a helmet and shield. "When the mother bomb exploded, the sky rained baby bombs. Each baby bomb hit the earth, bursting into hundreds of pellets, each one the size of a bike ball bearing. A direct hit would kill you, but if a baby bomb exploded nearby, this shield would stop the pellets. Here, try it on."

I took the shield, intrigued. Clumps of straw had been twisted to form a rope the size of my wrist. The rope had then been coiled around itself so tightly that a ray of sunlight couldn't penetrate. So this, I thought, was what Plum had made for her first graders. She and other Vietnamese peasants had deployed straw—their agricultural by-product—against our terrifying technology. I stuck my arms through the straps of the shield and patted the thick padding over my chest.

"No, no!" Autumn said, laughing as she took hold of the shield. "It goes over your back! Like a knapsack." She helped me into the shield as if dressing a child. Reaching up, she set the helmet on my head and tied the string under my chin. "See? When you hunker, the helmet and shield form a shelter."

"*Ruuuu, ruuuuuu!*" Uncle Beautiful made a rumbling sound.

I dropped to my heels inside a bunker of coiled straw.

"Rifle ready!" New Moon ordered. "Scuttle!"

There were whoops of laughter as I waddled to the corner, helmet bobbing, hands flailing, the shield bouncing against the dirt floor.

Giddy, I stood up, reasserting my equilibrium. "But are there still baby bombs?" I asked.

"Yes," Autumn said. "You read about them in the paper."

"I'm on the team to defuse bombs," Uncle Beautiful added. His voice turned somber. "A baby bomb killed my eldest son in 1984."

The swirl from gaiety to death threw me off balance. Nineteen eighty-four. That was nine years after the war. Twelve years after the bombing.

"I'm sorry," I said. "I didn't know."

A buffalo mooed. Uncle Beautiful turned the empty milk glass in his hands. "But the war," he said, "was fought by the American government, not the American people." He looked at me intently. "The American people are good. The American people are progressive."

I had heard this rhetoric in North Viet Nam during the war. Ho Chi Minh had subscribed to the Marxist distinction between the government and the people in wars of national liberation, with the United States government representing the interests of capitalists who enriched themselves through the arms industry. In order to benefit these higher classes, the U.S. government subjected the American people to war taxes and made the young men risk their lives in combat. The American people, Ho explained, were victims of the war much as were the Vietnamese. Therefore, he concluded, American and Vietnamese people belonged to the same side.

Ho's teaching explains in large part the reason Americans visiting Viet Nam today find so little resentment about the war. However, wearing a straw helmet and shield as I stood in front of Uncle Beautiful, I didn't have the courage to explain that we American people were not completely separate from our government and that we had not been totally ignorant when we paid for the baby bomb that killed his son. I chose instead to let Uncle Beautiful hold on to whatever comfort he could draw from Ho Chi Minh's teaching. In that moment, I chose silence over honesty.

The light shifted toward dusk, and the air took on the fragrance of falling dew. A woman pushed a cart of straw into the barn. The buffalo in the rear stall mooed. Another buffalo in a nearer stall picked up the beat.

"Milking time," Uncle Beautiful said, setting aside the helmet and shield.

That was the last time I saw Uncle Beautiful. He stood before me, arms folded, shoulders square, his face open to the world. He recited the same speech I would hear hundreds of times, but I believe he spoke it with honesty, on his own terms.

"When you return home," he said, "give my regards to your father. And give my best wishes to the American people."

It was two in the morning of my last night. I was dreaming about riding a bicycle alongside the rice paddies when Mrs. Beautiful appeared at my bedside as she had every night. Her lamp cast a pool of yellow light, illuminating a tiny cup. She held it out to me. I sat up, assuming she had brought tea. I took a sip.

Suddenly I was wide awake. Mrs. Beautiful had given me a dose of her health tonic, an elixir made from deer antlers and tiger bones. Its raw taste of whiskey seared my throat. Autumn slept on as I rose and followed Mrs. Beautiful to the table, where we sat side by side.

"I can't sleep," she said.

"Yes." I rested my hand on her shoulder.

"I miss my son," she said.

I nodded. "Uncle Beautiful told me about him."

She turned the demitasse of tonic in her fingers, then pinched her bottom lip between her thumb and forefinger. "I was ill." She sipped the elixir and offered me the cup. We passed the demitasse back and forth until we'd drunk it all.

"My son was with the army." She paused, watching the Siamese cat slip behind the family altar. "My son took leave to come home to see me. He was supposed to return to his unit the next day."

She rose and, lighting three joss sticks, set them in the incense urn. The sharp fragrance mixed with the biting odor of whiskey. She adjusted the wick on the tiny lamp made of dimpled, hand-blown glass, then returned to the bench we'd shared and poured another cup of tonic.

"The night before my son was to return to the army," she continued, "he went to visit friends. They'd found a baby bomb in a pond, but my son's friends didn't know what it was." She looked at me. "Maybe you've never seen a baby bomb. It's bright orange like your Malaysian sarong, pretty like a child's toy. When my son arrived, the baby bomb sat on the table, like this." She moved the demitasse cup to the edge.

"My son knew it was a baby bomb because my husband defuses them. Before my son could say anything, the baby bomb rolled off the table." She drew her knees up to her shoulders and hugged herself. "It killed my son, killed his friend's grandmother. Four people killed. Five wounded."

She looked at me. The frail light from the baby lamp accentuated her high cheekbones, making her seem even more gaunt. Her intensity turned to sadness.

"Do you think Americans understand?" she asked.

"Not yet," I said.

She set her hand on my knee. "You'll leave soon. I'll never see you again."

I offered her the cup of tonic. "If you agree," I said, "I'll come back."

"I agree." She sipped the elixir and returned it to me. "Finish it, Sister. It's late. We should rest."

"Tomorrow," I asked, "will you eat?"

"I will eat."

"Tonight, will you sleep?"

"Now," she said. "I will sleep."

XIV

In Motion

The sun goes down; my hair floats in the wind.
In the silence of spring, a snow-white egret
Wanders among rivers and lakes.

CAO BA QUAT
1809–1854

I returned to Khanh Phu in the summer of 1988, almost a year and a half after my first trip. By this time, the policy of *Doi Moi*—Renovation— had begun to take effect so that I had more freedom of movement. I was accompanied by Rose, a Vietnamese woman who worked for the Foreign Press Center. Rose's family was originally from Hue in the center of Viet Nam, where her father had been a famous poet.

In her early forties, Rose was the only woman in Khanh Phu with high-heeled sandals, short hair, makeup, and perfume. For all her softness, Rose could occasionally be prickly, and this made her interesting. I liked it that she didn't change her city ways. Rose was who she was and, like Autumn, she was invaluable.

UNCLE DUTIFUL'S COMPOUND

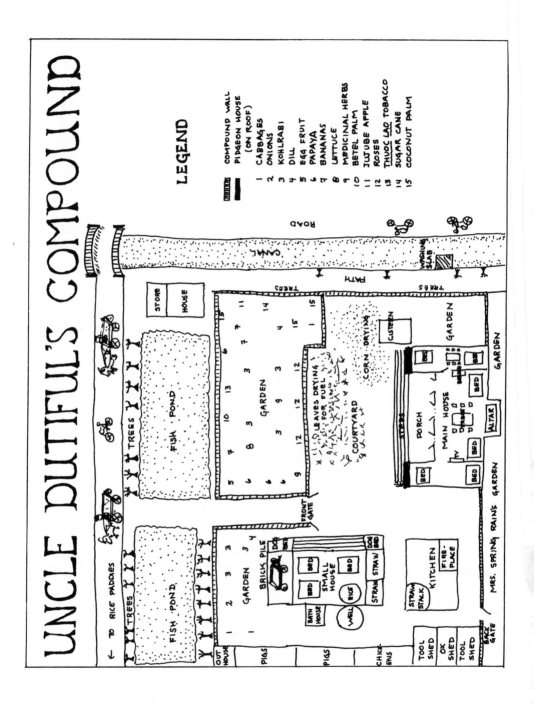

LEGEND

|||||| COMPOUND WALL
PIDGEON HOUSE (ON ROOF)

1 CABBAGES
2 ONIONS
3 KOHLRABI
4 DILL
5 EGG FRUIT
6 PAPAYA
7 BANANAS
8 LETTUCE
9 MEDICINAL HERBS
10 BETEL PALM
11 JUJUBE APPLE
12 ROSES
13 THUOC LAO TOBACCO
14 SUGAR CANE
15 COCONUT PALM

ROAD

CANAL

WASHING SLAB

PATH

TREES

TREES

STORE HOUSE

FISH POND

GARDEN

LEAVES DRYING FOR FUEL

CORN DRYING

COURTYARD

CISTERN

GARDEN

STEPS

PORCH

MAIN HOUSE

ALTAR

GARDEN

FRONT GATE

TO RICE PADDLES

TREES

FISH POND

GARDEN

BRICK PILE

SMALL HOUSE

BATH HOUSE

WELL

STRAW

STRAW STACK

KITCHEN

FIRE-PLACE

MRS. SPRING RAIN'S GARDEN

OUT HOUSE

PIGS

PIGS

CHICKENS

TOOL SHED

OX SHED

TOOL SHED

BACK GATE

Vietnamese etiquette required we stop at the house of Uncle Peaceful, head of the village. He looked robust as he greeted us over tea, but he had distressing news. Mr. Beautiful had died; Mrs. Beautiful, with whom we had expected to stay, was in mourning for her husband, who had collapsed six weeks earlier while feeding buffalo in the collective's barn.

I assumed Uncle Beautiful had suffered a stroke or heart attack, but one of his neighbors thought differently. She remembered an omen: Someone's water buffalo had strayed into the family's compound. According to the neighbor, Mrs. Beautiful hadn't burned enough incense and altar money for the ancestors to assist her in assuaging the evil spirits.

Now, with Mrs. Beautiful in mourning, nothing about this return visit seemed predictable. I felt even more apprehensive when Uncle Peaceful announced that we would stay with the family of Uncle Dutiful. I had not met Uncle Dutiful during my first visit, but I remembered seeing his photograph in the village hall. He'd served as chairman of Khanh Phu's Communist Party for forty years. In the photograph, Uncle Dutiful stood in the center of the village leaders, his shock of white hair formidable, his gaze intimidating.

With tea finished, Uncle Peaceful led us to Uncle Dutiful's house. Now seventy, Uncle Dutiful was engaged in another full-time occupation: raising a battalion of grandsons. The little boys swirled around their grandfather as he squatted in his courtyard, lashing new spikes to the frame of a bamboo fishing basket shaped like a woman's skirt hoop.

"Next door," he said in a gruff voice, glancing past his house, which was far smaller than Mrs. Beautiful's. He set the basket aside and, rising, removed a swatch of tobacco from behind his ear. Tearing off a plug, he popped the tobacco into his mouth and tucked the remainder back in place.

Moving quickly with his grandsons traipsing behind, he led Uncle Peaceful, Rose, and me down a narrow passageway alongside the kitchen and past an ox stall with a calf inside. Then we passed through a small opening in the back wall.

"Here!" Uncle Dutiful said, striding across the next-door courtyard and into the central room of the house. He pointed to a board bed with a reed mat, then to a grey-haired woman lingering in the shadows. "You'll stay with Mrs. Spring Rain, the widow of my younger brother. She's deaf." With that, he and Uncle Peaceful sat at the tea table in front of the family altar.

I hollered pleasantries at Mrs. Spring Rain. All the while she twisted a strand of grey hair. Her voice was soft. In her late sixties, she had wide-set eyes and a large mouth; wisps of loose hair added softness to her appearance. Smiling, she answered in the non sequiturs of someone who hasn't heard. I grew even more discouraged when I realized Mrs. Spring Rain was inaccessible. I watched her disappear into the side room, letting the grey curtain over the doorway drop behind her.

Rose and I joined the uncles at the table. "I report to you," Uncle Peaceful said, "we've made many economic advances since you were here." An active man, he shifted in his chair as if uncomfortable sitting still. "Last April we implemented Decision 10 from the Central Government and divided the paddy land by household."

"Families now own the land?" I asked, surprised. I drew up an armchair for Mrs. Spring Rain, who had returned with a saucer of peanuts.

"No, no! They have a fifteen-year lease," Uncle Dutiful said, pulling his knee to his chin. He leaned forward, watching the grandsons chase Mrs. Spring Rain's puppy across the courtyard. "The families profit according to how well they tend their land."

I couldn't believe what I was hearing. Surely these Communist revolutionaries realized they had turned Khanh Phu's collective paddies into individualized assets.

"And the harvest?" Rose inquired.

"The best ever!" Uncle Peaceful said.

"But what about the cooperative?" I asked, referring to the Communist economic unit.

"Stronger than ever!" Uncle Peaceful answered. "We've expanded the brick kiln and built a new and bigger carpet workshop with large windows and lots of light for the weavers. We've just started selling carpets to Romania," he added. His enthusiasm was contagious in those days before the collapse of the Soviet bloc and the quick end of its markets for Vietnamese products.

Uncle Dutiful's grandsons were peppering Mrs. Spring Rain's cistern with pebbles. "Enough of that!" Uncle Dutiful snapped. Jumping up, he called the boys and, excusing himself, left with them by the rear gate. Uncle Peaceful took his leave as well, but by the front gate.

"You should rest after your journey," Mrs. Spring Rain said, patting my shoulder.

Rose sat down on the arm of Mrs. Spring Rain's chair and, yelling into her right ear, talked about arrangements for our stay.

"I'm going down to Mrs. Beautiful's," I said almost beneath my breath. And then I did what in those days was revolutionary: Alone, I walked out of Mrs. Spring Rain's front gate.

A six-foot-wide canal separated Mrs. Spring Rain's house from National Highway 10. Whereas nearby National Highway 1 had one lane in each direction, National Highway 10 was a single-lane track. The water in the roadside canal had been used to cool a small electricity plant five kilometers away; warm even in the winter, it was used for bathing and laundry.

I nodded to three teenage girls scrubbing clothes against a washing slab by the footpath. One girl, who wore her braids in two sprightly loops, seemed particularly friendly. I did not know it at the time, but this was River, Uncle Dutiful's oldest granddaughter and older sister to the battalion of grandsons.

"You've forgotten your conical hat, Miss," River said, rinsing her print trousers in the brown water.

Having just slipped out Mrs. Spring Rain's gate, I was not about to return for a hat. "Thanks," I said, "but I'll be fine."

Delighted by my new freedom, I walked toward Mrs. Beautiful's house. The sun beat upon my shoulders; it burned my hair. Two boys playing Vietnamese checkers with pebbles looked up as I passed but then returned to their game in the dust. The two water buffalo they tended lolled in the canal. They had chewed each blade of grass on the bank down to its roots.

As I neared a crossroad, I recognized Mrs. Beautiful by her tall, slightly stooped frame. River must have acted as a quick-footed messenger, for Mrs. Beautiful wore a conical hat and carried a second. The tails of the white headband of mourning hung over her shoulder. I waved and walked faster.

"What are you doing out in this heat without a *non*?" Mrs. Beautiful demanded. She set the extra conical hat on my head. Grasping my elbow, she ushered me toward her house. A new iron gate had replaced the one made of bamboo. The gracious courtyard garden was abloom with roses and yellow flowers called *ly*, the same word as the name northern Vietnamese use for me. Mrs. Beautiful's dogs barked as soon as I came around the garden wall.

"Shhh!" she said to the dogs as we stepped inside the house. "You know Ly."

The stucco house was dark and cool, a respite from the glaring sunlight. Once my eyes adjusted, I noticed a new refrigerator and TV set. Then I turned toward the fragrance of incense and the special mourning altar. A white cloth with red Chinese characters covered the altar, which was crowded with urns of incense and trays of fruit. A photograph of Mr. Beautiful overlooked the display.

"Light some incense," Mrs. Beautiful suggested.

I removed three joss sticks and, lighting them, bowed.

Mrs. Beautiful poured tea at the table in front of the family altar. "You've come back for the Forty-ninth Day," she said.

"Yes," I answered, using the Vietnamese expression that means "I've heard" rather than "I agree" because at that time I didn't know about the Ceremony of Half-Mourning.

Vietnamese who follow Buddhism believe the deceased person's soul stays on with his family for forty-nine days before leaving for another destiny. During that period, family members burn incense and a lamp all day; they provide the deceased with dishes of food and ring a bell to announce each meal. Every week the family goes to the pagoda, asking Buddha to forgive the deceased person's transgressions. Vietnamese Buddhists further believe that those whose death was sudden need their family's prayers even more in order to depart in serenity. Then on the Forty-ninth Day, the family invites friends and relatives to a feast to send the deceased person's soul on its way.

Mrs. Beautiful nodded at her niece, who'd come in from the side room with three glasses of *che,* a snack made from green beans mashed with sugar. "Fragrance didn't make it back for the funeral either," she said of her niece.

Fragrance set the glasses on the table, then sat next to her aunt. In her early forties, she had a broad forehead and eyes the color of incense. It had taken three days for word of Uncle Beautiful's death to reach Fragrance at her husband's family's home near the Chinese border. Since she couldn't return in time for the funeral, she'd come back now for Half-Mourning.

"Please, drink!" Fragrance said. "We'll have to leave soon for the cemetery in order to return in time for the feast."

I was taken aback. I'd thought I was simply stopping by, but Fragrance and I gathered up incense and soon left by foot. As we walked along the road, bicycles passed, their chains squeaking. A bus barreled toward us, heeling to starboard, the chickens riding in baskets on top of the bus packed as tightly as the people inside. Three men hung onto the side door. When the bus slowed, the youngest jumped off. He carried a rucksack. A child called the man by name. Three women on bikes stopped, their voices excited.

"He must have just returned from the war in Cambodia," Fragrance said.

Just then New Moon pedaled up on her bicycle. "I heard you were back!" she said, stopping, one foot on the pedal, the other in the dust. She laughed, brushing back the hair that always slipped from her nape knot, then sweeping her hand toward the expanse of rice fields. "It was easy to find you," she added, her sturdy hands returning to the handlebars. "Even from a distance, you stand out like the village banyan tree."

We exchanged family news. "How was your harvest after the privatization of land?" I asked.

"Great! We bought an ox and a cart with rubber wheels!" New Moon beamed as she described the Vietnamese peasant's equivalent to my buying a brand-new car outright. "I've retired as head of the Women's Union," she continued. "But Apricot Flower will help you. I'll stop in to visit now and then. Forgive me if I'm in a hurry." With that, she turned and, waving, pedaled off.

Fragrance and I crossed the road to the cemetery, which doubled as a pasture. Half a dozen water buffalo grazed among the graves. A troop of barefoot buffalo boys raced around the closely chewed burial mounds. "Caught you!" one boy yelled, his tattered grey shirttails flapping as he tagged a younger child.

Fragrance located her uncle's grave. Kneeling, she lit incense. She spoke softly, saying the same phrases over and over, her words mixed with tears. "It's your niece, Uncle," she whispered, ". . . returning for your passage, Uncle . . ." "Uncle, your niece . . ." ". . . your journey, Uncle, to the land of the ancestors." She lit more incense and poked the sticks into the soft earth; the scent of cinnamon drifted over the grave.

As Fragrance and I walked back toward the road, I could hear snatches of conversations from the passing cyclists and then the distant toll of the pagoda bell. A nearby buffalo exhaled, an explosive sound spiced with the tang of chewed grass. The boys playing in the graveyard switched to soccer.

A thin youngster in a grey shirt kicked a ball of tightly wound bamboo strips. Another blocked the kick with his forehead and then dribbled the ball alongside a grave.

That visit, Apricot Flower, who had replaced New Moon as head of the village Women's Union, took Rose and me hither and yon, to the expanded brick factory and the swine barn, to the new carpet workshop, the ice-cream plant. But I felt like a restless tourist. I may have walked alone out of Mrs. Spring Rain's gate, but I was still living on glimpses.

One afternoon Rose, Apricot Flower, and I sat on our heels around the fire on the floor of Mrs. Spring Rain's kitchen. Apricot Flower was a demure woman with a clear face and eyes the soft brown of a deer's. She fed the flames with rice straw. Smoke curled upward, dusting the walls.

Rose tapped one of the tripod legs. "Do you know why the cooking trestle has three legs?" she asked me as she dropped a piece of fat into the wok. She added chopped garlic.

I shook my head, No.

"Once there was a man who treated his wife so badly she left him for a rich man." With chopsticks, Rose stirred the garlic, which sizzled, the heat releasing its aroma. She added pork, turning the pieces of meat with her chopsticks. "The cruel husband regretted his actions and left in search of his runaway wife. His was a long, arduous journey, but in time he chanced to arrive as a beggar at the house of the rich man. His wife recognized him, but he did not recognize her until she served him his favorite dishes."

Apricot Flower added cut green beans and fish sauce to the wok. "But then the second husband came home!" she said, taking up the story. While Rose stirred, I poked the fire, adding more straw. "The woman hid her first husband in her straw stack," Apricot Flower continued, "but then the straw stack caught fire. She jumped in to save her first husband! When the second husband saw this, he jumped in to save his wife. And so, all three burned up together."

"That's the reason," Rose said, spooning the stir-fry into a serving bowl, "the cooking trestle has three legs intertwined forever in the heat."

Apricot Flower lifted the pot of rice from the ashes. "Supper time," she announced.

In the evenings, we sat around chatting. One evening when it was oppressively hot, Rose and I moved a grass mat onto the front stoop. Apricot Flower brought out an oil lamp; soon we were joined by Uncle Dutiful and his wife, then by Apricot Flower's father, whose name was Uncle Firmness. He had been head of the district Communist Party during the French and American Wars. Silent Mrs. Spring Rain brought out the teapot and a plate of roasted peanuts.

The kerosene lamp threw a gold glow over the gathered faces. The village was quiet whenever the electricity went out. I could hear the voices of neighbors, the lulling of Uncle Dutiful's calf on the other side of the sugarcane and the plaintive sound of River singing her brothers to sleep.

"Dark of the moon," Uncle Dutiful observed, gazing into the blackness. He removed a stash of tobacco from behind his ear.

"Easy to slip through such darkness," Uncle Firmness added.

Uncle Dutiful nodded toward Uncle Firmness and then to me. "There were only a dozen of us guerrillas," he said. "Firmness here, my brother Spring Rain, Mr. Beautiful, Brother Peaceful, some others. During the late 1940s, we took on an entire company, over a hundred French and puppet troops." He chewed on the tobacco. "I was most afraid of the puppets."

"Why?" I asked in a low voice, fearful that I might be entering sensitive territory.

Uncle Firmness leaned forward. "The French couldn't tell us apart from their puppets," he said. He sat next to his daughter; the lamp highlighted the soft contours of their faces. "But the Vietnamese knew who we were!"

Aunt Dutiful poured another round of tea. Her back was so bent from osteoporosis that she looked at me by twisting her whole torso. "My husband could come into the village only at night," she said.

"By three A.M.," Uncle Firmness confirmed, "we'd leave again for the mountains."

"How could you survive there?" I asked. Two years before, I'd taken a tiny basket boat among the limestone buttes that rose directly from the marsh. I knew that the karsts' caves and crevices, although perfect for hiding, offered little for sustenance.

Aunt Dutiful cupped her hands, her gnarled fingers overlapping. "I'd take a small package of rice, as if I were going to market, and then I would leave it in some prearranged place."

Uncle Dutiful spat his plug of tobacco. "Then I'd slip into the village at night to pick it up. Ha! The French thought no one would dare swim the river when it was bitter cold. That's how we entered, with our clothes on our heads."

"They key was to be small," Uncle Firmness said. "We knew each other, just the twelve of us. And the women, too—"

Suddenly the electricity, which ran only at night, switched on.

"Ah ha!" Aunt Dutiful said, pulling herself up by the porch post. "Now the fan will run. We can sleep."

Mrs. Spring Rain rose, taking the teakettle inside. She turned on the fan and the single overhead bulb. All across the village, switches clicked: Stark white light broke apart clusters of neighbors gathered around their oil lamps. Then the one cassette tape that had been endlessly copied shattered the quiet. The Swedish rock group Abba blared forth, its insistent rhythms thrumming from stereo speakers dotting the village.

Abba usually subsided by ten in the evening. Then Uncle Dutiful's sister and River would come over to Mrs. Spring Rain's. In Viet Nam, to be alone is to be utterly desolate. Each night, the two women—one elderly, the other easing into adolescence—curled together with Mrs. Spring Rain on her board bed. Mrs. Spring Rain's dog curled with her puppy underneath.

Rose and I slept in the next room in the bed next to the family altar. We would talk late into the night, usually in English. Fluent in both English and French, Rose was translating *Catch-22* into Vietnamese. We would fall asleep with books and dictionaries piled around us, the conversation drifting from how to interpret Joseph Heller's slang to war itself.

One night after we'd turned in, Rose and I lay listening to River, who sang about a country girl who worked with a road crew in the Truong Son Mountains. It was a plaintive melody full of longing for the rice paddies in the Red River Delta.

"Since time immemorial," Rose said, toying with a seam in the mosquito net, "war has separated us from our native land and from each other. That's why our music is so full of sorrow. My family, too. For years we were separated from our *que huong*—our ancestral home—in Hue."

Rose turned toward me and ran a pen along the slats in the bed, making a rattling sound. "That's the sorrow of ordinary people," she said, poking at the wood. "But wars and governments can't keep gates up between us. They can't lock us up inside ourselves. You, for instance. The authorities worry about who you are. What trouble could you cause here?"

She pointed toward the grey curtain in the doorway leading to the other room. "The people here—Mrs. Spring Rain, the aunts, Apricot Flower, even Uncle Dutiful, Uncle Firmness, and Uncle Peaceful—they know you want to be friends." Rose laughed. "Here we lie together in the same bed. We talk all night, just the two of us. No one here can understand our English! But still," she said, turning onto her back and staring up at the mosquito net, "I can't yet invite you to come have dinner with my husband and son at my house in Ha Noi. Now that's silly."

Khanh Phu had three hamlets. Mrs. Beautiful and Uncle Dutiful lived in the two Buddhist hamlets along National Highway 10. The third hamlet, which was Catholic, lay along the river at the other end of the paddy road. A huge Gothic church overshadowed its houses of stucco and thatch. Since no one I asked knew when the Sunday service began, I cavalierly offered to find out.

I pushed my bike out the gate and pedaled past the washing slab to the road. I'd been off biking with Rose, but this was my first time bicycling alone. Or so I thought. I had pedaled a few hundred yards down the paddy road when I heard giggling. I looked over my shoulder to find River sitting on the luggage rack.

"Can you take me, Auntie?" she asked.

"Don't know yet," I said. "Aren't you afraid of crashing?"

I suppose Rose and Apricot Flower had sent River because they worried about my visiting a Catholic neighborhood. Catholics were still suspect in the late 1980s perhaps because Catholicism was identified with French colonialism and the American-backed Diem regime, which had drawn many Catholics to the South in 1954. Or maybe Rose and Apricot Flower feared for my safety on a bicycle. If so, neither could have imagined my anxiety: I had never before carried anyone on the back of a bike.

The paddy road was easy navigating until we neared the Catholic village. At a glance, I could tell that this village was poorer. Perhaps this was because of the greater distance from the main road, the lack of integration into the village leadership, or the lack of family planning. The courtyards were smaller, and many houses were made of mud and wattle instead of stucco. The road became rougher. With some trepidation I maneuvered us around a pothole next to a pile of manure leaning against the wall of the churchyard.

Suddenly, five boys tore down a narrow alley between courtyard walls. "*Lien xo! LIEN XO!*—SOVIET!" they shouted. The word spread like flames across straw added to a kitchen fire. Within moments, children blocked the road. As I pushed the bike, they pressed toward me, their warm bodies tinting the air with the smell of sweat. A year-old baby in the arms of a four-year-old stared at my face and screamed. Grabbing his sister's shoulder, he ducked his head under her arm.

The church was locked, but River found the sexton, an elderly man with a white beard that reached to mid-chest. The overlaid patches on his shirt rippled as he heaved open the carved doors. In 1968, American bombers had hit both the village temple behind Uncle Dutiful's house and the Catholic church. Now, holes in the church ceiling were like spotlights throwing jagged patches of sunlight across the pews.

The sexton shooed away the children who'd pressed through the door. A boy with freckles reached through a broken shutter and stretched to release the latch. The sexton rapped the windowsill. "Away with you!" he said. Then he turned back to me. "You must know Khanh Phu people in America."

"No, Uncle," I replied. In those days, logic collapsed when Vietnamese peasants met me. They assumed I either was or knew any American they'd heard of and that I knew any overseas Vietnamese with whom they'd ever been acquainted.

After we'd stepped back outside into the searing light, the sexton tugged the door shut. "Maybe the overseas Vietnamese will help us rebuild," he said, snapping the padlock. "We have services at five A.M. and five P.M. On Sundays a pastor comes from across the river for the seven A.M. service. You're welcome at any time."

The following Sunday, the church was jammed. Its vaulted ceiling with the jagged holes resonated with music. But now, standing with River in the sunlit courtyard, all was quiet except for the children's voices and a whispering sound the breeze made in a nearby mimosa. I felt something brush my wrist and turned to find the child who had ducked under his sister's arm. He reached out to pet the fine hairs on my wrist.

I thanked the sexton and unlocked my bicycle. The children pressed closer, laughing, their moist bodies brushing against mine. As I made my tremulous start, River settled onto the back of my bike. Her weight was so slight that I wouldn't have known she was there except for the gentle pressure of her hands at my waist.

The children's voices rose in an excited buzz. They swarmed around us, hanging onto the handlebars and fenders. Other children ran on ahead, blocking the road. I pedaled straight toward the pile of composted manure. The pressure of River's hands at my waist increased as, veering, I drove us up onto the side of the dung heap. Once we'd bounced back onto the road, I glanced over my shoulder. River waved, and I waved, too.

"*Lien Xo!*" the children called, waving back as this woman they called "Soviet" pedaled home.

XV

Demise of the Dragon

When peace was restored, I returned
To the old school, to the furrows, the sugarcane.
Again we met.
. . . .
Trembling, I took your hand so fine,
And you left it, burning there in mine.

FROM "Native Land"
GIANG NAM
1929–

"*E*veryone must know how to wrap *banh chung*," Uncle Dutiful said two days before Tet in February 1989. It was the end of the Year of the Dragon, the beginning of the Year of the Snake. Uncle Dutiful set a large, flat basket of taro leaves on the brick courtyard outside his house. The mist had turned the air raw. He tightened the collar of his tattered blue jacket and pulled his floppy green cap down over his ears.

I had first eaten *banh chung* in South Viet Nam during the war. Then,

Vietnamese friends I visited during Tet served the traditional square cakes made of glutinous ("sticky") rice, mung beans, onion, and strips of pork fat. The cake's taro-leaf wrapping turns the rice green. In those days, before I had acquired the taste, eating green sticky rice was like slogging through congealed oatmeal.

But by now a piece of ponderous *banh chung* dipped in *nuoc mam* sauce with its pungent, fishy aroma had become one of my favorite foods. Delighted by the chance to learn how to make the traditional cakes, I sat on my heels next to Uncle Dutiful. Aunt Dutiful brought a basket of sticky rice to her husband. She stood curved over herself like a walking cane. Her sister-in-law, who was tiny but erect, carried a basket of mashed mung beans the women had shaped into spheres.

Uncle Dutiful's daughter-in-law, who was the mother of the battalion of grandsons, brought out onion slivers and pork fat. Her name was Kindness. In her mid-forties, Kindness had the same soft features as her sister, Apricot Flower. Squatting next to me, she rested her arm across my shoulder, leaning her cheek against mine. Her hair carried the musky scent of rice-husk smoke.

"In a moment," she whispered, nodding toward Uncle Dutiful, "he'll tell the legend."

River looked up from sweeping the courtyard, her left hand held behind her back as she bent over the broom of bound twigs. Her two looped braids hung down like dangly earrings. "He's gonna tell the legend!" she called out as her younger brothers raced by. The twins, who were four years old, slowed like windup toys. The five- and six-year-old continued circling but slower and slower until they squatted near their grandfather.

Uncle Dutiful folded the shiny taro leaves to make a box six inches square. "King Hung Vuong had twenty-two sons from many wives," he began. "One son's mother had died when he was young, and so he was very poor." Uncle Dutiful spooned the thick rice into the leafy box. With pudgy fingers, the twins pressed the rice into the corners.

"Good," Uncle Dutiful said, adding more rice. "King Hung Vuong made a solemn announcement," he continued. "Whoever prepared the tastiest treat for the Tet festival would become his successor. And so his sons dispersed to the far corners of the empire and returned with delicacies—tiger steak, sautéed gecko, rare snakes. All except the poorest son." Uncle Dutiful broke a sphere of mung bean onto the bed of sticky rice. "He was too poor to travel. But then a genie appeared in his dreams and told him how to make a cake from peasants' food—glutinous rice, mung bean, onion, and pork fat."

"*Banh chung!*" the twins chorused.

Uncle Dutiful nodded at the six-year-old, who added pork strips to the square cake. The toddler dropped in onion slivers. The five-year-old added more glutinous rice, and the twins patted the rice into the corners. Then River helped her grandfather fold the taro leaves over the top and tie the square cake with a sliver of bamboo. Uncle Dutiful held up the cake. "This simple peasant dish," he said, "so touched the emperor that he chose the poor son to be his heir. Since that day, we Vietnamese have wrapped square cakes at Tet." Turning the cake in his hands, Uncle Dutiful inspected the corners.

"After you leave," Kindness whispered, her arm still around my shoulder, "he'll test his cake to see if it fits inside the wooden form they use at Aunt Spring Rain's. His cake will be perfect."

"When we were children," Uncle Dutiful's sister was saying as she handed her brother another taro leaf, "square cakes at Tet were a luxury for the rich. Who had sticky rice? Who had enough firewood to boil the cakes for twelve hours?"

"We were lucky to have broth from manioc leaves," Aunt Dutiful said, sitting by her husband. With her curved back, she came up to his shoulder.

"We starved under the French!" Uncle Dutiful added. He adjusted his wool hat and turned toward me, his gaze determined. "Better to die fighting."

One twin pulled the other's hair. "*Sssssst!*" Uncle Dutiful chided. "Help out, now. Sticky rice first." He creased the sides of another leafy box. "A Tet cake has everything," he added. "Carbohydrate, fat, protein. The taro-leaf wrapping will keep it fresh for a week. But if I set this cake in the pond, the cool water will keep it fresh for a month. Now, mung bean," he said to the six-year-old.

The twins began to wiggle and poke. "Enough," Uncle Dutiful warned. He folded the leaves on top of the cake. River slipped a bamboo string underneath.

"During the French War," Aunt Dutiful said, "whenever we had sticky rice, I'd make square cakes and drop them into the pond. At night Uncle Dutiful and the other guerrillas slipped down from the mountains to collect them." She looked at her sister-in-law as if wondering whether she should continue. "I don't want to make you sad," she added in a whisper, "but later, during the American War, the women in the South did the same thing. They hid sticky rice cakes in the ponds for their guerrillas, too."

Uncle Dutiful patted the pile of taro-leaf packages. "So many square cakes!" he said. "You can tell how wealthy a family is by how many cakes they wrap. See! We're rich already."

"What took you so long?" Rose called out in English from the front stoop of Uncle Peaceful's house. In her heeled sandals and jeans, she looked as stylish as a model. Rose had arrived ahead of me for the killing of Uncle Peaceful's pig. "Did you get lost?" she asked, laughing. "Or run from the execution?"

The pig was dead. That much was clear. It rested on a wide, flat basket in the middle of the courtyard, its head tilting at a rakish angle. The fatty flank, which had been severed from the rib cage, lay like a quilt around the pig's neck. One of Uncle Peaceful's cousins, a man in his fifties, reached under the flank, hacked off a cut of pork and shaved the meat, flipping the slivers into a huge granite mortar. A nephew in his twenties grabbed a pair of two-foot wooden pestles and began to pound.

"Faster," Uncle Peaceful ordered. The younger man pounded with such power that, even in the damp and bitter cold, he removed his sweater and then his shirt. Hot and breathless, he passed the pestles on to his brother, then sat back on his heels and added black pepper, fish sauce, and a touch of gluten to the mortar's meaty paste.

"Less gluten," Uncle Peaceful's son, Leader, said. "More pounding."

In his late forties, Leader's bristly hair made him look severe. He lived in Nam Dinh, the capital of Ha Nam Ninh province, where he was chief of police. Like Uncle Peaceful, Leader was a man to be heeded. However, that morning he was at his father's house and, according to Confucian Right Relationship, under his father's direction.

"Wrap the *gio*!" Uncle Peaceful said. By now the beaten pork had become so sticky that the men could no longer lift the pestles from the meat. Leader rolled the pasty pork inside banana leaves; then he folded the leafy edges over one end and thumped it against the bricks.

"Make it solid," Uncle Peaceful instructed.

Leader compressed the meat with his fingertips and folded the other end so that the *gio* was as crisply packaged as a roll of bologna. He tied the cylinder with a bamboo string and added a loop to hang the *gio* from the kitchen rafters, away from the dogs. Then he handed the banana-leaf package to his wife, a tall woman with a flat face and downcast eyes.

"Will you use incense?" Rose asked.

"No incense," Leader said. "Cook it by the clock."

His wife dropped the pork into a kettle of water heating over the wood fire in the corner of the low, dark kitchen. If she were to follow tradition, Mrs. Leader would light incense when the water boiled, then cook the pork roll until the last fragrance of the incense had faded.

Uncle Peaceful's son-in-law prepared *cha*. He beat the less tender pork and, adding fish sauce and gluten, arranged the beaten meat into a pancake spread on banana leaves in a flat, loosely woven basket. His wife set the basket to steam over another pot of boiling water. Their son cut pig skin into strips for roasting. Another son sliced the blanket of fat into cubes to be stuffed into sausages. Uncle Peaceful's two elderly cousins dropped the chunks into washed intestines. Then one cousin held up the intestines while the other poured in blood, squeezing each sack to force the blood from one intestine down into the next.

"It's time," Leader called, tapping his watch.

His wife emerged from the kitchen, holding aloft the dripping *gio*, its banana leaves a dull, grey-green. This first package, the tastiest of all, would be served to the first guest of Tet, who would eat with the men of the family. Leader tested the roll by bouncing it on the bricks. His father stood over him, watching.

"Done!" Leader said.

"*Hurmph,*" Uncle Peaceful said.

"Power with the eldest son," Rose whispered, reciting a famous Vietnamese saying. "Might with the father."

Even if I'd missed the killing of Uncle Peaceful's pig, there was no missing Apricot Flower's later that same day. Apricot Flower was a demure woman in her late twenties. As was customary for young couples, she and her husband, Honor, lived in the house of Honor's father.

Honor's father stood bent over in the low pigsty, his craggy features as striking as the limestone buttes that jutted from the rice paddies. He rubbed his hands together, then snatched the pig's hooves. The pig writhed on its back as father and son tied its legs to a bamboo pole and carried the pig out of the sty and across the courtyard.

"All right," Honor's father said to the neighbor, who had come to help because, by custom, no one kills the pig he has tended. Four men pinned the pig to the bricks. The neighbor's thrust to the throat was quick, the wail fierce. I recoiled as Apricot Flower held a basin under the neck, catching blood that spurted with each heartbeat. The pig rolled its head, straining and squealing. Then its jaws extended in a last fearsome wail before it expired in a gurgle of blood.

Apricot Flower waited for the last drops, then added boiling water to make blood pudding. Honor, who had his father's angular features, poured boiling water over the pig's back. I recoiled as the mist thickened with the cloying odor of steamed hair; the courtyard was silent except for the ominous scrape of the neighbor's knife against the hide.

Two hours later, we gathered to feast. Honor's father waved his hand over the table crowded with dishes: slices of pork fat; wedges of pork sausage; pork skin rolled in sesame seeds; pork nuggets and scallions wrapped in lettuce leaves; pork slices boiled with slivers of kohlrabi; boiled pork *gio;* steamed pork *cha;* and, for everyone, a garnished bowl of blood pudding.

"Please, eat as if at home!" Honor's father said. With chopsticks he deposited a soft cube of fat in my bowl. "This is the best meal of Tet."

"Everything is fresh," Uncle Firmness added, "and no one is tired of feasting!" He dropped a piece of sausage into my bowl.

"Ly's a vegetarian," Rose said, using my Vietnamese name. But even Rose could not separate herself from her own culture, for at that very moment she added a wedge of pork *gio* to the pile of food in my rice bowl.

After the meal, I sat with Apricot Flower's mother on the family's board bed. Aunt Firmness, who was a tiny woman with a large head and an ample mouth, was famous for speaking her mind. "You don't smell like a foreigner," she said.

"Mother!" Apricot Flower protested, looking sideways at me with a resigned smile.

"Foreigners smell like meat-eaters," her mother went on, popping a betel nut into her mouth. She chewed, releasing the betel's sharp, acidic odor. "But we smell like rice-eaters."

"Except at Tet!" Apricot Flower said.

Cheerful by temperament, Apricot Flower could sing the traditional ballad "Lover, My Love, Don't Leave!" in a plaintive voice that encircled her own story. In the 1940s, her father headed the district Communist Party, sparking the Resistance against the French. At that same time, Honor's father fought in France alongside the French and against the Nazis. Years later, Apricot Flower and Honor fell in love. Her father was distraught; her mother, outspoken.

In rural Viet Nam, marriage creates an economic bond tying two families together in the daily life of planting, weeding, harvesting, and feasting. Apricot Flower's sister, Kindness, had married Uncle Dutiful's son, and her brother had married Uncle Spring Rain's daughter. Both marriages had cemented Party connections. But since Honor's father had assisted the French, Apricot Flower's parents felt they couldn't trust Honor. Nevertheless he and Apricot Flower persisted until their parents gave in.

Now, Apricot Flower sat holding their two-year-old daughter. The child clapped her hands as Honor, puffing his angular cheeks, blew up a yellow balloon and released it without tying the end. Honor and Apricot Flower laughed as their daughter chased the balloon through its sputtering dips.

The two grandfathers—the one who had fought alongside the French and the other who had led the revolt against the French—sat laughing side by side on the same board bench, their backs against the same stucco wall. They clapped when their shared granddaughter caught the balloon. Hanging onto it, she climbed up onto the knees of the two elderly men. Scrambling from one lap to the other, she gave her balloon first to one grandfather to blow up, and then to the other.

Early that afternoon, I walked over to the village temple, which honored Tran Ton Linh, a famous literary master in Khanh Phu's early history. Inside the temple, I looked up through the gaping hole left from the 1968 American bombing. Drizzle cooled my eyes and cheeks. Drops of water slid down the temple walls, taking with it in slow decay the rearing jaws of the blue dragon painted over the door.

Through a shattered wall I could see the crater, now a fishpond, left by the bomb that had killed two people. Beyond the pond, two men digging a grave in the cemetery looked like specters who had risen through the mist from graves under the burial mounds. The grating sound of their shovels wrapped around me like a winding sheet. The grave they dug was for a woman of ninety-two, who had sipped warm buffalo milk during the night, then whispered, "I'm ready."

The crowd that gathered outside the woman's house for the funeral that afternoon was subdued. A drum took up an insistent rhythm as six men—the fathers of Apricot Flower and Honor among them—carried the red wooden casket, pushing through the throng toward the village hearse, which was a hand-drawn red wagon with gold trim. As soon as the elders had loaded the coffin, younger men pulled the red hearse out of the family's courtyard.

The procession started. First came the black and white funeral flags with wide, jagged fringes. Two men followed with a huge drum suspended from a shoulder pole. Then came two spirit houses, which looked like miniature temples with tiny flasks of rice whiskey inside. The long yellow banner connecting the two houses symbolized the road between this life and the next.

"If you've done evil," River explained, taking my elbow as we stood in the crowded courtyard, "in the Other World you'll be put into a huge urn and cooked."

I grimaced. "What's the worst offense?" I asked as the hearse passed us. The sons, bent beneath muslin hoods, followed.

"Stealing a water buffalo or the pagoda bell," River said.

Wearing muslin hoods, River's grandmother and great-aunt and the other elderly women of the village walked behind the sons. The women's wailing was moderate because the deceased's life had been long and productive: many harvests, four sons. Once the procession reached the cemetery, a double-stringed violin took up a mournful melody. With Uncle Firmness supervising, the men lowered the casket into the grave, using thin bamboo straps. The elderly women swayed, and the tails of their white muslin hoods swayed, too. Their wailing rose in pitch as the oldest son knelt at the grave's edge, his head bent.

"Forgive us!" he cried out to his mother's soul as clods of cold mud struck the casket. "Forgive us that we shortened mourning."

River leaned her head against my arm. Her hair, freshly shampooed for Tet, carried the sweet scent of boiled *bo ket* beans. "We would bury her tomorrow," she whispered, "but a funeral on Tet would ruin everyone's year."

"Pack the mound tighter," Honor's father said.

"More earth on this side," Uncle Firmness directed. He lit a bundle of incense and poked it into the muddy mound; the fragrance sliced through the chilling mist. Then the two-stringed violin switched to a cheerful tune for a woman with a natural death after a long life. Holding hands, River and I strolled with the villagers back out through the cemetery gate.

Several days later, the woman's two oldest sons came to visit. They presented me with bananas and apricot wine in a puzzling display of generosity.

"Our mother lived a happy life," the eldest son said after I'd invited them to sit down. He tightened the red plaid scarf around his head. His younger brother wore a green plaid scarf. "But Mother had one sadness. She had no daughter." The brothers leaned forward in tandem. "Will you be our mother's daughter?" the older one asked.

I was startled, and touched. I looked out the window toward the cemetery, where a water buffalo grazed near the fresh grave. "Yes," I said, accepting this rare gesture of affection. "I'd be honored."

On the eve of Tet, Mrs. Dutiful's sow gave birth to six piglets, a good omen for the New Year. The cold was so bitter that Mrs. Dutiful started a fire outside the pig pen. Because her back was so bent, she didn't have to stoop to poke the straw.

"Mr. Tao returns tonight," she said as the straw caught fire, the flames snapping.

"Mr. Tao?" I asked.

"The guardian of the kitchen. On the Twenty-third Day of the Last Lunar Month he leaves on the back of a carp to visit the King of Pearls in the heavens." She added rice husks, which smoldered, emitting a roasting aroma. The thick smoke rose, curling around the face of the ox which, grown now, stood munching rice straw.

Mrs. Dutiful fetched a basin of pig food she'd cooked from rice, arrowroot leaves, and slivers of banana trunk. The sow snorted through the warm slops. "On the Twenty-third," she went on, "wealthy families feast on carp to send Mr. Tao off on his travels. While he's gone, there's no guardian to prevent evil spirits from entering the house." She laughed as two piglets raced in circles, one trying to nurse on the tail of the other. "That's why we open the doors and windows and set off firecrackers at midnight on Tet Eve," she continued. "To welcome back Mr. Tao and our ancestors."

That night it was so cold that when Mrs. Spring Rain opened all the doors and windows just before midnight, Rose and I retreated to our bed. I already wore every piece of clothing I'd brought: a T-shirt, long underwear, turtleneck, two heavy wool sweaters, a quilted vest, rain parka, two scarves, and a wool hat. Nevertheless, my teeth chattered, and I was miserable.

Rose pulled the comforter tight around us. "Maybe the ancestors will bring back a warm wind," she said.

The sewing machine next to the bed stopped clattering as Fanciful, Mrs. Spring Rain's daughter, glanced up from the curtain she was rushing to complete by midnight. In her early twenties, Fanciful had taken Tet leave from her factory job sewing police uniforms in central Viet Nam. She laughed, her newly cut hair bobbing as she covered her toothy smile.

"Oh! I'd better hurry!" Fanciful said to herself. Turning the material under the needle, she pumped the treadle. Her teeth chattered as she sewed. Despite the bitter chill, Fanciful wore no sweater over her new, short-sleeved pink pajama suit made especially for Tet.

"It's almost midnight!" her brother, Steadfast, said, smoothing his hair as he checked out its wave in a cracked mirror. In his mid-twenties, Steadfast had returned from his job as a guard at the jail in the nearby town of Ninh Binh. With his chiseled jaw and wavy black hair, he looked debonair in the new blue shirt Fanciful had sewn him for Tet. He collected incense from the family altar and left for the nearby temple to welcome back his family's ancestors.

"Who'll light our firecrackers?" Fanciful asked, replacing the grey curtain in the doorway with the new blue one. The bitter breeze fluttered the soft material.

"How about Steadfast?" I asked, emerging from under the comforter. "Isn't he head of the family?"

"He won't be back in time," Fanciful said, holding out a string of a hundred firecrackers tied to a bamboo stick.

"Not me!" I said.

"How about your mother?" Rose suggested.

From Uncle Dutiful's house next door came a *ratta-ta-ta-ta-ta-tat.* Then the village exploded into blasts of light and such outrageous noise that even Mrs. Spring Rain heard it. She carried the firecrackers out to the front stoop and, touching a match to the wick, began to spin so that the firecrackers lifted away from the stick. The cuffs of her tattered trousers fluttered, and the tails of her old quilted jacket rose. Her soft expression turned into childish delight as the firecrackers exploded, *RATTA-TA, TAT TAT TAT TAT TAT.* The air filled with acrid smoke.

"A good year!" Rose said, glancing at the pink papers that littered the stoop. Every firecracker had blown.

"A plentiful harvest and many children!" Fanciful said.

Ka BOOM! The blast came from Mrs. Spring Rain's gate. In strode Steadfast, twirling a pistol that belonged to the district jail.

"Let's go," he said.

"Where?" I asked. I was shivering, it was past midnight, and we'd been busy since 4 A.M.

"To Uncle Dutiful's. I'm to be his 'first foot.' "

I'd been asked to be the first foot in Quang Ngai during the war and again on Pulau Bidong, the Malaysian refugee camp where I'd lived with Boat People, but in both places we'd had early evening curfews. It had never occurred to me that, in peacetime, the traditional visiting on the first day of Tet might begin at midnight.

In rural areas, custom dictates that the women stay behind for this visit. But since being a foreigner overrode gender, I joined Steadfast. Rose came along as well. Normally we used the back gate whenever we ducked between the two adjacent compounds. But this time we left by Mrs. Spring Rain's front entrance, then walked along the canal, around Uncle Dutiful's fishpond, and through his front gate. Handsome, debonair Steadfast entered first.

By my count, that day we had already been fêted at five pork feasts. Now, unexpectedly, here was a sixth along with, most important of all, the first bottle of rice whiskey to drip from the aunts' still. We sat cross-legged on the bed in a circle around the tray of dishes. Uncle Dutiful raised his tiny cup of whiskey.

"May the coming year bring you health, happiness, and prosperity!" he said.

"A wedding and children!" Rose said to Steadfast.

"But which girlfriend?" I teased.

"A wedding by next Tet!" Fierce echoed. He was Uncle Dutiful's son and the father of the grandsons. He pressed a pinch of hallucinogenic *thuoc lao* into the brass bowl of his ceramic water pipe. Inserting a small bamboo tube into the pipe, he touched a burning straw to the tobacco and puffed, emitting tiny clouds of smoke. The water pipe sang; Fierce exhaled, smiling. All the while his oldest son, then fifteen, stood in the doorway, scratching his cheek with a chicken foot.

We presented our gifts: crisp two-hundred-*dong* notes (then worth about three cents) for the children, warm socks for the adults, soap for the aunts, and a bottle of Johnnie Walker whiskey for Fierce and Uncle Dutiful. To each person we repeated our wee-hour-of-the-morning greetings for health, prosperity, and happiness in the Year of the Snake.

"Remember," Uncle Dutiful called out as we left by the front entrance. "Come early tomorrow!"

Soon we were home, and Steadfast was closing the bamboo gate. Mrs. Spring Rain's dog lay down under the bed. The newest puppy curled up next to his mother, settling his head on a teat. In the house, Rose set her books aside on a corner of the board bed, and she and I stretched out, a comforter under us, a comforter over us. The mosquito net hung all around like a filmy canopy. A frail light from the altar came through the netting and, with it, a trace of the incense Steadfast had lit for his ancestors.

"Sleep sweetly, Older Sister," Rose whispered in Vietnamese.

In house after stucco house, the villagers of Khanh Phu checked the tiny kerosene lamps left burning on their family altars. They spread blankets over the board beds on which, during the day, they had served their kin pork dishes and square sticky-rice cakes. They unhooked their mosquito nets and slipped underneath. In this way, each household folded in on itself like a single mimosa frond, its many tiny leaflets curling up for the night.

XVI

Debut of the Snake

The azure sky spreads its embroidery and brocade,
The days and months take on the color of hope.
The sun pours quantities of love into our hearts.
Villages fall asleep in the arms of rivers.

XUAN VIET
Contemporary poet

*I*t was 6 A.M. on Tet. Uncle Dutiful leaned across the tray of pork dishes on his board bed to refill my cup. "Bottoms up!" he toasted. The rice whiskey seared my esophagus. It smoldered in my stomach, warming me like the slow fire I had fed under Mrs. Spring Rain's rice whiskey still the day before.

I had been almost warm, squatting by that fire in Mrs. Spring Rain's dark kitchen. Big Dog and her puppy snoozed nearby; the hen made a nest for her chicks in the ashes, and the cat sat on the fire's one log just beyond the flames. Silent Mrs. Spring Rain dabbed a last bit of potato-leaf cement to make a seal between the bamboo condenser and the metal brewing flask of her still. Then she fed the fire with rice husks until the blackened flask gurgled on its tripod; the stark aroma of rice mash permeated the kitchen. Soon, the clear glass bottle at the end of the bamboo condenser began to fill, drop by drop.

Now, on the first morning of Tet, Uncle Dutiful held up a cup of the clear whiskey. "Drink!" he insisted.

Fierce picked up his water pipe. "The police chief's straw stack burned last night," he said.

"Did it burn or was it torched?" Rose asked.

"How would I know?" Fierce said, shrugging.

Rose turned to me, explaining in English. "If a farmer wants to—how do you say it?—zap someone, he burns his straw stack. Say the farmer is seen carelessly tossing a cigarette, then no one can accuse him of malice. He's reprimanded, but the deed is considered an accident. But if no one sees how the fire starts, then it's considered malice, particularly if the straw stack belongs to a police chief. Either way, this fire will ruin the police chief's Tet."

Uncle Dutiful refilled my cup. "One last drink," he said. "The whiskey will warm you up for the trip to the clan house."

Khanh Phu had four clans: Le, Dinh, Phan, and Trinh. The Le clan, which included Uncle Peaceful's family, was the strongest and richest. The Dinh clan, to which Uncle Dutiful belonged, was the largest and the oldest, dating back to the 900s, when one of Viet Nam's early capitals was established in nearby Hoa Lu.

The Dinh clan's temple was on the other side of the road. Delicate clouds of mist hung over the clan house, giving its rose garden and the gathering crowd a subdued appearance. Inside, Uncle Dutiful spread out grass mats before the altar. Then he adjusted the long, wide sleeves on the senior elder's lavender robe. The elders of the two lesser Dinh family branches stood waiting in yellow robes. In addition to ceremonial duties, each elder maintained the genealogy of his branch, preventing marriages between close Dinh relatives.

"Play the bell, the gongs and drum!" Uncle Dutiful began, reading the cantor's script. The clan house resonated with ringing and clanging. Children in the doorways pushed forward to watch the centuries-old ceremony.

In ancient times, Vietnamese believed spirits and demons surrounded them. They saw little difference between humans and animals, between the living and the dead. For Vietnamese, then as now, the dead pass on to another world close to the land of the living; since spirits of the deceased can easily return to assist or hamper those alive, honoring one's ancestors encourages the spirits to be helpful.

"Wash hands!" Uncle Dutiful directed. He watched the three elders prepare to pray. "Dry hands. On the mats!"

The second and third elders took their places behind the first in a triangle before the altar.

"Step in," Uncle Dutiful intoned. "Burn incense."

The musicians played their gongs and bells as the sharp fragrance of sandalwood filtered through the mist. The senior elder bowed three times before the altar, his arms folded inside his ample sleeves. Each time he rose, he lifted his folded arms up before his eyes so that the wide lavender sleeves hung over his mouth, keeping his own spirit inside.

"Pour rice whiskey," Uncle Dutiful instructed. The senior elder placed the whiskey next to a cooked chicken on the altar. The chicken—complete with wings and feet, tail and beak—held its head erect as it rested on a nest of rice.

"Hard to cook such a chicken," Rose whispered. "An overcooked chicken can't hold up its head."

"Bow down. Stand up!" Uncle Dutiful chanted. "Read the prayer!"

The elderly reader held the paper written in Chinese script two inches from his eyes. "On the first day of the Year of the Snake," he intoned, "in Khanh Phu village, Tam Diep district of Ha Nam Ninh province in the Socialist Republic of Viet Nam, we, the descendants of the Dinh clan, welcome our ancestors back on the occasion of Tet!"

The prayer went on to ask for health, prosperity, and happiness for clan members during the coming year. It ended by beseeching the ancestors to help preserve the fragile, new peace on the Chinese border.

"Ooooh! Almost time!" the boy next to me announced, elbowing his way out the door.

"Wine and betel nut!" Uncle Dutiful chanted. He waited while the senior elder chewed the betel nut, his arms folded, the broad lavender sleeves covering his eyes and his mouth.

"Burn the prayer," Uncle Dutiful called out, coming to the end of the ceremony. The reader held the prayer over a baby lamp; the paper curled, then ignited.

"Now!" The cry came from the courtyard.

There, a boy in a black beret spun, his arm extended over his head as he whirled, a string of firecrackers blasting. The pinching scent of burnt phosphorus mixed with the smell of prayer smoke and incense carrying New Year's salutations off into the air to honor the ancestors of the Dinh clan.

"Come visit for New Year's!" Dinh Van Chi said, stopping us on our way back from the clan ceremony. As his first (and family) name indicated, Dinh Van Chi was a member of the Dinh clan. His given name, Chi, means "will." Will owned the only aviator's cap in Khanh Phu. Wherever he walked, his ear flaps fluttered like small wings. He was Mrs. Beautiful's son-in-law.

Will led Uncle Dutiful, Rose, and me to his house, the oldest in Khanh Phu. Like other houses, his had three rooms in a row, with the central room's altar alcove interrupting the building's rectangular shape. Its carved folding doors were grey from a century of typhoons. I ducked under the low door frame and stepped over its high sill designed, like the sills in old pagodas, to make entry an overt act. Will's wife set out crisps of pork fat as we sat at the table. She had Mr. Beautiful's low cheekbones and quiet manner.

"Mother cried all night," Will said, when I asked about Mrs. Beautiful. "She won't get out of bed."

"So hard to start the New Year with Mr. Beautiful gone," Rose said. Her tone of voice acknowledged Mr. Beautiful's status change to that of ancestor.

"Please drink!" Will said, filling my cup. I sipped the golden liquor, which had a musty taste. He downed a whiskey and, beating his chest with his fists, made a rumbling sound, then leaned back against a huge, round post joined by wooden pegs to the rafters. "Tiger bones!" he said. "Makes you strong."

"In the mountains," Rose explained, "the ethnic minorities boil tiger bones until the bones dissolve." She had learned about traditional medicines from an elderly practitioner, a close friend of her parents. "Then they sell the condensed liquid for mixing with whiskey."

Uncle Dutiful held his cup aloft. "It will make you strong enough to take a Khanh Phu husband!"

"Can you find one tall enough, Uncle?" I asked.

Will shook his head, No, his ear flaps swaying. He knotted the flap strings under his chin and rubbed his toes. "Still too chilly to transplant," he muttered.

Everywhere in Khanh Phu farmers were gazing at the sky, feeling the air, and speculating about when they could transplant. During winters in northern Viet Nam, it feels as if there are no sunrises and no sunsets, as if there is no sun. There is only grey, a misty, clammy grey that penetrates the layers of sweaters and scarves and hats, shattering your bones.

At first I thought the villagers dreaded the unbearable cold of paddy mud. But during a later visit, when I learned to transplant, I came to see that their watching had nothing to do with pain. The decision of when to transplant was based solely on the rice, which depended on a certain degree of warmth to survive.

"Not yet," people kept saying over Tet feasts. "Not yet."

"Our old Vietnamese rice could survive this cold," Uncle Dutiful observed as he sipped more of Will's brew, "but not the new, short-term Indian hybrid. They transplanted the field near our house," he added, "the one next to the temple. It died."

"Maybe we can transplant day after tomorrow," Mrs. Beautiful's daughter said. She sat on the bed, gazing out a window at the leaden sky.

"Be sure to visit Mother," Will said when we rose to leave.

When I arrived at Mrs. Beautiful's house the afternoon of the first day of Tet, the mosquito net over her bed hung down like heavy, grey mist. She lay inside, facing the wall, a quilt wrapped around her. New Year's is a time for celebration unless there has been a recent death in the family. In addition to the death of Mr. Beautiful, the past year had brought Mrs. Beautiful another distress: the hasty marriage during mourning of the couple's remaining son to his pregnant girlfriend. And so on Tet Eve, as other villagers lit firecrackers and exchanged visits, Mrs. Beautiful had wept.

I tried rubbing her back, and I tried talking, but she remained silent, her back to me. I found this change alarming; I was accustomed to seeing her take charge. But when I returned two days later, Mrs. Beautiful seemed to have recovered. She took my elbow, once more asserting her grip as she led me to the "women's room." Closed and dark like a womb, this room in each house of the village had been the traditional birthing place before the midwifery clinic.

We sat on the edge of the bed, the mosquito net tossed up overhead. The room smelled dank. A blur of grey light coming through a slit in the closed shutters fell on a cabinet made of rough boards. Mrs. Beautiful drew up a wooden chair to hold teacups. Soon, the new daughter-in-law appeared with her newborn son wrapped in quilts and wearing a cap with tiny, red cat's ears. The daughter-in-law held her son out to me. I was terrified: Any baby I hold is bound to squall.

"Grandson, greet your auntie!" Mrs. Beautiful said. She made clucking noises while I held the child. Too young to know differently, the child stared placidly at me, as if I looked like everyone else. According to Vietnamese astrology, he would not have to work hard because he'd been born in the winter of the Year of the Dragon. The dragon is responsible for rain, but farmers are not looking for rain in the winter. And so, as a baby, he would sleep easily, which he did in my arms.

His mother, whose name meant Flowering Pear, carried a tray of pork dishes into the main room and set it on the bed away from the table reserved for the men. She was a quiet woman, almost transparent in the way she slipped in and out, disappearing with her son as quietly as she had entered. Given my feminist sensibility, this was a scene I found distressing. Following custom, Flowering Pear would serve Mrs. Beautiful's household until her baby son married, whereupon the cycle of servitude would shift to the next generation.

Mrs. Beautiful's sister and outspoken Aunt Firmness joined us. How alike we four looked, bundled in our scarves and sweaters as we sat cross-legged around the tray, our bare feet tucked under our black satin trousers. But how strange I must have looked with my russet hair and white teeth.

"We say people like you have ghost teeth!" Aunt Firmness said, laughing. Her perfect, black teeth gleamed.

"Does our life startle you?" Mrs. Beautiful's sister asked as she dropped a wedge of pork roll into my bowl. She had blackened teeth like her sister but low cheekbones.

"*They* startle me," I joked, pointing my chopsticks at the dogs, who eyed my wedge of pork, their tails swishing the floor.

"Burn more money!" Mrs. Beautiful ordered. She looked toward the door, where one of her daughters squatted by a pile of "paper money" bought at the Tet Market. Now that Tet feasting was almost over, the daughter prepared to send her ancestors back to the heavens.

"Why are you afraid of the dogs?" Aunt Firmness asked.

"The dogs attacked her," Mrs. Beautiful said, taking a betel nut. She loved to tell the story from my first visit, when I attempted to wear a bright orange Malay sarong to the outhouse.

Aunt Firmness smiled as she dabbed lime onto an areca leaf the way one might touch icing to a pastry. She rolled a betel nut in the leaf and set the tidy green package next to others she'd arranged on a tin plate. She offered me one.

I chewed the betel nut. It gave me an intoxicating rush, like fear itself. My heartbeat quickened. "What do I do now?" I asked, saliva seeping from my mouth.

"Like this." Mrs. Beautiful spat. A red plug of betel arced between two wooden window bars and landed outside at the base of a banana tree.

Apprehensive, I gauged the space between the bars. "I'll miss!"

"Come on, then." Aunt Firmness tugged my sleeve as she poked her bare feet into her plastic sandals. Outside, we leaned together over the garden wall: Our two betel plugs landed, *splat,* in one red puddle.

"Burn more money than that," Mrs. Beautiful called to her daughter, who held another piece of paper money over the baby lamp and waited as flames licked across the Chinese characters. She lit sheet after sheet of paper money until all that remained was a pile of ashes. The new daughter-in-law would sweep up the ashes on the fourth morning of Tet.

The people of Khanh Phu had spent days preparing for the village festival on the fourth day of Tet. The men carried the red palanquin once used by Ly Quoc Su, the founder of Khanh Phu, down to the river. They washed the sedan chair's high seat and its carved runners with clean water fetched from the center of the current. The women sewed special *ao dai,* the traditional long Vietnamese dress, for the eight virgins who would carry the palanquin.

A crowd filled the playing field across from the village hall. The voices sounded tumultuous like the river in flood; the greys and blues and drab greens of hundreds of hats and jackets looked like the changing colors of the Eastern Sea.

"No festival this big since 1954!" Uncle Dutiful yelled over the roar of the crowd. He was clearly enjoying himself. He'd replaced his tattered green hat with an old, black touring cap. "In the old days," he shouted, "the festival lasted from the fourth through the tenth day of Tet. The clans stacked trays of rice cakes from floor to ceiling, competing to see whose stack was most extravagant. But when we collectivized, we said the festival was feudalistic. Now we bring the festival back and call it 'traditional'!"

Uncle Peaceful loaded the palanquin with gifts for the ancestors: traditional square cakes, bananas that had been ripened by burying them in unhusked rice, and tiny flasks of rice whiskey. The eight virgins hefted the palanquin up onto their shoulders; the long silken panels of their dresses swayed over their black satin trousers in a wash of purple and red, gold and blue and green.

"To the temple!" Uncle Peaceful directed.

"Make way!" the police chief ordered.

The standard bearer lifted his red flag with the star of gold. Behind came great square flags of many colors, their dragon-toothed fringes flapping and, behind the flag-bearers, the eight virgins carrying the palanquin. The drummers joined the procession. An old man with a two-stringed violin and another with a bamboo flute followed. Then came the villagers, their new Tet shirts covered by jackets of grey and blue and olive drab.

The procession streamed past the market, the ice-cream factory, and the post office, then turned down the lane leading to the Garden of the Elders. I watched in dismay as children streamed over the temple wall, trampling the elders' flowers and fledgling cabbage plants. The rest of the procession followed the eight virgins, who set down the palanquin in front of the temple.

"Back! Back!" the police chief insisted.

But the crowd surged forward. Three teenage boys climbed into the jackfruit trees. Two younger boys in blue berets scrambled onto the temple roof. A young father lifted his son onto his shoulder to catch a glimpse of the village elders in their long satin robes. Executing steps like those at the Dinh clan ceremony, the elders shielded their eyes and mouths with their ample sleeves as they bowed down before the ancestors.

"Now, offer incense," the cantor read.

"Get back!" the police chief shouted. He flapped his arms to keep the crowd off the mats.

But the crowd pushed toward him, lifting up an old woman with one eye. She toppled onto the man playing the two-stringed violin. The police chief held back two little boys, but three more slipped by. He caught one barefoot youngster by the tail of his woolen scarf and twirled him around, rapping his knuckles.

Suddenly a white-haired man in a World War II French army jacket marched across the ritual mats, his brass buttons shimmering. He clicked his heels and pivoted; the crimson sash tied around his waist twirled. "Move back!" he ordered the crowd. He paced along the edge of the mats, brandishing a fan.

"He's crazy," Uncle Dutiful's son said to me. Fierce had wormed his way to my elbow. "His oldest son studied in Ha Noi. Became a government official. First one from Khanh Phu. The old man turned haughty."

"Offer tea," the cantor, who held the ritual poem, directed. "Bow down. Offer incense."

The gong sounded; a flute and two-stringed violin answered as the senior elder, who wore the embroidered patch for greatest scholarship, lit the incense. Pungent smoke floated on the mist until the pacing swashbuckler in the crimson sash fanned it away. Two young men pulled him off the ritual mats.

"Don't you dare!" he yelled.

"His son was corrupt," Fierce shouted. "Turned out of office. The son's disgrace drove the old man crazy. Otherwise, he'd be a village elder."

"Read the poem," the cantor sang. "Burn the poem!"

Soon, the ceremony was over, and the elders were lining up in front of the temple for a group photograph. Off to the side, the swashbuckler removed his crimson sash and World War II army jacket. He drew on a blue silken robe with ample sleeves. On his head he set a black turban. Straightening his shoulders, he crossed the ritual mats and silently inserted himself into the line of village elders.

With the cry of "Wrestling!" the crowd that had watched the temple rituals surged out the gate, the boys shortcutting over the wall to the muddy playing field. The contestants stripped to the waist in the bitter cold. Uncle Peaceful pulled his grey raincoat over his shoulders and sat behind the huge village drum, ready to serve as referee.

With the first drum roll, the entire line of wrestlers stepped forward, then receded, leaving behind two young men with bulging forearms and thighs. Then Uncle Peaceful took up a rhythm; the two men began an opening dance, then engaged each other. When one man hit the other in the groin, Uncle Peaceful rapped his stick against the metal band on the huge red drum. The contestants separated until Uncle Peaceful resumed the beat. When one man pinned the other to the mud, Uncle Peaceful hit the drum with a booming crescendo as the crowd cheered the victor.

There was plenty of cheering that day, but none with greater enthusiasm than when the two oldest wrestlers took on each other. One man was eighty; his white beard hung down to the middle of his bare chest. His opponent, perhaps seventy-five, was balding and had lacquered, black teeth. He wore a leaf compress over a sore on his thigh. The two began their match standing side by side, chatting, heads tilted toward each other.

Uncle Peaceful sounded his drum, and the wrestlers began to dance. They turned away from each other, approached, slapped hands, turned away, each move punctuating a drumbeat. They danced side to side, then grappled. The skin on their biceps sagged, but their moves were graceful, as if choreographed. The younger man grabbed his opponent's wrist. The older pulled back. Suddenly his face twisted with pain.

"Ouch!" he yelped.

"*Chet roi!*—Dead already!" the younger man teased. He laughed as he released his grip; by mistake he'd caught the elder's beard.

The two men began again to dance. Eventually the younger caught hold of the older. As the crowd cheered, the two went down laughing, tumbling together into the mud.

Rose and I were to have left for Ha Noi immediately after the festival, but I still sat on Mrs. Spring Rain's bed, my arm around her bony shoulders, screaming farewells into her ear. When I left the house, Apricot Flower took my elbow, but I turned back and whistled.

"Now what?" she said.

Out came Big Dog from under the wooden cart, the puppy chasing her swaying teats. Big Dog sat back on her haunches, her tongue lax, tail sweeping the bricks. I rubbed the inside of her ears. Then I took Apricot Flower's hand, and we left together through the bamboo gate.

"In the car now," Uncle Dutiful said, his voice gruff. He removed his dingy wool hat, once the resplendent green of newly transplanted rice, and smoothed back his formidable white hair.

A breeze came up, brushing the bamboo. The breeze felt almost warm on my cheek. An oxcart passed; the driver waved and pointed to the sky. "Look!" he shouted. "Spring at last. We can transplant!"

Apricot Flower looked up. She and Kindness saw the patch of blue sky and hugged each other. Honor tossed his beret into the air. Teenage River gamboled like a buffalo calf, and handsome Steadfast cheered. Uncle Peaceful straightened his shoulders as if he had just set down his heavy bamboo yoke.

I wished I could stay. I wanted to see Uncle Dutiful change that floppy green cap for his springtime pith helmet; I wanted to hear him urge his ox against the harrow. I could imagine the tangy smell of the ox's moist breath, could almost hear the gurgle of the wooden tines raking the mud.

I wanted to be with Apricot Flower and Kindness, with the aunts and with Mrs. Spring Rain as, bending over in a row, they poked rice seedlings into the paddy mud. The women would be talking about the joy of Tet feasting and the relief of no longer feasting. And they'd be sharing stories that, like the fragile green rice seedlings, would assume a life of their own.

XVII

A Blade of Rice

The higher the sun rises
The brighter grows the golden corn
The more beautifully shine
The drops of dew hanging from
    a blade of rice.

> FROM "Going to the Rice Field"
> TRAN HUU THUNG
> 1925–

*I*n *northern Viet Nam,* the first sunny day of spring in mid-February brings the beginning of a new planting season and high hopes. Particularly after the privatization of land, a good harvest could mean an electric fan, a cassette recorder, a TV, or maybe a refrigerator. In February 1990, the spring I learned to transplant, the paddies were bustling, as if the morning market had moved to the rice fields.

I had been back in Khanh Phu for a week. One afternoon I walked down the paddy road to join Mrs. Beautiful's daughter-in-law. This was the road

Mrs. Beautiful had cited as the most important civic improvement in Khanh Phu. Like all roads and house foundations in the Red River Delta, it had been built by digging buckets of mud from the paddies and laying up the chunks of mud by hand. The resulting raised base is reflected in the Vietnamese expression *len duong,* "to go up onto the road."

That afternoon, I passed two-wheeled oxcarts creaking under heaped dung. The returning, empty carts rattled. I paused at a place where pig dung had been unloaded onto the road, cutting traffic to one lane. A woman in a grey blouse, her trousers rolled up over her knees, shoveled manure from one of the piles into yoked baskets. Leaving the shovel poked into the dung, she stooped under her yoke and lifted the baskets. Then she stepped from the road onto the narrow foot dike. Two carts approached her pile of dung.

"One cart at a time!" the woman warned. "Oh no," she added. "Trouble."

An empty ox wagon failed to yield to a loaded buffalo cart. As the driver of the buffalo cart veered around the manure pile, his right wheel slipped off the raised road, tipping the cart. The dung slid. The driver seized his cart's hitching yoke, tugging. He jabbed his buffalo's flank. Snorting, the buffalo tossed his head and dug his hooves into the road.

"Too late," the woman with the yoked baskets said.

"*Chet roi!*—Dead already!" the buffalo driver muttered as the other wheel slid into the rice field. Paddy water slapped the wheel hubs. The driver removed his pith helmet and ran his fingers across his scalp, separating his hair into furrows.

By now the cart's wheels stood flush against the raised road; the hitching yoke stretched across the road like a security guard's gate. To the driver's right stretched a line of empty carts, to his left a line of loaded ones. The waiting buffalo and oxen chewed their cud, their tangy breath rising in small clouds.

The driver unhitched his buffalo and led him to the roadside to graze. Two other drivers jumped from their wagons into the paddy. They set their shoulders against the rear board of the stuck cart and, jamming their feet into the paddy mud, shoved. The cart remained stuck.

Uncle Peaceful had been building a dike between two fields. "Come on!" he called, beckoning to other drivers. He joined the men behind the cart. Soon a dozen young men in pith helmets and rolled-up trousers pressed their shoulders against the rear board. Uncle Peaceful, forty years their senior, took the most vulnerable position beneath the tilted dung.

"Ready?" he said. "Two-oo. Three!"

"*Ummmph!*" the men grunted.

The wheels rocked. Water sloshed between the wooden spokes as the load shifted, radiating its racy smell. Uncle Peaceful stood up and stretched. A smudge of dung creased his shoulder like a yoke. He gauged the wheels, which had settled farther into the paddy mud.

"Should we rock it?" the driver suggested. He and several other men had been tugging on the long wooden hitch.

"Rock it back, then forward," Uncle Peaceful directed. The men bent again to the rear board. "Ready?" Uncle Peaceful called. "Two-oo. Three!"

With a sucking sound, the wheels broke free of the mud; like a lumbering beast, the wagon rose up onto the road. The driver tugged on the right side of the hitching yoke until the cart stood aligned with the traffic. He led his buffalo to the cart, backed him over the yoke, and with the help of several others, lifted the curved wooden crosspiece onto the water buffalo's shoulders.

"My apologies," the driver said to the others. "My thanks."

The empty carts waited while the driver of the rescued wagon led a slow procession of laden carts down the paddy road. I followed, walking along the edge of the raised bank.

"Ly, Ly!" Someone called from across the rice field. "Come help."

Mrs. Beautiful's daughter-in-law, Flowering Pear, was transplanting in a line of four women. In front of the women stood two rows of seedlings ordered as neatly as village children lined up for school. In the paddy water behind the women lay scattered bundles of tender green shoots ready for planting.

I shed my sweater and rolled up my *quans*. An older woman at the end of the line laughed, her eyes dipping behind her wrinkles. Her upper lip covered the gap from a missing tooth. "Do this work and you'll turn into an old hag like me," she teased.

The man in the next paddy yanked his buffalo's traces. "Stop! Turn!" he yelled, pulling a stake from the mud. He lifted the harrow, tines dripping. The buffalo swung with a sloshing sound. Dropping the harrow, the driver reset his marking stake and snapped the traces.

"*Di! Di!*" he ordered. "Go! Go!"

I kicked off my flip-flops. As soon as I stepped from the grassy bank, the earth turned alien. Muck oozed between my toes. It swallowed my feet, engulfed my calves, tugging at my balance. The mud gave off a swampy smell. I lurched toward the women, arms flailing.

"She's tippy as that oxcart," one of the women said, looking at me in amusement. She was about my age. I recognized her by the birthmark on her cheek and the patched sleeves of her blouse. I'd noticed her and a teenage daughter in the market that morning. The woman had handed two soiled bills to the vendor, then added a cabbage to lettuce she already carried in her conical hat. Later I'd seen her at a wedding of a neighbor I knew casually. The wedding had been a simple affair with traditional packages of tea and betel nut exchanged between the families followed by tea and cigarettes for the guests.

Now, she wiped her forehead, her patched sleeve jiggling the tattered hat. She smiled and introduced herself; her name meant "damsel." She resumed planting the third row of rice. I picked up a bundle of seedlings and took my place in line between Damsel and the old woman.

"I saw you at the wedding this morning," Damsel said. With her right hand, she thrust rice shoots into the mud as quickly and evenly as a sewing machine stitching fabric.

"Did you see that groom?" Flowering Pear said. She reached for another bundle of shoots. "He wore an old brown shirt. Not even a white one."

"Is your son back home?" I asked Flowering Pear. Three days before, she had left her year-old son at her mother's for weaning.

"Not yet," she answered, smoothing her blouse over her breasts, which were full of milk. "I miss him. Everyone else gets to see him but me."

"Not so close together," Damsel said to me. "Here, like this." She spread her fingers. With her thumb pivoting on a seedling, she spanned to the next rows.

I separated a shoot with five thin blades. Mrs. Beautiful's son-in-law, Will, had dug the seedbed in clumps, making the hairlike roots harder to separate than when his wife pulled the seedlings one by one. I tucked the roots into the mud, which felt smooth and cool against my fingers.

"Ly doesn't know about rice," Flowering Pear said. She had none of the reticence I remembered from when we'd first met at Tet the year before.

"So how would the bride and groom meet?" I asked, returning to the subject of the wedding.

"In the haystack!" the old woman said.

Flowering Pear, who'd been a hasty bride, bent toward the paddy, fingers quickening. I felt a pang of regret that I'd asked the question.

"Perhaps they'd meet in the market," said a young woman, whose name meant "oriole."

"Oriole might know," Flowering Pear teased, her tone lighthearted.

Single and shy, Oriole blushed and looked away.

"Now, you're planting too far apart," the old woman said to me. She took my hand and placed hers against mine, palm to palm. "No wonder you can't measure. Your hand is too big."

"Suppose the boy sees the girl first in the market," Damsel explained. The water gurgled as she stepped back for the next row. "She's buying noodles. He notices her eyes. 'How are you?' he says. The girl looks down."

"She's shy, you know," Flowering Pear added, finishing a bundle.

"Suppose the next time they see each other," Damsel continued, "it's on the paddy road. It's the first warm day, like today. She's walking back from the fields, carrying her conical hat in her hand. She sees him coming in his oxcart."

Damsel stopped planting. We all stood, stretching our backs. Flowering Pear waved to her brother-in-law. Will had replaced his aviator's cap with an olive green hat that had a floppy brim. Now, he looked like the other men leading buffalo carts laden with dung.

"You must need more seedlings if you have time to chatter," he called from the road.

Damsel removed her conical hat, its stitched leaves curling with age, and held it in front of her face. She gazed into the tip of the hat's cone as if the scratched circle of metal there could still function as a mirror. I laughed as, exaggerating each gesture, Damsel smoothed her hair, tucking a strand back into the knot at the nape of her neck.

"The girl returning from the fields," the old woman said of Damsel's theatrics, "prepares to act casual. She fears work has smudged her beauty. The young man in the oxcart nears."

Damsel lowered her hat until her eyes and lashes appeared over its ragged rim. She let her gaze fall to the side. Flowering Pear and I both giggled. The old woman reached for a bundle of shoots and continued her scenario. "He says, 'Maybe I'll come see you.' She looks away and says, 'Perhaps.' "

"The girl doesn't say 'yes,' " Flowering Pear said, starting another row. "She doesn't say 'no.' "

"And then?" I said, reaching for a bundle of shoots. My heel dropped into a buffalo's hoof hole, making me stagger. I swore silently at the long-absent buffalo.

"Find out about the boy's mother!" Flowering Pear said. Flowering Pear waved to three women carrying yoked baskets of brilliant green seedlings along the paddy dike. "Transplanting, are you?" she called to them.

"Transplanting, are you?" the women called back. Throughout the day, that phrase echoed between women in the paddy and those on the paddy dikes.

"No family plants early," Flowering Pear said, "or their field will be gobbled by rats."

"We call them 'paddy chickens,' " the old woman said, twitching her nose in imitation.

"How come you can't plant straight?" Damsel asked me.

I was feeling embarrassed about my ineptitude when Flowering Pear rescued me. Fingers dripping, she pointed to her hips. "Ly can't grow rice because she has snow up to here."

"Then how can you live?" Damsel stood up, perplexed. Her hat threw a jagged shadow across the birthmark on her cheek. "You can't survive if you don't grow rice."

"Still chattering, are you?" Will called, returning in his empty cart. The brim of his olive green hat flopped every time the cart jounced.

"Is Mother cooking rice?" Flowering Pear asked him. "You'll have supper with us, won't you?" she said to me.

"I'd like to," I answered, "but tonight is the death day feast for Uncle Dutiful's father."

The man harrowing the next field slapped the buffalo's traces. "Turn!" he ordered.

"Can't your water buffalo plow in that snow?" Damsel asked.

"Americans have red buffalo," Flowering Pear said, separating the last seedlings in her bundle. She nodded toward the red tractor rumbling in the distance. Its steel paddle wheels churned, leaving behind a foamy wake as the tractor rode over the low dikes separating each family's paddy.

"The black buffalo eats grass," the old woman muttered. "The red buffalo prefers chicken." She smacked her lips.

I laughed. During collectivization, the tractor mechanics were also the drivers of the cooperative's three "red buffalo," which had been imported from Czechoslovakia. The red buffalo seemed always to break down unless the drivers had been treated to noodles with chicken for breakfast.

"I don't have a tractor," I said, joining the other women on another row. "But my neighbors do. I hire theirs."

"The way we hire Uncle Peaceful's grandson," Flowering Pear said.

Uncle Peaceful's grandson and two partners had bought one of the red buffalo when collectivization ended. The partners' investment, equal to six hundred American dollars, was four times a Ha Noi civil servant's annual salary at that time. I found the irony startling: The grandson of the Communist revolutionary who had collectivized Khanh Phu led its budding entrepreneurial class.

"Now instead of chicken," the older woman said, "the red buffalo eats money!"

We continued moving backwards as did the other groups of women working all across the flat expanse of paddy land that stretched as far as I could see. Each group transplanted an individual family plot in accordance with the long-term leases of 1988. We moved as if we were dancers, left feet stepping behind the right as, again and again, each woman separated one fragile green seedling from her bunch and set it into the mud.

"Is your back tired yet?" the old woman asked.

"It is," I said. I was beginning to feel how the endurance of Vietnamese women had grown from the mammoth task of transplanting so many acres of paddy, seedling by seedling.

"You will transplant with us for days," she added, "but we'll do this for weeks. And then for years."

"If you let me stay here for years," I teased, "I might even get so I can set out a straight row."

We had reached the end of the paddy by the road bank. There remained only the small section of the field where we'd been standing. The light had faded, turning the sky to grey. An empty cart creaked up the paddy road, its driver sitting on the buffalo.

"Look, Oriole," Flowering Pear said, climbing from the paddy. She set her hat on the grass. Sitting on the bank, she began to wash her legs. "Here comes Resilience back from his last load. He would look handsome in a white shirt and groom's makeup!"

"Oooh!" the old woman said, pointing to my ankles as I stepped from the paddy. "The leeches like white meat!"

I looked at my feet and shuddered; bending over, I scraped off the leech clinging to my ankle. With morbid fascination I watched a tiny stream of blood pour down my foot over skin heavily wrinkled from the water. I knew a protein in the leech's saliva prevents coagulation, but I also knew the peasant's trick. I tore off a bit of leaf from my conical hat and dabbed it onto the bite; the bleeding ceased.

Damsel dropped her tattered hat with its scratched tin mirror on top of Flowering Pear's. She nodded at the approaching buffalo cart, then winked at Oriole. "Resilience has strong arms," she said.

"Wonder where else he's strong!" the old woman teased, tossing her hat onto the pile. Her laugh was raucous. All around, within earshot, women stood up, laughing, their seedling bunches dripping into the paddy. Only Oriole continued working.

"Almost done, are you?" Resilience said to her when he came within speaking distance. He smoothed the wave in his hair. He rode sideways on his buffalo's back, one leg hanging down the flank, his broad shoulders dipping with each *clippity-clop* of the hooves.

Oriole smiled, inserting each seedling with extra care. When the cart had passed, she stood up and gazed at Resilience's receding silhouette. Then she washed her feet, rolled down her trousers, and gathered up our conical hats. We all walked together down the paddy road, past a preteen girl in ragged trousers. She set her yoked baskets down at every buffalo plop and, with a banana-leaf scoop, gathered up the fresh manure.

A gentle spring wind blew from the river. The iron pines along the dike road rustled with that haunting sound the villagers called "the voice of ghosts." A gust spread across the freshly transplanted rice. With a graceful flutter, each seedling bowed to the breeze.

That evening, Uncle Dutiful stood before his family altar. He removed his knit hat, smoothed back his white hair, and adjusted the collar of his blue worker's jacket. Then he withdrew three joss sticks from the package lying between dishes of food on the altar and lit the incense by dipping the sticks inside the chimney of the baby lamp. He clasped the smoldering sticks between his palms.

Bowing, Uncle Dutiful invoked his father's spirit. "On the Fifteenth Day of the First Lunar Month of the Year of the Horse," he said, chanting in the hushed voice appropriate for the departed, "I, your son Dutiful, stand before the family altar on the anniversary of your death. Oh Virtuous Father, you labored—sturdy as a mountain—to nourish me, your child. Come now and join these guests whom I, your son, have invited to a feast in your honor."

Uncle Dutiful set the burning incense into an altar urn. One by one he removed the dishes of food: potato soup with dill, snails the size of a fingertip, chopped chicken, fresh fish from his pond, and scallions wrapped in coriander leaves. These he arranged on a tray, which he set in the middle of the board bed. From the altar he lifted a bottle of rice whiskey made in his wife's still. He pulled its banana-leaf stopper.

"Please," Uncle Dutiful said, inviting Uncle Firmness, Rose, and me to sit on the bed. He held his hands out over the tray, palms up. "Come drink to my father's honor."

"To your father's honor!" Uncle Firmness said, echoing the toast. His oldest daughter, Kindness, had married Uncle Dutiful's son, Fierce, merging the families of the two revolutionaries. Uncle Firmness and Uncle Dutiful shared six grandchildren, including teenagers River and First Son and the battalion of small grandsons.

Uncle Dutiful topped off Uncle Firmness's cup of rice whiskey. "A wealthy man would invite many friends," he said. "My guests are few, but all the more precious."

Fierce pressed PLAY on the borrowed cassette recorder he'd set on the altar. A soprano sang of sunlight glancing over transplanted rice seedlings. He pulled a chair up to the corner of the bed and set his water pipe on his knees.

"Have you been to the fields?" I asked Uncle Firmness, dropping a snail into his rice bowl.

"No," he said, shaking his head. "I watch the grandchildren, old men's work. The kids drive me crazy. So many questions."

" 'Why, Grandpa, why?' " Uncle Dutiful imitated. He laughed, glancing across the room, where Kindness hovered over the little boys, who squatted at a low table made of lashed bamboo. With inch-long thorns, the boys pried the flesh out of the tiny snails; their discarded shells rattled like beads.

"But when the children grow up," Uncle Firmness went on, nodding at First Son, "it's my turn to ask, 'Why, Grandson, why?' "

At sixteen, First Son had the compact build of a wrestler. Whenever he smiled, his curling eyelashes erased any conceit he might have shown about his good looks. Rose thought First Son was spoiled. "But then," she would add, "he's the oldest grandson. You watch, though. Number Two Grandson does the work."

Grinning, First Son handed me two snapshots—one of himself, the

other of his girlfriend. The photos had been taken on either side of a potted chrysanthemum.

"This is the idea of First Son's girlfriend," Rose said. "Shoot two pictures. First Son sits on the left of the potted plant, Girlfriend sits on the
right. If they don't marry, each person has a picture. If they marry, then
they can put the two snapshots together into one picture."

"He's too young for one picture," Uncle Dutiful muttered, refilling our
cups. He emptied his own.

"Father's old-fashioned," Fierce said. He lit his water pipe and drew
on its stem until the pipe sang. The smoke had a silky smell. Fierce's voice
rose in pitch. "Years ago I brought bell-bottom trousers back from Ha Noi,
but Father wouldn't let First Son wear them. Said bell-bottoms weren't
revolutionary."

"How can you labor," Uncle Dutiful protested, "in trousers with cuffs
wagging like fish tails?"

"You can't make a security checkpoint in the mind," Fierce said, drawing
on his pipe. "This time when I came home to stay, Father said to me, 'You
think you're so smart, having worked in Ha Noi. Prove it in the paddy.' But
who wants to grow white-haired like Father laboring in a rice field?"

I smiled, remembering an afternoon two years before. Fierce had lain
across the board bed, the top of his head toward the door, gazing at himself
in a mirror. The battalion of boys sat behind him on low stools, removing
his grey hairs strand by strand. Over the years I had never seen Fierce
work; however, the advance of grey hair had proved unstoppable: With
each visit, Fierce looked more and more like his father.

"What was my father's life?" Uncle Dutiful went on, his cheeks rosy
from rice whiskey. "A slave to the French, that's what he was! The French
were locusts. They consumed everything."

"Sometimes your grandsons *whir* like locusts," Uncle Firmness observed. "Just when I want to listen to the news."

"What news do you get?" I asked.

"Radio Ha Noi. BBC. Voice of America." Uncle Firmness deposited a
section of cleavered chicken leg into my bowl. He nodded at the borrowed
cassette recorder, his shoulders squaring. "Dutiful is too poor to have a TV.
Dutiful chaired the village Party, but I chaired the district. You should
come watch my TV."

I'd stopped by Uncle Firmness's house several days before. For the first
time ever, I'd seen the grandsons sitting still, their fists pressed into their

Autumn (center) joined me in Khanh Phu in early 1987 before the changes that would come with Renovation. The woman on the left led the Khanh Phu Women's Union during the American War. The woman on the right was a guerrilla against the French.

Mrs. Beautiful, a guerrilla during the French War and a trainer for the Khanh Phu women's militia during the American War, was the first Vietnamese peasant to welcome an American into her home to stay. Mrs. Beautiful's daughter-in-law and grandson tend her altar following her death in 1993.

Autumn was a child in September 1945 when her mother took her to Ha Noi's Ba Dinh Square to hear Ho Chi Minh read his Declaration of Independence (below). Ho had modeled his text on a copy of the U.S. Declaration of Independence. In 1953, Ho Chi Minh and General Giap (right) examine plans for the battle of Dien Bien Phu, where the Vietnamese defeated the French. *(Ngo Vinh Long Collection)*

Many of the women I played badminton with in Ha Noi's Lenin Park carried supplies to Dien Bien Phu. The trip took three months by foot. *(Ha Noi Women's Museum)*

Women were responsible for much of the North Vietnamese defense against American bombers. *(Ngo Vinh Long Collection)*

When the men went south during the American War, the women learned to plow as well as run the large irrigation pumps. Both jobs had previously been done by men. *(Ha Noi Women's Museum)*

A formal ceremony on January 1, 1955, celebrated the total liberation of North Viet Nam from the French. *(Ngo Vinh Long Collection)*

Uncle Dutiful had recently retired as chairman of Khanh Phu's Communist Party when I first stayed at his house in 1988. During the French War, he, Uncle Spring Rain, and several other guerrillas captured the French garrison after spreading a rumor through the Market Mouth that a large number of Viet Minh soldiers had encircled the village.

Uncle Dutiful's son, Fierce, enjoys a toke of hallucinogenic tobacco. Uncle Dutiful's sister looks on.

Uncle Peaceful lights incense for his father's altar at the ceremony commemorating the anniversary of his father's death.

Mrs. Spring Rain serves rice along with soup made from greens and small crabs caught in the rice paddies. *(Photo by Autumn)*

New Moon facilitated my first visit to Khanh Phu in early 1987. During the American War, she had led Khanh Phu's women's militia. She and her husband courted when changing watch.

Khanh Phu's carpet workshop thrived during 1988, when the cooperative received a large contract to sell its handmade oriental rugs to Romania. However, the workshop was forced to scale back after the market collapsed with the disintegration of the Soviet bloc.

The hand-pushed bicycle used to supply Dien Bien Phu and the Ho Chi Minh Trail is still a common means of transport in rural Viet Nam.

Roadside cafés are new since the policy of *doi moi* (Renovation) in late 1986 allowed free enterprises.

With Renovation has come renewed attention to traditional arts. Craftsmen in Khanh Phu did the renovation work for the Temple of Literature in Ha Noi.

Uncle Dutiful's grandsons at work tending the family's water buffalo.

jaws as they watched Soviet cartoons. By now, a fifth of the people in
Khanh Phu had television. Three years before, no one owned a TV. The
change in consciousness had been stunning. Now, adults had images in
their minds of Western wealth. For the first time, they spoke to me about
their own poverty.

"I've seen Moscow and Tokyo," Uncle Firmness said. "I've seen your
Beverly Hills. Automobiles as long as my house. You should have seen TV
last night! The palaces of the deposed Czech Communist Party leaders. A
marble staircase as big as our river dike just to go upstairs. We don't even
have upstairs." With his chopsticks, he clipped a tiny snail Mrs. Dutiful had
caught in the pond. "Whole rooms of pork for the leaders!" he continued.
"No wonder they were fat!"

"Once I assisted a Czech delegation visiting Ha Noi," Rose said. "The
Czechs brought all their food. They even brought their own water. And
servants, too. The servants had to bow before the visiting diplomat, like
slaves to an emperor."

Uncle Dutiful poured more rice whiskey. "Like my father to the
French," he said. "My father couldn't feed his own children."

Uncle Firmness pulled a yellowed photograph from his shirt pocket
and handed it to me. "The peasant guerrillas after a meeting with their district managers," he said.

His oldest grandson leaned over my shoulder, pointing at two of the
earnest, youthful faces. "There's Grandfather Firmness," First Son said,
"and there's Grandfather Dutiful."

"But you had no weapons?" I said.

Uncle Dutiful sat up straight. His white hair wavered. "How could we
have weapons? We were poor!" He pointed to his temple. "Our weapon
was our wits."

With that, Uncle Dutiful climbed off the bed and took down from the
rafters a fish trap, which was made of lashed bamboo slivers. It looked like
a small dress hoop. That morning, Uncle Dutiful and Number Two Grandson had plunged the basket into the pond mud. Reaching through the top
of the hoop, they caught the fish trapped inside. Aunt Dutiful then fried
the fish for the death-day feast.

Uncle Dutiful turned the hoop upside down and tested his thumb
against one of the bamboo spikes. "The French would stomp across our
seedling beds and crush the season's potential harvest in a few minutes! We
built special traps." He reached inside the hoop, pointing to a circle of cane

used as a brace. "We added bamboo spikes here, pointing up from inside toward the rim. So easy! We dug up our seedbeds, set the traps deep underneath. Then we set the seedlings on a flat basket atop the trap."

Uncle Dutiful rested the fish trap on the floor; stepping back, he marched toward it, his steps exaggerated in imitation of the French. I chuckled.

"The Westerner stomps across our seedbed," Uncle Dutiful explained. "He steps on the flat basket, falls into the trap! He tries to climb out, but the bamboo spikes pierce his flesh. He thrashes, sinking, sinking until he gags on paddy muck."

I gulped, no longer amused.

Uncle Dutiful hung up the fish trap. "Or sometimes," he said, "we hid a banana stake in the paddy."

"What was that?" I asked, wary of what would come.

"We carved a bamboo spike with barbs like a porcupine quill, embedded it in a banana trunk, and buried the trap." He spread his arms to illustrate the banana trunk's length. Then he ran his forefinger from his ankle to his knee. "When a French soldier stepped on the spike, it went through the sole of his boot and up into his calf.

"It was impossible to break off the spike there in the rice paddy. The soldier couldn't stand the pain of the vibration from cutting the spike. So, the French needed six soldiers to rescue the wounded man—two to carry the man, two to haul the banana trunk, one to carry their weapons, and one to guard the procession."

Uncle Dutiful removed the wad of tobacco from behind his ear. "We would surreptitiously mobilize the Vietnamese soldiers inside the French garrison," he said. "Once we mounted a rumor campaign that there was a large Viet Minh unit surrounding the French fort." He tore off a piece of tobacco and popped it between his teeth. "We fought with our mouths!"

"But you can't just fight with your mouth," Uncle Firmness explained. "You have to act."

"Indeed!" Uncle Dutiful said. "We asked one family to kill a pig. We asked other families to cook huge pots of rice so the French would think a large Viet Minh unit was nearby. Then we let it be known that if the Vietnamese garrison leader didn't want to talk to us, the French would be defeated and he would be killed. We sent a message for the garrison leader to come out and meet us on the far side of the river across from the Catholic church.

"We were only three guerrillas—my brother Spring Rain, another man, and myself. We brought along four peasants to act as escort. That's all we had—three guerrillas, four masked peasants, and a rumor. The Vietnamese garrison commander was a very tough man, but he was afraid because of the rumor we'd spread. We had only one pistol. How could we three guerrillas fight? We had to fight with our mouths."

Uncle Firmness leaned forward. As district leader of the Party, he had been responsible for strategy covering a number of villages. "The guerrillas told the garrison commander, 'We'll fight to our last gunner!'" he explained.

Uncle Dutiful reasserted his reign over the story. "'Think carefully,' Brother Spring Rain said to the garrison commander. 'If you don't surrender, we'll attack and a lot of Vietnamese will be killed.'

"'But if I surrender to your demands,' the commander said, '*I'll* be killed. I'll die either way.'

"'You haven't even heard our demands,' we said.

"'What are they?' he asked."

Uncle Firmness sipped his whiskey. "We always had the same three demands," he explained. "First, you must release all your prisoners. Second, you may not conscript Vietnamese laborers. Third, you may not assist any French operations."

Uncle Dutiful tapped the edge of the feasting tray with his forefinger. "The garrison commander didn't know what to do. 'But the French will be suspicious if we don't have Vietnamese workers,' he complained.

"'All right,' we answered. 'You may have two laborers if you'll slip us two machine guns.' And so we agreed. We asked guerrillas from other villages to help us," Uncle Dutiful continued. "Seven days later, we pretended to fight. It was all pretend! What did we have? Maybe twenty of us in all! But we captured the French garrison guarding the river.

"We sent our French prisoners to Nam Dinh, but we educated the Vietnamese puppet prisoners about the French oppressors. Once they were converted, we added them to our force. Everything else in the garrison—the food and other supplies—we gave to the people. That night, we got drunk.

"But the weapons!" he went on. "All made in America! U.S. carbines. Remingtons!" He nodded at Uncle Firmness. "We passed the weapons on to the district. According to our thinking, a guerrilla makes traps, lays mines, maybe at most uses a grenade or a pistol to escape or kill himself to avoid capture. The United States had supplied the French with weapons. Ha! The United States supplied us!"

"You Americans paid for seventy-five percent of the French War," Uncle Firmness said. "Then after we won our independence in the North from the French in 1954, the war continued in the South." He tapped his temple the same way Uncle Dutiful had. "When the Americans invaded the South in 1965, our guerrillas had to turn the same Weapon of Wits against your GIs. That's one way our Resistance fighters in the South supplied themselves during the American War. They stole American weapons from your puppets."

I nodded, feeling bleak. The folly of it all seem staggering.

"Excuse us," Uncle Dutiful said. "We don't want to make you sad."

"Here is one of our customs," Uncle Firmness explained. "During a thousand years, whenever we beat the Chinese, we sent a delegation to China to apologize. You see, the Chinese had lost face in the defeat. We should have apologized to the French and the Americans after their defeats. After we break our heads against each other, we must recognize we are family."

"Please," Uncle Dutiful said, gesturing to the food. Threads from his cuff brushed the feasting tray. "More chicken. Snails. Fish."

"Time for Americans and Vietnamese to drink tea together," Uncle Firmness said as he motioned us to a table in the center of the room. His small grandsons, having eaten their fill of snails, tumbled onto the bed in a pile of interlaced legs and arms. Fierce turned the tape over. He moved the baby lamp from the altar to the table, then sat on a stool, his *thuoc lao* bong on his knees. A zither played a melody as delicate as the dew settling on the day's transplanted seedlings.

"My father was a slave," Uncle Dutiful said. With tea, he rinsed the tiny cups in which we'd drunk his wife's rice whiskey. Then he filled the cups with green tea harvested from his garden. He offered us each a demitasse. "This is the proper way to honor my father on his death day," Uncle Dutiful said. "Now I can serve a feast of greater splendor than any meal my father ever ate."

XVIII

A Bowl of Rice

The lark raises its song.
The rice ripens season after season.
Rake in hand, I work the fields.
The heavy grains pour joy into my heart.

FROM "Visiting the Rice Field"
TRAN HUU THUNG
1925–

A peasant's years pass in a rhythm of seasons: transplant, weed, harvest, rest; transplant, weed, harvest, rest. By chance, I learned to harvest six months before the visit I spent transplanting. The day in June 1989 when I arrived in Khanh Phu to harvest, tanks rolled into Beijing's Tiananmen Square, crushing pro-democracy Chinese students.

As Rose and I sat on Mrs. Spring Rain's stoop, listening to the BBC news in English, Uncle Dutiful squatted nearby. Chewing a toothpick, he cocked his head toward the radio's strange sounds. Fanciful looked up from the embroidery she was finishing in the waning daylight. Banana leaves in the garden rustled with a breeze that smelled of rain.

"The demonstrations in Beijing," Rose explained. "A live report."

As soon as the news finished, I switched to Radio Viet Nam so Uncle Dutiful could listen, too. "Will something like this happen in Viet Nam, Uncle?" I asked, a little worried about approaching a touchy topic.

Uncle Dutiful shook his head; his sheaf of white hair fluttered. "Never! We Vietnamese don't follow the Chinese." He struck his left palm with the side of his right, as if to split his hand into two. "Our Renovation is different. Ours will be peaceful."

Rose lifted her curls up off her neck, then refastened the pink foam hair roller she used as a barrette. "Mr. Do Muoi met with Vietnamese students the day after the Chinese demonstrations began," she said, alluding to the Vietnamese Communist Party general secretary and Viet Nam's most powerful leader.

"What did he say?" Fanciful asked. She was in her early twenties.

Rose touched the fine lines at the corner of her eyes. "How should I know?" she answered. "Do I look like a student?"

Uncle Dutiful laughed, a rumbling sound. "We Vietnamese have had enough fighting!" he said, poking the concrete stoop with his toothpick. "That's what Mr. Do Muoi would have said to the youth. We Vietnamese must follow our own way."

The Radio Viet Nam broadcast moved on to the weather, predicting rain. "Bah," Uncle Dutiful muttered, glancing toward the *prit prat* sound of drops hitting the banana leaves. Just then his sister came through the garden gate, carrying a spray of cut rice. Handing the rice to her brother, she sat nearby.

"What do you think?" she asked.

Uncle Dutiful turned the stalks over with one hand; the kernels, which had a greenish tint, made a *whisp whisp* sound as he rotated them across the creases in his palm.

"Not yet," he said.

"But the radio says it may storm," his sister countered.

"Not yet," Uncle Dutiful said.

"*As soon as I* finish this rose," Fanciful said one morning several days later, "I'm going to the market for some more needles." She looked up from her bamboo embroidery frame set on two stools in the doorway. Her bent needle glittered in the sunlight. "Want to give me a ride?"

"Sure," I said, sitting on my heels to wait.

Instead of returning to her factory job sewing police uniforms in the south, Fanciful had stayed on to grow rice and pursue a sideline. "Sideline" was the current economic buzz word. Whereas the Vietnamese Communist Party had suppressed private enterprise during collectivization, the Renovation that began in early 1987 encouraged entrepreneurs. By mid-1989, sidelines were common even in the countryside.

Fanciful pulled the needle through the cloth, flicking her thumbnail against the cotton. Her stitches formed a glossy surface as smooth as a rose petal. "There!" she said. "One more flower done."

"How long does it take you to finish a whole tablecloth?" I asked. I knew tourists on Ha Noi's Silk Street would pay twenty dollars for a piece like the one Fanciful embroidered.

"Seven days," she said. "I can sell the tablecloth for twenty thousand *dong* (about three dollars in American money). A simpler pattern with fewer roses takes four days and pays half that, or ten thousand *dong.*"

I did some quick arithmetic. Fanciful earned less than ten cents an hour.

"You haven't seen our new market!" she said, spreading a muslin dust cover over her work. "When we privatized the buffalo and pig barns, Mr. Beautiful's daughter and son-in-law won the contract to sell the buffalos. We tore down the buffalo barn and used the bricks to build the market."

Remarkable, I thought, as I turned the bicycle around and pushed it out the gate. Here was another example of how the descendants of the Communist leaders who had collectivized Khanh Phu now managed its capital assets. I climbed onto the bike and started off. Fanciful jumped aboard.

"Are you going to harvest?" a young woman with long hair flowing down her back called as we passed. She had come several times to embroider with Fanciful.

"Not yet," Fanciful answered over her shoulder. "We're going to market to buy more needles."

I parked the bike under the banyan tree. Traditionally in northern Viet Nam a banyan tree marks the entrance to a village so that, returning from the rice fields, villagers can see the tree and begin to relax at the thought of visiting with friends in the banyan's shade. Khanh Phu's tree was several hundred years old; its first tendrils had long since grown into massive trunks. New tendrils grew from the branches high above me. They reached down toward the earth, where they would soon root.

Standing under the banyan, I paused to watch a blacksmith tuck his white goatee up under the chin strap of his conical hat. His shop was new since my last visit. "Out of the way now," the blacksmith said to his grandson, who was about eight years old. The boy was beating at the anvil with a hammer. With tongs his grandfather removed a piece of metal from the coals and, carrying it to the anvil, shaped the metal into a curve.

"During collectivization," Fanciful said, nodding toward the pile of finished sickles, each tagged with a name, "we were discouraged from making and selling goods privately. We had to buy everything in the State Store. The quality was awful. Crafts like this disappeared. It's not just the children who have to learn the old trades," she confided, pointing to the boy's father, who spun the bicycle wheel that powered the bellows, "but the adults as well." She tapped the watch she'd bought with her embroidery money. "I'll meet you here in a half hour."

The new market was two rows of brick and stucco stalls. Women jammed the open expanse between the stalls, their conical hats bobbing amidst the greys and blues of their blouses. I followed a woman pushing a bicycle with two large baskets hanging from either side of the luggage rack. Three piglets rode in one basket, a toddler in the other.

"Are you the American?" a stranger in her mid-fifties asked, stopping me. She wore a maroon blouse and a conical hat with a worn chin strap of black velvet.

"Yes," I said.

A man selling ice cream pressed by me, honking the horn on his bicycle. The child riding on his luggage rack held a rice cake in one hand, an ice-cream stick in the other.

"Remarkable," the woman said, fingering the material of my shirt. "Do you know people from Khanh Phu in America?"

I shook my head, No.

"They're rich!" the woman said, moving on.

Another woman with a mole on her right cheek bumped my conical hat as she lifted a basket from her head. Squatting, she removed the basket lid. Four crabs scrabbled out of the basket and scurried away, but she snatched them back and sold them to a woman wearing a patched grey blouse. Pocketing her money, the vendor set the basket on top of her hat and moved off into the crowd.

"Ly!" The sound came from my left. I turned to find a woman smiling from behind her spread of wares. For a moment I couldn't place the face.

Then I remembered. Here was Plum, who had taught first grade during the American bombing. I hadn't seen her in over two years.

"Buy some fish sauce!" she said, holding up a beer bottle stoppered with a banana leaf. "How about some MSG? Kerosene?"

"Are you no longer teaching?" I asked, sitting on my heels.

"I retired last year," Plum answered. "After twenty years. Forgive me if I tend a customer," she said, pouring *nuoc mam* into the empty beer bottle a buyer presented. The air filled with the heady odor of fermented fish. Plum pointed across the crowd. "New Moon is selling over yonder."

I soon found New Moon, who had facilitated my first visit to Khanh Phu. She sat behind an array of sundries: pens, school notebooks, three barrettes, blue glass beads, and a half-dozen flashlight batteries.

"What good luck!" she said, offering me a four-inch-high stool. "I heard you were in the market, but I couldn't leave my stall to find you."

"So you're buying and selling, too?" I asked.

"Yes, as a sideline." She held the glass beads out to a teenage girl in a blue blouse. The girl fingered the beads and moved on.

"And your family?" I asked.

"Fine, but we're so busy!"

"Have you begun to harvest?" I asked.

"Not yet." New Moon took a thousand-*dong* note—then worth about fifteen cents—from an elderly woman wearing a tattered conical hat. The woman dropped two size-C batteries into her market basket. "But we're ready," New Moon continued. "Maybe tomorrow." She leaned toward a young woman, who'd picked up a school notebook. "I'm selling notebooks cheap," she said to her.

The woman selling next to New Moon lifted the cloth off her basket, releasing the aroma of fresh French bread. "Buy a small loaf," she said to me.

A man standing nearby on a crate held aloft a small package. "For anything that ails you!" he called out. His vest, black fedora, and fast-paced patter marked him as an itinerant salesman. "Headache, backache, stomachache, toothache." His voice rose in pitch as he opened the package. "These herbs cure all. Step right up, step right up, here's your chance, don't take too long, tomorrow's too late . . ."

"So will you be in the fields tomorrow?" New Moon asked as I rose to leave. She winked at me. "When I was in charge of your visit, you were always so anxious to *do* something."

I laughed, feeling a little like a schoolgirl meeting a former teacher. "New Moon," I said, "there's no stopping me now."

The house wrens were singing at 5:30 A.M. the next morning when Uncle Dutiful led his untrained ox to the cart waiting on the paddy road. The battalion of grandsons swirled around him, then ran ahead, climbing into the cart. They jumped out and scrambled in again. Second Son lifted the yoke, and Uncle Dutiful pushed against the ox's flank.

"Get on over there!" Uncle Dutiful yelled at the ox.

Second Son dropped the yoke. Startled, the youthful ox tore down the paddy road with the rattling cart in tow, the grandsons tumbling inside.

"*Ach!*" Uncle Dutiful yelled. He ran alongside, tugging on the lead rope. The ox halted, snorting, twisting his head against the lead as Uncle Dutiful climbed inside the cart. "*Di di!*—Go!" he yelled, shaking the rope as he ordered the animal to get going. The ox began to plod. The metal cart wheels with strips of tire tread wired around the rim clattered as Uncle Dutiful and his tumble of grandsons rode off toward the paddy fields.

Fanciful, Kindness, teenage River, Uncle Dutiful's sister, and I followed. River carried strips of bamboo to bind the sheaves of rice. Kindness, Fanciful, and I carried the sickles, and Senior Auntie carried a kettle of green tea. As we passed a courtyard wall, a cock flew up onto the glass fragments embedded in the top. He stretched his neck, and crowed. By the time we reached the paddy, sunlight brightened the mist rising from the river. It cast a gold glow over the fields of ripe rice, over the oxcarts beginning to line the paddy road, and over the people spreading out over the fields.

Uncle Dutiful stopped the ox, and his grandsons piled out of the cart. Second Son lifted the yoke while Uncle Dutiful led the ox free. He handed the lead rope to one of the small grandsons, who followed the ox as it grazed along the paddy road.

"Two dews," Uncle Dutiful said.

"How's that?" I asked, confused. I handed a sickle to Senior Auntie. Her *ao ba ba* and *quans* were both patched, her face webbed with wrinkles.

"We have a legend," Senior Auntie said, "about an older sister who forced her younger sister to haul manure from dew until dew while the older sister sat at home and did only light housework at midday."

"During collectivization," Kindness added, kicking off her sandals, "we farmed communally." She rolled up her trousers and adjusted the leggings that protected her calves from leeches. Taking a sickle, she stepped into the paddy.

Fanciful joined her. "We came to the fields after the sun was overhead," she said, "and then we left early. We worked one sunshine. But now that we farm our own plot, we start before the dew lifts and stay after it settles. Now, we work two dews."

I rolled up my trousers and followed Fanciful and Kindness into the paddy. Although technically not related, the two women were part of the web of family relationships that spread over the paddy land. Fanciful was first cousin to Kindness's husband and, through her sister Serenity, was sister-in-law to Kindness's brother.

"Here's how to harvest," Kindness said, taking the place on my right. Her light brown eyes made her pupils distinct, giving her face a sense of transparency. With her left hand she gathered two clumps of rice, twisting a few stalks around the clump. Flicking her wrist, Kindness cut the grass, *whish*. Gathering two more clumps, she sliced the stems.

I tried to grab two clumps but was too clumsy. Already frustrated, I settled for one.

Fanciful took the place on my left. "Cut where the stalks are dry and crisp," she cautioned.

"Always above the mud," River added. Her braids, which hung in loops, swayed as she worked.

Senior Auntie took her place next to River. We worked as a line of five, moving right to left and back again: wrap, *whish*, set aside; wrap, *whish*, set aside.

Uncle Dutiful leaned against the cart on the bank, watching us work. "We weren't close to the land like this during collectivization," he said.

I stood up, surprised. It was one thing for youthful Fanciful to critique collectivization, but Uncle Dutiful had helped implement Khanh Phu's cooperative after the French defeat. I knew that peace after the American War had brought the challenges of rebuilding when the mobilizing energy possible during the American bombing dissipated. As I watched Uncle Dutiful chewing on a stalk of rice straw, I realized these factors must have challenged collectivization.

"We were strangers to the land," Uncle Dutiful went on. "Every day a different plot of land. It was like sleeping in a strange bed every night."

Senior Auntie flicked her sickle against another clump. "The enthusiasm for harvesting disappeared," she added. "We had slogans instead of rice."

"But in the old days, way back when Auntie and I were children," Uncle Dutiful said from his post by the oxcart, "people composed poetry to honor the harvest. They sang the poems back and forth as they worked."

"And now?" I asked, perking up at the thought of the songs.

"The poetry will return," he said.

"Be sure the stems are even," Senior Auntie warned.

"Like this," Kindness said, setting her pile of rice aside so quickly that I couldn't differentiate her motions.

"Can you do it slowly?" I asked, trying not to whine.

"Maybe!" Kindness said, laughing. She stood up, wiping the sweat on her broad forehead with her sleeve. Then she bent again and, cutting two clumps, lifted the heavy heads with the blade of her sickle in a gesture as soft as a caress. She set the clumps aside in a pile, the stems even. The grains of rice made a gentle rattling sound.

Uncle Dutiful began to work behind us. He wrapped a bamboo string around a pile of rice, then twisted the string and tucked in the end. When he'd caught up to us, he went back to the oxcart and retrieved a bamboo pole sharpened at each end.

"Do you have this tool in Ohio?" he asked, jabbing one end into a sheaf of rice, then the other end into another sheaf.

I stood up, the sweat running down my forearms and onto the sickle handle. I shook my head, No.

"It's a *don xoc*," he said as, shouldering the pole, he carried the rice to the cart. "That's what we call a person who causes trouble on both sides."

"Like you sometimes, Uncle?" I teased. I bent over again and cut a swatch of rice. "Sometimes," I said, "we'll compare a person to an animal. Do you do that?"

"Sure," Kindness said, her sickle flickering in the sunlight. "We say someone who's only out for himself wriggles like an eel. Or we say a person is stubborn like a crab. A crab crawls sideways, never forward."

"Or complains like a cow!" Fanciful, who was given to merriment, added. She set aside another clump of rice. "A cow regurgitates everything and chews it all over again."

"So many caterpillars . . . ," Senior Auntie complained.

"Complains like a . . . ," Fanciful teased her elder.

Senior Auntie laughed, covering her toothless gums. She stood up, a green worm on the end of her sickle blade. "See?" she said to me as if I might arbitrate.

"Last harvest," Kindness said, her hands busy with wrap, *whish,* set aside, "the caterpillars ate the trunks of the rice stems. The rice fell over into the paddy mud before it was ripe. People stared at their fields and cried."

Uncle Dutiful speared one sheaf and then, rotating the *don xoc,* speared a second. "You women talk all the time," he complained, shouldering the pole. "Five women working, but it takes only one old man to keep up with you!"

"But Uncle," I protested, determined to keep up with my share of the verbal prodding, "you forgot to count the ox and the cart."

"*Pshaw!*" Uncle Dutiful said, his laughter making that deep rumbling sound. "The ox eats only grass. And the cart doesn't eat at all!"

We reached the end of the paddy. Turning, we started back, each cutting a swath and laying the rice atop the brown stubble. Out of the corner of my eye I could see two men pushing bicycles up the paddy road. The bamboo slat shelves lashed to the frame of each bicycle were loaded with rice.

"Good harvest?" one of the men asked.

"Good enough!" Senior Auntie called back.

"Mother!" one of Uncle Dutiful's small grandsons called. He waded knee deep in a nearby paddy sluice, a crab in his tiny fist. "Look!"

Kindness stood up, sickle in hand. "Good!" she called back. "Bring it here. We'll save it for supper." She bent again to her work. "Of all those years we were hungry," she said, "the worst was 1980."

"Nineteen eighty," I said, remembering the Boat People pouring that year onto Pulau Bidong, the Malaysian refugee camp where I'd worked as health administrator. "But wasn't the hunger worse during the war?"

"No," Senior Auntie said, "the Chinese and Soviets gave us food then. But after we ousted the Khmer Rouge, few countries would help us."

Kindness's six-year-old son ran up, his expression triumphant as he held out the crab. Kindness removed a handkerchief from her pocket and wrapped the crab inside. She nodded toward her only daughter, River, who bent over the rice, her looped braids swinging against her cheeks. Then she looked at me, her light brown eyes steady. "We adults could stand the pain that comes with an empty stomach," she said, "but no sound tugs harder at your heart than hearing your child cry from hunger."

Senior Auntie stepped up onto a paddy dike and, pouring green tea, offered me a glass. I joined her on the dike. Just then Uncle Precious, who was Mrs. Spring Rain's next-door neighbor, came by. He sat perched on the front board of a cart laden with sheaves of rice.

"Ah," he said, pointing to my ankles, "I see the leeches are having lunch."

Stopping his cart, Uncle Precious leaned over to watch as I cut the leech loose with the tip of my sickle, then tore a snippet of leaf from my conical hat. "I'll tell you a story about leeches," he said. "During the bombing, we harvested at night. One night we stopped to eat rice and soup. I couldn't see what I was eating. I thought my wife had put a tiny red pepper in the soup to invigorate me for the harvest." He held up his hand as if clasping a morsel between his chopsticks. "I held the red pepper in my chopsticks and bit it in half. I chewed."

Uncle Precious tilted back his pith helmet and laughed, displaying his tobacco-stained teeth. "It was a leech! Half chewed in my mouth. I wanted to puke. I couldn't eat for a week. So don't you worry, Ly, if the leeches like American meat. You'd rather have them eat you than you eat them." Chuckling, Uncle Precious slapped the lead rope against his buffalo's flank and waved as the buffalo plodded on.

"So Uncle Dutiful," I said, nodding toward Uncle Precious as I returned to the paddy, "what's better, an ox or a buffalo?"

Uncle Dutiful set a sheaf of rice into his half-filled cart. "The male buffalo. It's the strongest and so the best, but the ox is more versatile because it can take the heat. All a buffalo wants to do is loll around in a fishpond."

I bent again to the rice, wrapping, cutting, setting aside; wrapping, cutting, setting aside. My back ached. The sun seared my skin. My shirt was soaked. Sweat dripped from my chin into the paddy mud.

I could sense how Vietnamese endurance is tied to their labor season after season, year after year, birth to death. Through my hands and feet I could feel how Vietnamese are as rooted to their land as their village banyan tree. Bending over, the mud oozing between my fingers and toes, I began to feel that no American military technology—no matter how massive or how sophisticated—could have subjugated the villagers laboring in the fields around me.

When we reached the end of the paddy, I stood up, looking out over the gold rice in the still-uncut fields. The breeze brushed over the ripe grains. The air smelled sweet with their fragrance. We turned and waded back and forth, crisscrossing the finished field, picking up any stalks that had strayed into the mud. They would be good for pig food.

I nodded toward the stacked cart. "But do you pay some of your harvest in taxes?" I asked.

Uncle Dutiful restacked a sheaf that hung out over the sideboard. "Fifteen percent for seed, irrigation fee, and taxes," he said. "The rest is ours."

"Are you tired?" Fanciful asked.

"Yes," I admitted, removing a last leech and washing my legs in the paddy sluice.

The grandsons came running, the youthful ox cavorting behind them. Once again, Uncle Dutiful urged the ox in place as Second Son, River, and I lifted the yoke. Then down the road Uncle Dutiful went, leading the ox and the loaded cart, his grandsons racing along behind.

That afternoon we spread the rice over Uncle Dutiful's courtyard. Fierce pulled a large stone roller from a shed next to the kitchen. With the little boys in pursuit, Fierce and First Son pulled the heavy roller over the stalks, knocking loose the grains. Soon Fierce and First Son dropped the roller handle and sat on the stoop. First Son lit a cigarette. Fierce gathered his water pipe into his lap. He leaned back, blowing smoke; its odor was dizzying.

"Enough of threshing," he said.

"*Bah!*" Uncle Dutiful grumbled. "You young people won't do the hard work of farming." He picked up the handle; Second Son joined him. They ran in circles around the courtyard, the great cylindrical rock rumbling along behind them. Soon they, too, collapsed on the stoop.

"*Whew!*" Uncle Dutiful said, running his hands through his shock of white hair. "I'm getting too old for this."

River and I took a turn. Pressing our waists against the worn wood of the handle, we started with a walk, then quickly moved to a trot. The stalks of rice cut into my bare feet; the loose grains underneath were like tiny rollers. Round and round we went as the sun beat down, drying the rice. Beads of perspiration gathered on River's upper lip. Sweat ran down my back; it dripped from my elbows as we ran, the great rock rolling behind us.

"Enough!" we chorused, gasping. The dropped handle bounced against the trampled stalks as we, too, collapsed on the stoop.

Fierce leaned over and picked up a blade of rice, examining the head. He tossed it back onto the courtyard. "We're not done yet," he said. "Guess it's our turn again," he added, setting aside his pipe.

For several hours we took turns. Then Second Son raked aside the straw, leaving the light brown kernels of rice in the sun to dry. At the end of the afternoon, River and I swept up the threshed harvest. We walked back and forth over the courtyard, searching for missed grains.

"Time to eat," Aunt Dutiful said, emerging from the smoky kitchen. She bent over a huge blackened kettle of steaming rice she'd cooked over the tripod. Senior Auntie followed with a bowl of soup made from greens, tiny red peppers, and the captured crab. Kindness carried chopsticks and bowls. With a wooden paddle, she filled the bowls with rice from the blackened pot.

"Please, eat as if at home," Kindness said, offering me a bowl of rice. I held the bowl in my hands, feeling the heat of the rice warm my palms. Steam rose from the rice, carrying with it a delicate, almost bland aroma which at that moment smelled more enticing than any feast.

Leaving the Bicycle Age

Within wood lies the essence of fire.
If hidden, this fire will spring to life.
Why deny it is there?
Ignore the embers, and flames will soar.

"Wood and Fire"
Ngo Chan Luu
950–1011

*B*y early 1990, the peasants of Khanh Phu had reaped huge profits on their privately held paddies. The village had a zest I'd never felt before. I sometimes found myself feeling wistful as I watched Khanh Phu's exuberance. I felt like I was in a community on a binge. Like much of Viet Nam, Khanh Phu had entered the consumer age. Motorcycles, nonexistent in the village three years before, were common. The oppressive odor of exhaust hung over the paths. I wondered how long before plastic bags would litter the grass.

One day the week after I arrived, Apricot Flower pedaled her bicycle through the bamboo gate to Mrs. Spring Rain's house. "Honor and Steadfast are on their way!" she announced. She leaned her bike against the cistern.

"Did they get the motorcycle?" Fanciful asked, her feet pausing on the sewing-machine treadle. She was hemming one of her tablecloths. The *clickity-click* of the needle stopped.

"Ooooh, I can't wait," teenage River said. She gathered the last ears of corn drying atop the cistern into a round-bottom basket. Then she sat on the bottom step, the basket between her bare feet, her outgrown trousers riding up her calves.

Rose, Mrs. Spring Rain, and I sat on the stoop, shelling the corn that Mrs. Spring Rain had been drying for days. My fingers ached from pushing against the kernels that seemed soldered to the cob. The balls of my thumbs had turned milky with blisters. But River's fingers moved quickly. Her kernels showered the basket with a *pip-pip* sound.

"Auntie," River said, looking up at me, "why don't you wear earrings?" River's tiny gold earrings jiggled as she worked.

"Don't you keep savings, Auntie?" Fanciful asked me, referring to the earrings. Six months before, Fanciful's satin peasant trousers and straight hair had resembled the style of other village youth. Now, her tight jeans and curls made her look as if she'd come from southern California. She wore a set of delicate gold earrings that dangled against the side of her neck.

Rose, no longer a fashion anomaly in her jeans and short hair, shooed away chickens pecking at the shelled corn. "In Auntie's country," she explained, "they keep money in banks, like the one Serenity runs."

Serenity was Mrs. Spring Rain's daughter, Fanciful's sister, River's cousin, and Apricot Flower's sister-in-law. When investment groups proliferated throughout Viet Nam, Khanh Phu opened its own bank with Serenity as treasurer. Interest on one-month deposits ran 5 percent per month. Three-month deposits earned 7 percent. Borrowers shelled out 8 percent interest per month for loans.

"They're here!" River shouted. From outside the bamboo gate came the racing sound of an engine revved in neutral. River dropped her half-shelled ear of corn and raced to the gate. The sewing machine stopped clattering. Fanciful jumped from her chair.

Steadfast and Honor, astride a shiny black motorcycle, careened around the corner of the compound's stucco wall. With a screeching of brakes, they stopped in the middle of the courtyard, scattering the chickens. Mrs. Spring Rain's newest puppy darted under the pull cart.

Debonair Steadfast dismounted and, grinning, flipped a switch. A siren wailed. Even dear, deaf Mrs. Spring Rain jumped.

"We settled the loan!" Steadfast yelled into his mother's ear. Confused, she fingered a loop on her quilted peasant jacket.

"What do you think?" Honor said, straightening his beret. Angular features gave his face a French look. He ran his fingers over the silver HONDA CD 50 seal on the gleaming fuel tank.

"Look at this," Fanciful said, jumping in and out of the beam cast by the headlight.

"The end of peaceful times," Rose murmured to me in English.

I chuckled, but with sadness as I recognized the truth in Rose's comment. Steadfast and Honor had been in anxious conversation all week. For some months, Steadfast had been part of an investment club at the district jail, where he worked as a guard. Now, he and Honor were investment partners in Khanh Phu. The two were brothers-in-law by association since Steadfast's sister Serenity was sister-in-law to Honor's wife, Apricot Flower.

Late the night before, Rose and I had tried to sleep while Steadfast and Honor haggled in the other room with a friend, a sullen youth in faded Lee jeans and Czech tennis shoes. Steadfast and Honor had lent their friend 2.9 million *dong*, then worth $690. The debtor wanted to renegotiate his loan.

"You've had extensions," Steadfast insisted. His voice carried none of the provincial shyness I'd known years before. "Time's up. We'll take your Honda."

"But my bike's worth four million," the debtor countered.

Rose ran her fingers down the inside of our mosquito net. "In old days," she whispered in English, "peasants used to talk about a hundred or a thousand *dong*. Now, they talk millions."

"We'll give you the Simson for the Honda," Honor said, referring to the East German motorcycle Steadfast had picked up in an earlier bankruptcy deal. Honor had been agitated all week. Wheeling and dealing aggravated his ulcer. "We'll call the loan settled," he added.

The debtor resisted. "But you bought your Simson for only four hundred!" he argued.

"See?" Rose whispered, "Nowadays when people say 'hundred,' they mean 'hundred thousand.' "

"But the Simson's worth a million now," Steadfast said. His voice had a jail guard's authoritarian edge.

It was true that in six months the price on motorcycles had doubled; still, the negotiations made me intensely uncomfortable. The frenzy was like the money pyramids at home: Sooner or later the buying-and-selling frenzy would crash and someone would be badly hurt.

"The difference is interest," Steadfast added, pushing the deal to a close. "You have until ten tomorrow morning to pay."

"Easy to borrow," Rose had murmured. "Hard to pay back."

The next morning, Steadfast and Honor left on the sputtering Simson. Now, they stood amidst the shelled corn, their arms folded across their chests, admiring their newly acquired Honda. Its engine idled with the even sound of precision parts perfectly timed.

"Do they have Hondas like this in Ha Noi?" Honor asked Rose.

"Can I go for a ride?" River asked. She straddled the seat, earrings bobbing. "Please!"

"Teach me to drive!" Fanciful said, laughing.

"Whose motorcycle is this?" deaf Mrs. Spring Rain asked. As bright as anyone else, she missed much of what happened.

"In Ha Noi, that bike would bring five million," Rose said.

Honor nudged Steadfast. "You're going to Ha Noi for the police exam," he said. "Take the bike."

"The bus is cheaper," Steadfast said, polishing the fender with his shirttail.

"Take the bike!" Honor repeated. "Sell it. We'll make a million."

"How do you call it in English?" Rose said to me. " 'Junk bond dealer?' "

Steadfast nudged River off the Honda. As soon as she dismounted, he climbed aboard and revved the engine. The muffler gave off a thin cloud of acrid fumes. As Steadfast turned the cycle around, Honor hopped aboard. Steadfast popped the clutch, and the two young men roared out of the compound.

We returned to shelling corn. Rose tossed aside her bare cob and took another. "I'm a civil servant," she said to me in English. "My whole year's salary isn't enough to buy that old Simson motorcycle even if its price were still four hundred. I work two, three extra jobs—writing, teach English, translate *Catch-22*, translate *The Class*." She sighed. "How can I keep up with a peasant businessman?"

Despite the frenzy of buying and selling, age-old traditions continued. Shortly after daybreak several days later, Mrs. Beautiful's second daughter came to fetch me for the ceremony of "change the shirt." Her husband's senior uncle, who had died three years before, was about to be exhumed.

We guests gathered at the widow's house to share a jug of rice wine with silk cocoons steeping in the bottom, the worms still inside. To my partial relief, the worms were not served in the cups of wine but remained instead in the bottom of the blown-glass demijohn.

Soon we walked behind the widow and her two sons to the graveyard. The sons carried an earthen urn of perfumed water and a tiny terra-cotta box. They set these down amidst the grassy burial mounds.

"Which grave?" the older son asked, shovel in hand. "The floods make everything look so different."

His brother pointed to a grassy mound that looked like every other grave. "This one!" he said.

"No," a guest countered. He was an elderly man, who had suffered a stroke. He often wandered around the village. Every once in a while he grew disoriented; when this happened, one of the children led him home. He pointed to a mound two graves over. "That one."

"We'd better wait," the older son said.

In time Uncle Firmness arrived. Surveying the site, he designated a grave. He turned up the collar of the same brown plaid coat I'd always seen him wear year after year. His soft, round face seemed at ease as he watched the younger men dig. The clods of earth made a dull, slogging sound as they fell off the shovels. Soon the men had cleared the earth from a wooden coffin. They dug out a shelf to stand on, then pried open the lid. I turned away in dismay: The coffin was full of black, rancid water.

Uncle Precious, the neighbor who'd mistakenly eaten a leech, was standing by my right side. He shifted his grandson to his other hip. "We have a saying about our life in the rice paddies," he said. " 'Both the skins of the living and the bones of the dead are soaked through.' "

At that moment, the widow plunged forward. *"Aw—ooooh!"* she cried out.

Two young men grabbed her elbows, holding her back as she tried to hurl herself into the coffin full of dark water.

Uncle Precious nodded. "This is the widow's last chance to see her husband," he explained.

The widow wept as her older son removed a femur from the coffin. The man rinsed the femur with perfumed water and set it in the terra-cotta box.

"Only the immediate family can do this work," Uncle Precious explained. "An outsider washing the bones might take a tiny bone, say a fingertip. If so, generations thereafter will have trouble with that joint."

A stranger on my left nudged my elbow. In his thirties, he had soft hair that flowed in waves away from his forehead. "I tell them it's unsanitary to change the shirt," he muttered. "But they won't listen."

"People can play a trick on you," Uncle Precious continued. He edged closer when the second son poured a bottle of rice whiskey into the coffin. Islands of white foam floated in the black water. The searing fumes of alcohol mixed with the odor of rancid coffin water. "That's why we use rice whiskey," Uncle Precious added. "It makes the tiny, forgotten bones rise to the top. The son can collect every one of them."

The man on my left tugged my sleeve, his voice hardly more than a whisper. "I've been to East Germany, the Soviet Union," he said. "I've learned about the new ways."

"Where does this bone go?" the older son asked. Squatting in the mud, he turned a black rib in his hands, then set it alongside a thigh bone in the crypt.

"No!" Uncle Firmness insisted. He patted the right side of his jacket. "On the other side. It's this rib!"

"I used to think the way these people do," the man with the wavy hair continued. "Then in 1987 I was sent to the labor force in East Germany. I learned their language. West Germany bought out my work contract when the Berlin Wall came down. Five thousand dollars! I came home a rich man!"

The older son lifted the skull from the wooden coffin. I recoiled as he rolled it over, emptying the dark, foul water. Then he dipped clear, perfumed water from the urn and poured it over the blackened skull.

"When the skull is black," Uncle Precious said, "it's a sign the person was buried in good dirt and that the water rose to melt his flesh."

Uncle Precious's voice dropped in pitch, the way it did when he was about to launch into a story. "Once," he said, "there was an old man who took care of the Buddhist pagoda. He was buried by the monuments in the rice paddy next door to my house. But when they dug up his coffin three years later, the skin was still on his bones. It was shriveled! The fingertips moved, as if alive!"

I tightened the scarf around my neck, intrigued and horrified. "What did they do?"

"They buried him again!" Uncle Precious tweaked his grandson's chin. "But for another four years, just to be sure. Then they dug him up again, but the skin was still there. They had to scrape it off! Terrible! Who knows if his bones were ever clean?"

I grimaced as I imagined the sound of scraping.

"Wash the skull clean!" Uncle Firmness directed.

The older son held the skull like a bowl while his brother filled it with herbal water. The older son moved his cupped hands holding the skull in a slow circle until water sloshed from the eye sockets.

"If you don't clean the skull," Uncle Precious said from my left side, "future generations will suffer from mental instability."

"I may be the richest man in Khanh Phu," the man on my right muttered, "but I live amidst old ways."

The older son reached into the coffin, his arm up to the elbow in black water. He felt all across the bottom. Then he swept his hand through the islands of foam. He set two tiny bones in the terra-cotta crypt.

"That's all the bones," Uncle Firmness announced. "Close the lid."

"No!" the widow sobbed. "NO!"

Together, her two sons set the terra-cotta lid in place. Then they lifted the box and carried it to the spot where two masons waited, ready to build a permanent tomb.

Several days later, I was startled awake at 6 A.M. by a radio blaring news from Ha Noi. A floor bolt scraped against the concrete portico as deaf Mrs. Spring Rain opened the double wooden doors to the courtyard. I could hear her water bucket made from truck-tire tubing slosh in the cistern. The radio continued on to news of the province and the district and then the villages. That morning, there was no news from Khanh Phu.

"How about the hearing aid you brought?" Rose said at breakfast. She dipped a translucent rice cake into fish sauce.

"Maybe it can save us from the radio," I said, eating a rice cake. The cake was as bland as porridge but with a slippery texture like raw oysters.

"You brought a hearing aid?" Fanciful said, gathering the chopsticks and stacking the rice bowls. "I'll call Mother." Leaving with the tray, she returned with Mrs. Spring Rain. She led her mother to a wooden armchair in front of the ancestors' altar.

"This will help you hear, Mother!" Fanciful yelled.

"What?" Mrs. Spring Rain said. She looked confused. Her gnarled fingers toyed with the top snap of her gray *ao ba ba*. It was hard to believe that only one generation separated this woman in loose black satin *quans* from her daughter in snug jeans.

Rose hooked the hearing-aid amplifier over Mrs. Spring Rain's ear and attached the earpiece.

"From Ohio, Mother!" Fanciful shouted. She turned on the tiny switch atop the hearing aid.

"Heavens!" Mrs. Spring Rain said. She sat up straight, her back rigid.

Just then Steadfast roared into the courtyard on his new Honda. He parked the motorcycle and, stooping, checked the wave of his hair in its rearview mirror. Then he came in and sat on the arm of his mother's chair. "How are you doing, Mother?" Steadfast asked, yelling into Mrs. Spring Rain's ear.

"Quiet, Son," she answered. "I can hear!"

That visit, the craze was pool. The day I arrived, carpenters were building the first pool table, which was about a third the size of the standard model. By midweek, there were three tables; by the end of the week, a half dozen. First and Second Sons made up their own version, combining an empty beer can, a table-tennis ball, and a small stick. Whenever they came to Mrs. Spring Rain's house, they set up their pool hall on the bed Rose and I shared.

In one week, three new VCR players arrived in the village. The families that owned the VCRs sold tickets to see videos they rented in nearby Ninh Binh. There were over a hundred TVs, and a plentiful supply of electricity kept cassette players running all day long.

But with the individualism of Renovation had come the demise of socialized services. Throughout the country, the quality of education had dropped and, with it, the literacy rate. Health services, no longer free, were beyond the reach of the poor.

Although I didn't know anyone who wanted to return to the time before Renovation, my wistfulness for the old days grew. Now it was only in the early morning or late at night that I heard the delicate sounds—an ox sighing, chicks peeping, the rain on banana leaves.

One evening, after a day of transplanting, a group of us sat on a grass mat on Mrs. Spring Rain's bed, shelling corn. The power was out. A kerosene baby lamp atop the pile of shelled corn illuminated Steadfast's handsome face. He added honey to an elixir made from dried venison and rice whiskey and then poured his brew into demitasse cups, which he offered around. The brownish drink tasted sweet and smooth. For a snack, Mrs. Spring Rain brought in corn kernels she'd roasted.

"Where's your hearing aid, Mother?" Fanciful yelled. She tossed a bare cob into a basket and reached for another to shell.

"I'm saving the battery for a party," Mrs. Spring Rain answered. She sat on the edge of the board bed and, rubbing her callused fingertips over a cob, popped off the kernels.

"But you have lots of batteries, Auntie," I said. "Anyway, the party is right here, now."

Mrs. Spring Rain retrieved the hearing aid. As soon as she did so, Steadfast tucked it into his own ear and turned the switch. Rose leaned close to Steadfast's ear.

"Hon-DA!" she whispered.

"*AKkkkk!*" Steadfast yelped, laughing at the sudden power of the word.

Mrs. Spring Rain, deaf since birth, inserted the hearing aid into her own ear. She looked at her son and daughter shelling corn. "I never knew Fanciful laughed so much," she said. "Or how much the pig grunts. I can hear Steadfast coming home on his motorcycle. Oh my!" She looked at him. "I can even hear your teeth crunching corn kernels."

By 10 P.M., we had dumped the shelled corn onto a huge, flat drying basket that took up a quarter of the floor. Before long, the last person was back from the outhouse, and Steadfast was closing and locking the front doors. Rose let down the mosquito net, which settled around our bed.

In the next room, the radio summarized the day's events at ordinary volume. When the broadcast came to local news, I heard a high-pitched whine. Mrs. Spring Rain had raised the power on her hearing aid, attentive for news of Khanh Phu.

X X

Dew's Glint

Life is lightning, so briefly there, so soon gone.
Green in spring, the tree sheds its leaves in autumn.
Why fear the course of splendor and decay?
Rising glory and quick decline are but dew's glint
upon a blade of grass.

"Advice to Disciples"
VAN HANH
?–1018

I'm embarrassed to admit that I lost touch with the news of Khanh Phu. Sometimes, as much as I may think of friends at a distance, I fail to remind them that they are in my thoughts. But Vietnamese are more considerate; they often write letters asking after every person they have ever heard me mention. For Vietnamese, as one of their proverbs says, "The greeting is more important even than rice."

And so, chagrined, I returned to Khanh Phu in the spring of 1994 after not having written my friends there during more than three years away.

My embarrassment was compounded by the way everyone I met immediately asked after my father. I could report that my dad sent his greetings and that now, in his mid-nineties, he continued to tend fruit trees in his community's Garden of the Elders.

But the news I heard of Khanh Phu was less comforting. I had assumed that Mrs. Beautiful, hearing I'd invited Autumn to join me, would insist we stay with her as we had during our first visit together more than seven years before. And so I was all the more distressed to hear the news when Autumn and I stopped by Uncle Peaceful's. We found Uncle Peaceful's house full of guests. He stepped outside to greet us. As we chatted, it seemed to me that his shoulder tilted a little more. His hair now had flecks of silver.

"We 'lost' Mrs. Beautiful," he said, using a Vietnamese idiom for death. With his fingertips, he lifted the tip of a branch of a bonsai tree. "She couldn't eat, even went to Bach Mai Hospital in Ha Noi, but they couldn't do anything so they sent her back home. She had cancer. She died last year several days after Tet."

"And the others?" I asked, taken aback and afraid I might hear of other losses. "Your wife? Uncle Dutiful? His wife and sister? Mrs. Spring Rain?"

Mr. Peaceful rubbed his palm across his face in a flat-handed gesture Vietnamese often use. "Everyone's fine," he said, leading us into his son's house across the courtyard. "Now you must join the feast commemorating my father's death. Afterwards you can take your things over to Mrs. Spring Rain's."

Little had changed in Mrs. Spring Rain's house, yet everything was different. There were the small signs: The garden wall was gone, replaced by a few stacked bricks that had turned green with moss. A picture frame displaying a photo of Steadfast in a policeman's uniform told me he'd passed his exam.

"Steadfast is married," Mrs. Spring Rain announced, pointing to the trail of bricks where the garden wall had been. "We needed more courtyard space for the wedding so we took down the wall."

Although Mrs. Spring Rain's hair was greyer, a new orange *ao ba ba* made her seem younger. She was excited to share other news. Steadfast's wife was expecting a child. Fanciful had also married and had a son. But Mrs. Spring Rain's best surprise came in through the gate in the arms of her daughter Serenity. Serenity was a solidly built woman with a large mouth. She laughed, displaying perfect, white teeth.

Serenity was the only member of Mrs. Spring Rain's family whom Autumn and I had met in 1987. She was married then and distressed that she had no children. Autumn had referred her to doctors in Ha Noi, and in subsequent visits Rose did so as well. Still, the years passed in the sad absence of children.

Now, in her arms, Serenity carried a son of fourteen months. She held him out to me, jubilant. As terrified as I am of babies, there seemed no choice but to take this child in my arms. He laughed as if my holding him were another of his life pleasures.

"And your name, Little One?" I asked, looking into his eyes. They were shiny and deep black like longan seeds.

"His name is Happiness," Serenity said.

Autumn touched the boy's cheek. A few days before, she had finished a book for Vietnamese parents on the developmental stages during early childhood. "I've hardly ever seen such a happy child," she said.

During our time at Mrs. Spring Rain's, Serenity and her baby often stopped by, as did many of the neighbors. Autumn and I came and went as well. Now that Uncle Dutiful's household had a television, Autumn and I slipped next door each evening to watch the news. In the days before predictable electricity, Uncle Dutiful's family had spent evenings chatting over the frail yellow light of a kerosene baby lamp. Now, conversation ceased; we turned away from one another, our attention focused on the TV.

Uncle Dutiful sat with his knee pulled up to his chin; he ran one hand through his shock of white hair. His sister and the battalion of grandsons had settled onto the board bed. Kindness turned on the bamboo slat bench to face the screen. She had cut her hair since the last time I'd seen her. Apricot Flower, who still wore her hair long, toyed with her older sister's curls. Mrs. Dutiful came in, bent over a plate of rice fritters, which we nibbled throughout the news and a special program about nearby Hoa Lu, an early capital of northern Viet Nam.

Only River, who had grown from a teenager into a self-assured young woman, seemed oblivious to the television. She was embroidering a tablecloth stretched over a four-foot-wide frame that rested on stools immediately below the TV. All the while, she studiously ignored the young man who watched her every stitch from his seat on the other side of the frame.

Whenever River left the room, the young man followed; as soon as she returned to her embroidery, he took his place across from her.

"We'll have a wedding soon," Fierce said. Now, his white hairs, too many to pluck, made him look like Uncle Dutiful. Fierce set a pinch of *thuoc lao* into the bowl of his water pipe and lit the dried leaves. The pipe gurgled as he drew on its bamboo stem.

At that moment, First Son entered the room. In his early twenties, he had been laid off from the district beer factory. First Son strode over to the TV and, without a word, switched the channel, his thumb rolling over the dial. His thumbnail was long like those of the ancient mandarins, whose tapered nails served to announce their distance from hard labor. But unlike the mandarins, First Son had painted his thumbnail crimson. He switched the channel back to the history of Viet Nam's first capital and left the room. All the while, his elders and younger brothers stared at the flickering grey screen, which seemed to have temporarily stolen their minds and their souls.

If material goods are to be a gauge, almost every household in Khanh Phu seemed better off than in late 1990. Uncle Dutiful's family not only had a TV but had replaced the rambunctious ox with a sedate water buffalo. Mrs. Spring Rain cooked over a charcoal stove instead of an open fire; Apricot Flower and Honor had built their own house of brick and stucco. The younger men wore colored shirts, and the women wore new Western slacks, print blouses, and hair ribbons; the road sported a few more shops. Nevertheless, the wheeling-and-dealing exuberance of 1989 and early 1990 had given way to solemnity.

"So what happened?" Autumn asked Serenity one day over lunch. Serenity sat with Happiness on her lap. The boy continued to giggle, but Serenity's face turned somber.

"We made a lot of money in those days," Serenity began.

Indeed, the 1988 privatization of both paddy land and rice sales created a sudden increase in yield, thrusting northern Viet Nam into the world market for the first time in almost forty years. Unauthorized trade in rice and other commodities across the Chinese border flourished.

Serenity clipped a piece of egg between her chopsticks and fed it to her son. "We could borrow and lend," she went on. "Steadfast bought a Simson motorcycle and turned it in for a Honda! We had an investment group here in Khanh Phu. I was accountant, until it went bankrupt."

"Bankrupt?!" Autumn said, her chopsticks poised.

Autumn knew as well as I that during the late 1980s, over seven thousand investment clubs had formed across Viet Nam. However, by the end of 1990, most had gone bankrupt. During an earlier visit, I had heard the story of Khanh Phu's bankruptcy from a number of villagers. I turned to Autumn, hoping to lift any embarrassment off Serenity. "Someone you and I didn't know ran off with the funds," I said.

"Oh dear," Autumn said, leaning against the back of the bench. "How much was lost?"

"Millions." Serenity brushed back her son's hair with the tip of her forefinger. Her nail was short and ingrained with dirt. "Steadfast lost millions, Mrs. Beautiful's family lost millions."

Millions. I did some quick calculations. These were heavy losses. Two million *dong* was roughly two hundred dollars, at that time slightly below the annual per capita income.

"Where did they go with the money?" Autumn asked.

"Who knows?" I said. "Maybe to the south. Maybe they left the country."

Serenity shifted her son to her other arm and opened her blouse for him. "It was like when a typhoon strikes," she said. "What could we do? We had to start over again from nothing."

I was prepared for loss when I visited Mrs. Beautiful's house, but not for desolation. That day, the sunshine that brightened the rest of Khanh Phu seemed not to reach into her family's courtyard. I stepped inside the gate and stopped short. The flower garden and the wall around it were gone. Villagers were always knocking down walls and reusing the bricks but, looking around, I saw no new structure.

"Ly!" called Flowering Pear, Mrs. Beautiful's daughter-in-law. Carrying a baby in her arms, Flowering Pear ran down the steps of the house where Autumn and I had first stayed. She invited us inside. I introduced Autumn as we sat at the table where, years before, Autumn and I had shared so much tea. On first glance, the room with its two beds was much as I remembered, but then I looked again. The cabinet inlaid with mother-of-pearl was gone. In its place sat a huge crate made of rough lumber. There was nothing on top of the crate: no brass incense urn, not even a baby lamp.

As Flowering Pear sat next to me, I set my hand on her forearm. "I came to 'share the sorrow,' " I said.

Flowering Pear began to weep. I thought with sadness of her youthful whimsy when we'd transplanted together. Now, shifting the baby to the crook of her arm, Flowering Pear looked used-up.

"Would you like to visit Mother's altar?" she asked.

We crossed the courtyard to the other house. I stepped with care around a beehive blocking the doorway. Once inside, I felt an air of depression. The furniture inlaid with mother-of-pearl was gone; the room was bare except for two small altar tables. Tinted photographs of Mr. and Mrs. Beautiful taken when they were in their forties looked out over a barren room.

Autumn lit incense sticks and bowed before the side altar; I did as well, bending before the photograph of Mrs. Beautiful. In the photo she wore her hair wrapped in a piece of black velvet and wound around her head in the traditional style of women from northern Viet Nam. Her eyes spoke determination.

"I'm sorry I wasn't here for you," I murmured into the pungent smoke that drifted across her gaze. I was remembering the night when she woke me up to drink her tonic made from tiger bones. She had told me then about her son killed by a baby bomb long after the end of the war.

Autumn and I moved over to the central altar for the son and Mr. Beautiful. We lit more incense and bowed. In the "women's room," we lit even more incense and placed it on the altar over the doorway to honor the daughter who had died of a heart ailment. Like the central room, this one was empty except for a beehive facing the window. The third room, which had once housed Khanh Phu's first refrigerator, was empty as well.

The baby whimpered, and Flowering Pear wiped the boy's nose as she led us from the vacant house back to the tea table. "He's feverish," she explained.

"Oh!" Autumn said, "I have some medicine from China."

Whenever we traveled, Autumn took along a small cloth bag from which she would produce clean clothes, extra sweaters and scarves, a pen knife, the rasping flashlight, or even a snack. And always there was some small gift that was perfect. Now, Autumn set in the middle of the table the most exquisite box I've ever seen. It was the size of a ring case and covered in red silk embroidered with dragons. Inside, on a bed of silvery satin, rested a tiny glass vial with a gold cap.

"Use just two drops," Autumn instructed. "Mix the medicine with rice."

But Flowering Pear seemed not to hear. Carrying the baby on her hip, she rummaged in a corner of the room and, returning with a spoon, shook the vial over it. She tried to insert the spoon into the child's mouth. He resisted, squalling.

"Try banana or rice," Autumn repeated. She stood up as Mrs. Beautiful's second son, Sturdiness, rode up on a bicycle. He carried half a bag of newly hulled rice strapped to the luggage rack.

Sturdiness was a pleasant young man with sad eyes. Though clean shaven, the stubble on his face was thicker than that of most Vietnamese, giving his narrow jaw a grey, beleaguered look. Mrs. Beautiful's daughters had long since married into other families in the village, leaving Sturdiness to manage the family's affairs.

We chatted over tea. "What happened to the cassette player?" Autumn asked after a while. Seven years before, the family had owned the largest boom box either of us had ever seen.

"Sold it," Sturdiness answered.

I brushed a fly from my forearm, another from my ear. I didn't remember so many flies. These were large and sluggish, and they buzzed loudly.

"So you're tending the beehives," I said, making conversation. I nodded toward the other house.

Sturdiness shook his head, No. "They belong to a friend from another village."

At that moment, the young man's desperation struck me. As the second son, Sturdiness had been raised to follow, not to lead. He had been unprepared for the role thrust upon him when the baby bomb killed his older brother. Sturdiness would have done fine under the old system, where the collective took care of everyone, but now support of the State had given way to private enterprise. Saddled with three children, he and Flowering Pear were supporting themselves by selling off his family's assets.

A year after Mrs. Beautiful's death, there remained little to sell. As we left that afternoon, it seemed to me that the only tangible objects of color that remained behind were Autumn's tiny box sitting on the table and the glowing tips of incense burning on the altars.

Our last day, Autumn and I bought a packet of incense from the owner of the new corner shop near Mrs. Spring Rain's house. Then we walked to the cemetery to visit Mrs. Beautiful's grave. New Moon, who had helped host our first visit, joined us. That morning, the village was like a silk painting in which "floating rain" obscures the mountains and fields, concentrating the viewer's eye on some small scene rendered in exquisite detail.

As I walked among the unmarked burial mounds, I could see the rain yet I felt nothing on my face. Removing my sandals, I followed New Moon along a narrow dike between puddles. The moisture had softened the earth. The mud squished between my toes; with each step there was a burbling noise and the subtle scent of humus. New Moon paused between two burial mounds.

"Maybe that one," she said, pointing. The light blue plastic she wore as a rain cape rattled. Then she shook her head, No, and looked out over the mounds that rose like small hills from the graveyard. "You know," she said, "I can't tell which one is hers."

Coughing, Autumn wrapped her scarf tighter around her neck. She had trouble breathing when the humidity was so high. "Let's find Mr. Beautiful's tomb," she suggested.

"That's easy," New Moon said, "Mr. Beautiful has 'changed his shirt.' " She pointed to a cement tomb with Mr. Beautiful's name and dates etched on its face.

Autumn lit three sticks of incense and placed them before the tomb. She bowed three times, then stepped back and, turning, lit the rest of the incense in the packet. One by one, she pushed each stick into the top of a different, unmarked mound.

As I breathed in the drifting fragrance I could almost feel the grasp of Mrs. Beautiful's fingers on my elbow. Haunted, she had ignored collective wisdom in the days when Viet Nam was still closed. She'd reached out to me, and then she hung on.

Mrs. Beautiful's life may have been but dew's glint upon a blade of grass but, standing there among the burial mounds shrouded in floating rain, I found myself planning ahead. Several days after Tet of 1996, the Year of the Rat, would be the third anniversary of Mrs. Beautiful's death. I would return then to honor her soul with a proper farewell. It would be the time then when Sturdiness would change my friend's shirt.

Book III

Ha Noi
Viet Nam's
Largest Village

Rice Pounding

How terribly the rice suffers under the pestle!
But it emerges polished, as white as cotton.
The same process tempers the human spirit:
Hard trials shape us into polished diamonds.

FROM *A Prison Diary*
HO CHI MINH
1890–1969

XXI

At Home by the Red River

Impetuous energy and gentle calm
Rumbling roar and spreading hush,
The river cannot hold its waves;
They seek the open sea.

FROM "The Waves"
XUAN OUYNH
1942–1989

*T*raffic thickened as our airport van entered Chuong Duong Bridge. Below, the Red River, rich in iron oxide, swept by in a graceful curve, giving Ha Noi its name, "Inside the River." But whereas the river moved at a stately pace, we had stopped. Two trucks—battered veterans of the American War—blocked the bridge, their hoods raised.

"Welcome to the Ho Chi Minh Trail!" Flower joked in English. Her face was full for a Vietnamese, soft and exuberant, like a peony in full bloom.

I relaxed, relishing the sound of Flower's laughter. We hadn't seen each other for fifteen years, not since my first trip to Ha Noi during the war. By

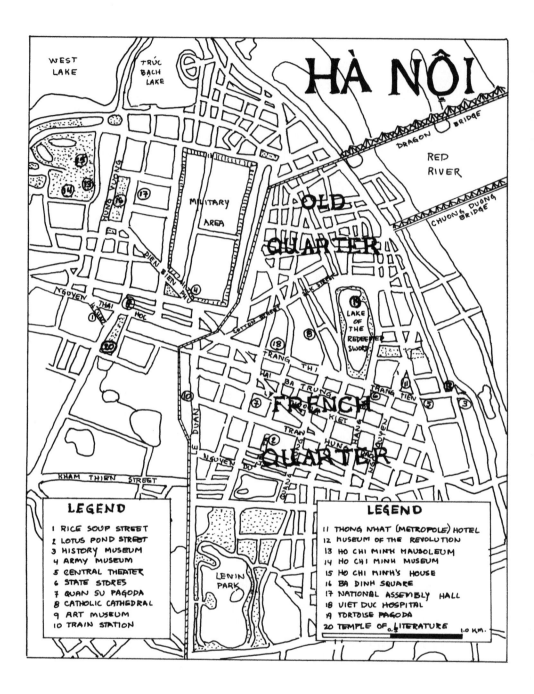

HÀ NÔI

WEST LAKE

TRÚC BACH LAKE

DRAGON BRIDGE

RED RIVER

CHUONG DUONG BRIDGE

OLD QUARTER

MILITARY AREA

LAKE OF THE REDEEMED SWORD

FRENCH QUARTER

NGUYEN THAI HOC

FUNG VUONG

DIEN BIEN PHU

TRANG THI

HAI BA TRUNG

TRANG TIEN

LE DUAN

NGUYEN DU

TRAN HUNG DAO

KHAM THIEN STREET

LENIN PARK

LEGEND

1 RICE SOUP STREET
2 LOTUS POND STREET
3 HISTORY MUSEUM
4 ARMY MUSEUM
5 CENTRAL THEATER
6 STATE STORES
7 QUAN SU PAGODA
8 CATHOLIC CATHEDRAL
9 ART MUSEUM
10 TRAIN STATION

LEGEND

11 THONG NHAT (METROPOLE) HOTEL
12 MUSEUM OF THE REVOLUTION
13 HO CHI MINH MAUSOLEUM
14 HO CHI MINH MUSEUM
15 HO CHI MINH'S HOUSE
16 BA DINH SQUARE
17 NATIONAL ASSEMBLY HALL
18 VIET DUC HOSPITAL
19 TORTOISE PAGODA
20 TEMPLE OF LITERATURE

0.5   1.0 KM.

now, it was the summer of 1990; I'd returned for a four-month assignment to set up an office for the American Friends Service Committee. As interim director for Quaker Service, I would be among Ha Noi's first American residents; Flower was to be my Vietnamese partner.

"Remember the first time we crossed Dragon Bridge?" Flower said, pointing upriver. "It's used only for bicycles and cyclos now."

I glanced at the lacy French artifact, which looked as frail as a child's Erector-set model. Dragon Bridge—once the sole road link between Ha Noi and Beijing—had been a prime U.S. bombing target during the war. Back then in 1975, stuck in traffic on Dragon Bridge, I had watched lines of women carrying yoked baskets of earth that weighed some eighty pounds per load. They emptied these into the craters.

But now in 1990, the riverbanks below Dragon Bridge were verdant with cabbages and greens; the bridge itself was a blur of bicycles. Everything looked different from the way it had looked during the war except that motorized traffic entering Ha Noi was still in gridlock. Up ahead of us, a man inserted a steel shank into the crankcase of his truck and gave the rod a twirl. Soon the truck lurched forward, its engine spewing acrid smoke.

"*Whew!*" Flower said, waving at the air.

I had made a dozen trips to Ha Noi since the end of the war and had often asked after Flower; I knew that she'd married and had a daughter. Still, despite my inquiries, we never met after my first trip to Ha Noi during the war. But intimacy can grow across a void. Now, by chance, the agency that provided AFSC's contact with the Vietnamese government had assigned Flower to Quaker Service.

Flower and I were like old roommates reunited in giddy friendship. My one worry—what Vietnamese colleague I would work with—dissolved. And so I relaxed as our van made its way through downtown Ha Noi to Rice Soup Street, where I settled into the room that would double as office and living quarters.

When Flower left that first day, I asked her to swing by Cotton Street and tell Rose I was in town. On previous trips, I had grown so brazen that I would stop by Rose's house unannounced. But the relations between the United States and Viet Nam were like a road checkpoint with a levered bamboo pole and a guard to raise and lower the gate. Sometimes the gate would be up; sometimes, down. Whenever you found a gate down, it was wise to chat with the guard in Vietnamese. When it was up, you could wave and ride through, but with caution because you never knew when the bamboo pole might bop you on the head.

Every time there was an opening in the relationship between the United States and Viet Nam, the gate lifted a little higher and it became easier to pedal back and forth underneath. However, a slight closing usually followed any opening. The bamboo gate had recently dropped; an American teacher and an American journalist caught by its swing had been deported. For that reason, I was not about to chance dropping in unannounced on Rose.

Minutes after Flower left, Rose arrived. She parked her bicycle in the narrow alley by the house. In her white sweater, snug jeans, and high-heeled sandals, she looked as stylish as ever. Her hair curled gently around her face, but her eyebrows had gathered into a fretful line.

"Why did you send Flower?" she asked. "Why didn't you come yourself? I thought we were sisters!"

I smiled at her, shrugging. "I didn't want to get you in trouble."

I led Rose up the narrow staircase that circled the outside of the stucco house. Soon we were sharing news. I told her that I'd been asked to select poems by Vietnamese women for an anthology by American women veterans of the American War. Since the Ha Noi Post Office had a fax machine, I could make the final deadline, which was two weeks away.

"Want to work on this together?" I asked Rose.

"You remember Xuan Quynh?" she answered.

"Of course."

Xuan Quynh, a close friend of Rose's, had been Viet Nam's foremost living woman poet until her death almost two years before. She and her husband, the dissident playwright Luu Quang Vu, and their twelve-year-old son had been killed in a car accident. I was there in Ha Noi at the time. Rose and I rode with Luu Quang Vu's theatrical troupe in the funeral procession, the largest spontaneous outpouring since Ho Chi Minh's death. Afterwards we went to the Central Theater, a French colonial structure in the center of Ha Noi, to see the actors' last performance of Luu Quang Vu's satire *The Disease of Pride*.

"Do you know 'My Son's Childhood'?" Rose asked. "It's Xuan Quynh's poem about her first son during the bombing. He's grown now." She began to recite,

What do you have for a childhood
You smiling in the bomb shelter?
At three months you turn your head,
At seven you crawl.
You toy with the earth,
You play with a bomb shelter.

"Perfect," I said, remembering how much I enjoyed the way Vietnamese recite poetry. "We'll fax around the embargo."

The U.S. embargo against North Viet Nam began in 1964 and was extended to the entire country after the collapse of the Sai Gon regime in 1975. In 1994, thirty years after it began, President Clinton lifted the embargo. But in 1990 the embargo was still on, and it forbade telephone contact. Even so, I could fax from Ha Noi to the States because overseas calls went by way of Australia. When calls from Viet Nam arrived in the United States, they were indistinguishable from other Australian transmissions. I explained to Rose how friends in Bangkok had agreed to forward any faxes sent to me from the States.

"So, you are my sister after all," Rose said. "Stop by tonight to pick up your bicycle. You are always welcome at my home."

Within days of my arrival in late 1990, it was clear that, at least for me, the bamboo gate remained raised. During years of visits from 1983 until 1989, my talking alone with one person had been as unthinkable as a visit to the United States by an ordinary Vietnamese. But now I was able to speak freely with strangers on the street and could even accept spontaneous invitations to their houses. The period of strain from 1975 to 1990, what I call the "Years of Silence," had eased.

Vietnamese friends soon were dropping by my room on Hang Chao. *Hang,* meaning "wares," is common among street names within old Ha Noi, where merchandise is still grouped by street; *Chao* is "rice soup." Thus Hang Chao is Rice Soup Street, having earned its name during medieval times, when scholars gathered for rice gruel outside the Temple of Literature, Ha Noi's first university. From my window, I could see the arching eaves of the Temple.

An ageless medieval erudition had permeated the neighborhood when I first visited the Temple of Literature during the war; this feeling had lasted through the 1980s. But by late 1990, *Doi Moi*—Renovation—had arrived. Peddlers sold blue jeans from Thailand outside the Temple. Despite the embargo, others hawked Coca-Cola and Wrigley's gum.

The late twentieth century dominated Rice Soup Street as well. At daylight, vendors strung tarps across the sidewalk and set out displays of motorcycle parts. "Ball-Bearing Market," Flower said, aptly renaming the street. Indeed, Hang Chao, a shortcut between two major thoroughfares, had turned into a racetrack with motorcycles tearing past, horns blaring. Flower and I closed the shutters whenever we wanted to talk, but nothing could keep out the street's fine, metallic grit.

"This office is not permanent," we promised each other.

Between 1975 and 1990, Quaker Service administered its Viet Nam projects from Laos. During that time, the American Friends Service Committee was one among only four U.S. organizations with relief, reconstruction, and development projects in Viet Nam. As tensions between the United States and Viet Nam eased, the Vietnamese government allowed two American organizations—the Mennonite Central Committee and Quaker Service—to base staff in Ha Noi.

Part of my job was to set up smooth systems. Within four months, I would finish up old projects, start new ones, and arrange for my replacements' basic needs: a house, someone to cook, bicycles, banking, mail systems, and enrollment for their two children in Ha Noi's United Nations International School. These were administrative tasks: a thousand bicycle jaunts, none glamorous but all necessary.

From the outset, I loved the duck-and-dive of Ha Noi traffic. Oncoming bikers must have thought it strange to see a lone Caucasian in the mass of Vietnamese. But those coming up behind me would have assumed from my conical hat, drab parka, and baggy *quans* that I was just another Vietnamese. However, in October 1990, on the day of the sixtieth anniversary celebration for the Women's Union, I startled traffic in both directions: I wore an *ao dai.*

The *ao dai* is perhaps the most gracious and also the most uncomfortable garment created. The bodice—tightly fitted with long tapered sleeves and a high mandarin collar—precludes breathing. The skirt—two long flowing panels slit to the waist—is a hazard. Only the satin trousers make sense. Although the *ao dai* I wore was twenty years old, its embroidered white roses looked fresh, as if still dappled with dew. Taking care to keep myself free of the alley's grime, I pushed my bike into Hang Chao.

"Watch out!" called the ball-bearing vendor across the street. "You'll catch your *ao dai* tails in the spokes."

I clasped the rear panel of my *ao dai* against the handlebars and climbed aboard my bike.

"Hold both panels!" yelled the vendor to my left.

"Hang your bag over the handlebars!" shouted the vendor to my right. "Someone may steal it."

Off I went, thinking I had everything under control. But I'd forgotten that my hair hung in a foot of russet curls below my conical hat. A motorcycle coming from behind sped past. The driver, turning his head to gawk, didn't notice an oncoming cyclist, who had also turned to stare. They collided. I stopped and, pushing up the sleeves of what would pass for an evening gown in the United States, bent the woman cyclist's fender back into shape. Then I raced off to Viet Nam's National Assembly Hall.

"Please," the usher said in rehearsed English. "Invite you climb stairs, sit with foreigners."

"Please," I answered in Vietnamese, "if I sit with your foreign guests, I'll feel awkward in an *ao dai*." I pointed to an empty seat several rows away. "Couldn't I sit with my Vietnamese friends?"

The usher nodded, Yes, showing me to the empty seat. I settled into a lush garden of *ao dais* made from brilliant brocades and silks embroidered with delicate flowers. There were traces of perfume in the air and, all around, the soft sound of women's voices.

"And your work?" I asked the woman on my right after we'd introduced ourselves.

She spoke about family income-generation projects for rural areas. Good. I had promised some colleagues that I would help locate Vietnamese women to attend a Quaker Service conference in Laos on income-generation projects. Here, without looking, was my crucial contact. I wrote down her name as the band heralded the entrance of dignitaries, including Nguyen thi Dinh, president of the Women's Union.

Mme Dinh had been deputy commander of the South Viet Nam Liberation Forces when Sai Gon fell in 1975. It was she who had organized *Dong Khoi*, the 1960 Uprising. She had recounted for me once how, with homemade explosives and guns made from wood, she and other women had liberated three districts in Ben Tre province from the American-backed Diem government. News of the Ben Tre Uprising then traveled by the Market Mouth to Vinh Kim, where Second Harvest, Fifth Harmony, Sixth Rice Field, and others organized the Uprising that liberated Ban Long.

Mme Dinh spoke in a rush of southern Vietnamese dialect with a sound that was broad, flat, and rich like the Mekong Delta. Then she paused and, in the style of Communist Party congresses, raised her hands to chest level and clapped. The audience, bedecked in the vibrant colors of Renovation but still versed in the old ways, applauded in unison.

But except for speeches at similar formal celebrations, the rhetoric pervasive until the late 1980s had faded. I rarely heard the word *dong chi*— "comrade" anymore. In Ha Noi, socialist language became more moderate, shifting like Vietnamese musicians who, finishing an opening drum roll, set aside their drumsticks and, picking up bamboo flutes, capture the pathos of generations in trill after trill.

Even Huu Ngoc, one of the famous Vietnamese Marxist cultural workers, surprised me. His office was on the second floor of the old French villa that housed Ha Noi's Foreign Languages Press, also called World Publishing. Although retired, Huu Ngoc worked half days as editor emeritus and also chaired the press's advisory board. I had seen him many times before, but our meetings—formal and ceremonial—had always been held in a conference room.

By 1990, I was enough of a regular that one of the employees simply pointed to Huu Ngoc's office door. That day I knocked and entered a tiny room, where every surface was piled with books that gave off the musty smell of decaying, high-acid paper. Motes of dust thickened the air. Huu Ngoc looked up from a manuscript he was writing in longhand. In his seventies, he was a gaunt man with a triangular face accentuated by dark glasses, sunken cheeks, and a narrow chin.

"Senior Uncle—," I said after we'd exchanged pleasantries.

"Call me 'Older Brother,' " he suggested. "It's more intimate."

"You speak French so well," I continued. "You must have been born into the Vietnamese administrative class." I had always wanted to hear Huu Ngoc's personal story, but I had never asked during the Years of Silence because in those days answers to personal questions inevitably came in the form of "speak in general." This time I pushed on. "How did you make the transition from bourgeoisie to Communist, Uncle?"

" 'Older Brother,' remember?" he corrected with a smile.

Huu Ngoc was always attentive to words. "Vietnamese is a dangerous language," he was fond of saying. "Take my name, *Ngoc*, for instance. Say it with the low, hard tone and it means 'Pearl.' But say *'Ngoc'* with a circumflexed *o* and a rising tone and you have 'idiot!' For myself," he would add, his hand opening in a gesture of humility, "I prefer to be called 'Idiot.' "

But Mr. Pearl was no idiot. He told how he had grown up on Ha Noi's Silk Street among retired scholars, who printed their Chinese texts with wooden blocks. His father had been an administrator for the French electric company. As a member of the privileged class, Mr. Pearl had attended French schools.

"When I was a young man," he continued, "I decided I didn't want to work for the French. I left Ha Noi in 1939 and taught secondary school in Vinh and Hue until 1945. In Hue I came to know revolutionaries, who invited me to join them. By 1946, I had started a Resistance newspaper, *L'Étincelle.*" He looked at me, squinting. "That newspaper, *The Spark*, was directed toward soldiers drafted from the French colonies in Africa to fight here against us Vietnamese."

"But how did you get the newspaper to them?" I asked.

"Special emissaries." Mr. Pearl tapped the table with his pen. "We smuggled the newspaper into the restaurants and hotels frequented by the French legionnaires. We even smuggled it into the French military quarters! Then later I became chief of the army office responsible for reeducating French prisoners of war. We arrested soldiers from Morrocco, Senegal, Algeria! And soldiers from France, too. We taught them about nationalism, then released them. Oh, they were dangerous! They organized for our cause *within* the French regiments!"

After the American War, Mr. Pearl coedited the thousand-page anthology *Vietnamese Literature*, which was published in Ha Noi in both French and English in 1981 and sold internationally. Its contents ranged from poetry written in the late 900s to short-story excerpts from the American War. He had also edited *Vietnamese Studies*, a journal in English and French begun in 1964 and reaching close to a hundred volumes by 1990.

In 1988, I had agreed to seek an academic publisher in the States for excerpts from the *Vietnamese Studies* series. By 1992, I was able to make an arrangement with the editor of the Yale *Lac Viet* series. But in 1990, I was still looking for a publishing partner, and World Publishing—like all Vietnamese institutions facing the demise of government subsidies—was looking for money.

"We thought we'd renovate part of our publishing house into apartments for foreigners," Mr. Pearl said as he poured tea. "What do you think?"

Whew, I thought: pure capitalism.

"You're right downtown," I said. "You have a good location." I couldn't resist a bit of mischievousness. "You know the capitalists say there are three essentials for a profitable business—"

Mr. Pearl leaned forward. He spoke excitedly. "What are they?"

"Location. Location. Location."

"And goods to sell!" he added. From a stack of books, he chose a copy of *Vietnamese Studies.* He blew off the dust and then, removing his dark glasses, held the book an inch from his left eye. He scanned its contents. "Wouldn't Americans want to read this: 'The Irremediable Crisis of the Puppet Regime'?"

"Well, Senior Uncle . . . ," I hedged.

"Remember?! Call me 'Older Brother.'" He chose another volume. "Then how about this legend?" he countered. "You know I keep trading culture—importing and exporting. Here, 'The Toad Which Lodges a Complaint before the Heavens!'"

"Now that's a possibility," I said, pulling out the American books I'd brought for Mr. Pearl to use as source material for a volume he wanted to write about American culture for Vietnamese readers. My American books with their glossy jackets were as conspicuous among the yellowing Vietnamese texts as the fancy clothes of the first visiting overseas Vietnamese had once been amidst the drab dress of Ha Noi residents.

Mr. Pearl took hold of the *Benét's Reader's Encyclopedia,* a one-volume reference work of world literature. "Oh, look at this!" he said, removing his dark glasses and holding the book against his left eye. "Splendid!"

"Older Brother . . . ," I said.

"Good." Smiling, he turned to the entry on Steinbeck. "You remembered."

"If I'm a younger sister," I said, "would I be rude to ask about your eyesight?"

Peering over the book, Mr. Pearl spoke in a factual voice as if listing dates of Party congresses. "My right eye is farsighted, four-and-a-half-diopter correction. I use it when walking. When I read, I use my left. It needs fourteen-diopter correction but in the opposite direction. The difference is too great to correct with glasses." He returned to the Benét, his sunken cheek against the print.

So this, I thought, is the scholarly equivalent to peasant persistence. I leaned forward. "An ordinary magnifying glass," I said, talking to the glossy book jacket, "decreases the light, countering its own effect. Maybe I could get a magnifying lamp from the Thai Blind Association. Then you would have both magnification and light. Would that help?"

Mr. Pearl set down the text. His eyes gleamed. "Indeed it would."

Over the years in Viet Nam, I have shied away from personal gifts beyond a few small mementoes. But here, it seemed to me, the effect on an institution could be as helpful as the books I'd brought.

"Let me see what I can do about a lamp," I said.

"We should nickname you 'Hyphen,' " he replied.

"Hyphen?"

"Ours is a language of monosyllables. But sometimes we put two words together, as in *Viet Nam* and *Ha Noi*, to make a new word. In the old days—you remember how it used to be—double words were hyphenated. The hyphen appeared insignificant. But don't you see? For years it aided understanding."

Flower and I often joked that Ha Noi was Viet Nam's largest village. In 1990, Ha Noi did not have a functioning phone system; it was easier to telephone the States than to call across town. To meet someone, Flower or I had to bike across the city to make an appointment—which of course could be booked only if the person we sought was in. Then we would have to return, biking again across town to keep the appointment.

While in Ha Noi, I learned to carry the file for every current project, whether Quaker Service or personal, in the cloth bag I slung over the handlebars of my bicycle. In those days, the chance was good that everyone I needed to see was on the street. I conducted much of my business from the seat of my bike, using the handlebars as a desk.

One afternoon I was pedaling in a knot of bicycles when I heard my name. It was Tran Viet Son, who pedaled in the other direction. A painter,

Mr. Son was director of the Fine Arts Department of the Ministry of Culture. We'd been working together on his upcoming trip to the States for the opening of "As Seen by Both Sides," an exhibition of paintings by Vietnamese and American artists.

"Have you heard from Mr. David?" Mr. Son called. David Thomas headed the host organization, the Indochina Arts Project.

"I'm going for the mail now!" I yelled over my shoulder. I backpedaled, my left foot down, my right up, ready to accelerate. "If there's a letter, I'll bring it by. When will you be in tomorrow?"

"Eight sharp!" he shouted into the mass of commuters.

I jammed my right foot forward, passing two men outside a day care center. One set his tiny child on his luggage rack; the child grabbed his father's belt as the two took off into the blare of horns. The other man loaded his son into a bamboo baby seat. He unfolded a red mosquito net, shielding the child as if he were a prince. Both men swerved around a man whose toddler had slipped from the luggage carrier. The child clutched her father's thigh while he steered toward the curb.

I followed a new Toyota Landcruiser. In 1990, cars were still rare in Ha Noi. Flower and I called the white Landcruisers popular among United Nations staff "the white buffalos." This buffalo was spotless, its windows closed tight. I could have swooped around the car, but instead I coasted, aware my conical hat fused me with the crowd.

Like me, the people inside the Landcruiser were Caucasians. The mother sat with her arm across the father's seat-back. From the father's posture, I could tell he was attentive to traffic. The children, a boy and a girl, faced backwards. They looked flawless in nanny-starched shirts, their hair stiffly parted. They stared at the pedaling mob, their eyes wary.

For me, rush hour was a favorite time. I would savor the smell of charcoal and kerosene cooking fires that enriched the afternoon air. I loved the bustling intimacy of Ha Noi traffic, the four-way conversations between two bicycles, each with rider and passenger. And I loved the way two women or two men would ride separately, side by side, chatting and holding hands. And yes, I relished the anarchy of it all.

And so, at that moment, coasting behind the sealed Landcruiser, I wanted to reach inside and release those children. I wanted to pop them both onto the back of my bike, and take them into the hurly-burly world of Ha Noi.

XXII

Toasts and Tea

We took up arms, fought and won.
All the four seas are now serene.
Great changes are forthcoming.
Let everyone everywhere be so informed.

FROM "Proclamation of Victory
Over the Invaders"
NGUYAN TRAI
1380–1442

One afternoon I heard the distant whistle of the four forty-five and pedaled harder to beat the train to the crossing. Just as I arrived, guards hauled
two rusty gates across the road, but still a motorcycle sped through the
gap. Two boys in school uniforms dragged their bicycle under the barrier,
into the fury of the train's whistle and then under the far gate; they sped
off. I waited, my front wheel pressed against the rusty barrier.

A Landcruiser pulled up on my right, a Rumanian bus on my left. A
Soviet Lada swerved onto the wrong side of the road, stopping at the gate.

A tractor hauling sand came alongside it, further blocking the oncoming lane. The four vehicles waited side by side like the starting lineup for a stock-car race. On the other side of the crossing gate, a similar lineup jammed the road. Then second tiers formed on both sides of the gate. And then third.

The train rumbled through, whistle shrieking, its car roofs stacked with bicycles, windows crammed with faces. As the crossing guards rolled back the gate, the cars and motorcycles pressed forward until they stood nose to nose, blocked four abreast, engines revving. But we cyclists kept moving. Like the others, I lifted my bicycle frame onto one shoulder and walked through the press of cars and motorcycles. My handlebars grazed the roof of a white Landcruiser. The driver, a blond woman, rolled down her window.

"What's wrong?" she asked.

"It's a stampede of white buffalo," I answered.

"Oh no!" she said, cranking her window shut.

Oh Lady, I muttered to myself, why did you say that?

The woman and her Landcruiser were guests of Viet Nam; the evening stampede was but a symptom of a nation in transition. For years, Right Relationship had defined bicycle etiquette. Everyone yielded to loaded cy-clos and bicycles carrying huge saddle baskets filled with cabbages. Beyond that, the rules followed social status, so that regardless of who was at fault, I would apologize to a senior uncle but might chastise a nephew. However, in 1990, rules for cars had not yet entered the Ha Noi consciousness.

The electrical system was equally chaotic. People tapped into it at will. When typhoons came, officials shut down the entire city, worrying that live electrical wires might drop into the flooded streets. In the early evening, the power sometimes dropped to 80 volts but later surged to 360, frying appliances. Housing starts and additions were just as unregulated, with little attention to demands on water and sewage. And buying and sell-ing was as much a free-for-all as the cyclists lifting their bikes over the cars.

One afternoon, while in the midst of evening commuter traffic, I met Flower headed the other way. "We received a fax about the poetry book," she called across the *whir* of spokes. "I'll leave it on the desk. Rose says she's moving to her new house next week, and Autumn can come for tea tomorrow."

"Thanks, Watcher!" I teased.

"Watcher" was my nickname for Flower. Each morning, we divided the day's errands. Then we took off, I on my bicycle, she on her brother's motorcycle. Ha Noi was then such a small town that we invariably ran into each other, even when plans changed and I went somewhere not on my list.

One morning at the end of my stay, I was biking over to see Mr. Pearl to tell him that the magnifying lamp was on its way. How strange, I mused as I pedaled, I haven't bumped into Flower. At that moment, I heard a *beep, beep*. A motorcycle pulled alongside. There was Flower, exuberant, her hair lifting in the breeze.

"Watcher," I muttered.

"Wanderer!" she teased.

Flower and I spent much of our time outside of Ha Noi working on clean-drinking-water projects and irrigation systems. To improve primary health care, the most important project work is to provide clean drinking water; to improve nutrition, at least in Viet Nam, the crucial work is irrigation, since irrigation not only helps control flooding during the rainy season but also provides water for a second crop and sometimes even a third during the dry season.

Nam Ca Nang was one of the many villages where we worked. To reach Nam Ca Nang, we traveled twelve hours by jeep to Son La town, the capital of Son La province in the mountains west of Ha Noi near Viet Nam's border with Laos. It was another half day by jeep to the district town and then several hours by small boat up the Da River to Nam Ca Nang. But as remote as Nam Ca Nang may have seemed to us, the village was not remote to the people living there.

Viet Nam has some fifty ethnic minorities, all with different cultures, customs, and languages. Nam Ca Nang was White Tai, an ethnic group also present in China, Laos, Thailand, and now the United States. Like many ethnic minorities living in the mountains of Viet Nam, the people of Nam Ca Nang used roving "slash and burn" agriculture, cutting trees on the mountainsides in order to grow upland rice.

After one season, when the soil was too depleted for rice, the White Tai grew corn. The third season they planted manioc. Then they moved on to cut and burn another slope. Their slash-and-burn agriculture was not a cultural choice but a necessity for food. However, control of water through irrigation could make it possible to use land for crops year after year.

Together with a Vietnamese engineer, Flower and I walked along the irrigation canal to the broken dam that had once fed Nam Ca Nang's rice paddies. We agreed to cover the engineering costs, provide the cement and reinforcing bar, and pay the masons to rebuild the dam if the villagers would contribute the unskilled labor.

Although I made subsequent trips to Viet Nam, I did not return again to Nam Ca Nang until three years later, in 1993. I was startled by the changes that had come from the project. Nam Ca Nang could feed itself. The village paths were clear of buffalo dung because manure for the nearby paddy land had become precious. Villagers raised more pigs, and they'd started vegetable gardens.

That trip in 1993, the village leader led me into his house on stilts, where he served lotus tea in thimble-sized cups. Then we toasted each other with rice whiskey he'd brewed with medicinal herbs harvested from the forest. The spacious wood floors and tidy sleeping section in the leader's house were much as I remembered from 1990. But everything had changed. Now, with increased paddy yields, three quarters of the villagers had electricity. Each evening, television brought the rest of the world to Nam Ca Nang.

The process of opening throughout Viet Nam came by small steps. Until the mid-1980s, Ha Noi's sidewalks had been bare, but in 1987 I began to see occasional tea stands. By 1988, the tea stalls were selling cookies and bananas, and then came noodle stalls and other small businesses.

In 1989, Rose took me to Ha Noi's first private beauty parlor. The beauty parlor was in one of the first Ha Noi houses to be purchased with the proceeds of private enterprise. I sat with Rose on a bench in a room so narrow that the knees of the women on the opposite bench interlocked with ours like the spines of hair rollers jammed into a box. The smell of cream rinses, conditioners, and moisturizers constricted the air.

I could see how the owner had made so much money. Her scissors clicked, *snip snip snip.* "And your son?" she would say to one customer, *clip clip clip.* "And your daughter?" she would say to another, *snip snip snip.* For years, most Vietnamese women had worn their hair tied back into a knot or wrapped in a strip of black velvet around their heads. Now, instead of the same traditional style, the beautician coiffured customer after customer in an identical stylish swirl.

"How about you?" she asked me.

"Oh thanks," I said, "I don't think so."

"Yes, do!" the other women cheered. "It's old-fashioned to wear your hair in a nape knot."

"Maybe a trim," I said, opening my thumb and forefinger like calipers. "A centimeter [about half an inch] or so."

As soon as I sat in the beautician's chair, I knew I'd made a mistake. She sank her fingers into my hair, which hung well below my waist. I could feel her hands delighting in an exotic texture. Her scissors began, *clip clip clip.*

I took one look in the mirror but, seeing myself, recoiled as I remembered the mirror effect of the "bottle babies" born to women from areas of the Mekong Delta sprayed with Agent Orange. I turned instead toward the women on the benches. They sat, shoulders wedged, their faces framed by curlers.

"You'll soon look much younger," a woman wearing pink hair rollers said to me. She worked in the Ministry of Culture.

"We'll find you a Ha Noi husband!" an older woman added, removing her curlers. She dropped them into a box on her neighbor's knees.

"Will you have a permanent?" the woman next to her asked me.

I laughed, pointing to my head. "You want me to have more curl than this?"

The women laughed. Suddenly I realized the beautician had been busy all the time we'd been talking. Her scissors were too close.

"Just a centimeter!" I protested.

But it was too late. What hair remained was so short that I could no longer wind it into a knot. Still, I feigned pleasure as I removed two thousand *dong*—then about thirty cents—to pay the going price for a haircut.

"Oh no! No charge," the beautician said, sweeping long swirls of russet hair into the day's shearings of black. "It's a pleasure to make you look so young."

By the fall of 1990, there were fifteen Americans including two children living in Ha Noi. We figured we couldn't be Americans anywhere without celebrating Thanksgiving. Thanksgiving was Bob's idea. He was an American mapmaker who had worked as a United Nations volunteer in Ha Noi for more than a year. Lisa, Jim, and Peter—three English teachers with Volunteers in Asia—pitched in to help.

By then, we Americans had too many Vietnamese friends to fit into one room, so we settled on an exclusively American event. Nevertheless, none of our American evening could have been possible without Bob's wife, Mai. She and Bob had been married two months. Trained as an interpreter in Ha Noi, Mai spoke exquisite English. She was a Vietnamese citizen and intended to remain so. It was Mai who, with the help of her mother, found us a "Western chicken," as turkey is called in Viet Nam.

Jim made the stuffing with Russian bread. Lisa prepared applesauce, mixing Chinese apples with Vietnamese cinnamon. Peter picked up some Bulgarian wine. Jan, codirector of the Mennonite Central Committee program, produced a can of Thai pumpkin. Stan, her husband, hand-cranked that American wonder—ice cream—using Vietnamese condensed milk.

Sitting there at one long table spread with all the fixings, we might have passed for Norman Rockwell's famous painting. With the addition of several American consultants, our ranks had swelled to twenty-three. Jan's parents, retired college professors, lent a silver-haired dignity. The two children provided the essential touch of impishness.

"We have much to be thankful for," Stan said when the blessing had been given.

Stan's comment made me smile. My Quaker grandfather used to say those very words at Thanksgivings when I was a child. I had said them myself at annual gatherings in my farm kitchen. Now, Stan had transplanted to Ha Noi that one small tradition from my own family.

The dishes began to circulate; praise for the cooks quickly followed. There weren't enough forks to go around, but to me it felt just right to eat Thanksgiving in Ha Noi with chopsticks. And I was selfishly glad for the custom that chopsticks allow: I could reach into the serving dishes bite by delicious bite. I could also play with the Vietnamese custom of dropping delicacies onto my compatriots' plates.

When our Thanksgiving feast was finished and it was time to leave, we all lingered around the table, as if something more remained.

"Think how much has changed," Stan said, looking at the faces in the waning candlelight. "Who of us was here last year?"

We each cast back to where we had been the year before: Indiana, Vermont, Kansas, California, a rustic farm kitchen in Appalachian Ohio. We shook our heads: "No." "No." "No, not me." Soon our gaze settled on the newlyweds, a Vietnamese interpreter and an American mapmaker.

"Yes," they said, holding hands. "We were here."

My Quaker Service tasks included the paperwork for a shipment of prosthetics equipment to the Rehabilitation Center in Qui Nhon in central Viet Nam, where the project I'd worked with during the war had moved in 1976. When I wrote to the center director, requesting signed arrival notices, I asked after our former staff. I received a warm reply from the director but no arrival notices.

A month later, I met the director at a conference in Ha Noi. I'd brought along another set of forms, but he insisted on coming to our office on Hang Chao that afternoon rather than sign the forms I'd brought. I was annoyed. I'd counted on finishing my monthly accounts before the weekly mail pouch left that evening. I suspected the director wanted to propose another project. I would have to give up an hour's work just to drink tea and say No.

That afternoon, I grumbled over spreadsheets as Flower set out teacups.

"Time for chitchat," she teased.

I looked up and saw the director at the door, his grin impish. I'd been had. There, peeping from behind the director's shoulder, was Quy, who had been our head prosthetist in Quang Ngai. And from behind Quy peered Hoang, our mechanic and driver. We hadn't seen one another in twenty years.

"*Troi oi!*—Good Heavens!" I said, laughing. I clasped Quy's hands and then his shoulders and then Hoang as well. Then I turned to the director. "Now," I said, teasing, "I understand why you were so uncooperative!"

There *was* lots of chitchat. Quy and Hoang wanted news of other Quaker Service wartime staff, and I was anxious for stories of our Vietnamese colleagues and of our patients. Quy and Hoang asked Flower about our work in Son La and Thanh Hoa provinces, and she asked all about their work in Qui Nhon.

During our months together on Hang Chao, Flower and I served plenty of tea. But for me, that afternoon was the most precious. Two parts of my world connected: On one side were Quy and Hoang, friends from the wartime South; on the other, Flower, a friend from the wartime North. Once they had been as separate as two nations; now they were as near as the two words in *Viet Nam*.

XXIII

The House on Lotus Pond

This blue sky is now ours.
Ours also these perfumed plains,
These streams heavy with brown silt,
This homeland—it is ours.

NGUYEN DINH THI
1924–

Flower was a blessing. I had worked in Viet Nam long enough to know that my white face handicapped me for many tasks, particularly finding a permanent residence to replace the room on Hang Chao. Flower and I asked everyone we knew. If Flower asked, the rent might be three thousand dollars a month; if I asked, it was five thousand. Yet our budget was one thousand.

"How about if we keep my American face out of this?" I suggested. "Why don't you take charge of finding a house?"

By Flower's count, she checked out more than thirty houses in varying states of mildew. Then one afternoon she dashed into our room.

"My aunt has a friend with a house!" she announced.

"Not another friend," I teased. Whether we needed a veterinarian or an engineer, Flower always had a friend who knew someone to ask.

"They want fifteen hundred dollars," she said. "If the house is OK, I'll see if I can talk them down."

"Talk fast," I said.

Flower left to scout; she returned, giddy. "It's perfect! On Lotus Pond Street, across the Thien Quang Lake from Lenin Park. Two rooms upstairs, each with a small balcony, two baths, large living room and kitchen, patio, even a garage. I talked them down to twelve hundred dollars. I was ruthless!! Want to look?"

Look we did. Even I talked fast. We were pushing limits to rent from a family rather than from the government. I wanted the owners to know that Quaker Service wartime work had included the Saigon-controlled South as well as the Viet Cong-controlled South and the North. I also wanted to be sure they knew I had worked with Boat People. We parted cordially, and I left Flower to work out details. Flower bargained the rent down to nine hundred dollars. A week later, we biked over to sign the lease.

"There's something I should tell you," Flower said. She rested her hand on mine the way women in Viet Nam do when pedaling side by side. "Last night my mother told me the landlady is our cousin."

"If you don't have a 'friend,' " I said, "it's a cousin."

Flower laughed. "About as near a cousin as here to America! But it's a good thing I didn't know. Else how could I bargain so brutally?!"

Over tea with the landlords, I arranged to pay our deposit. In Ha Noi at that time, everyone—Vietnamese and foreigners—paid major expenses in green dollars. This transaction would require that I wait several hours at the bank for the money and then bike across town with the greenbacks padding my middle.

"We can't meet you Tuesday morning," Flower said, showing our landlady the schedule for Quaker Service staff visiting from Bangkok. "But we could come here after *Nhan Dan*."

"*Nhan Dan?*" the landlady said, perplexed. *Nhan Dan* is the Vietnamese Communist Party's newspaper.

"Our guests organized a conference," I said, still wanting to educate her about our work. "It was in Cambodia for editors from Southeast Asian newspapers. They want to visit the two *Nhan Dan* staff who participated."

"My sister-in-law went to Cambodia," the landlady said, looking over Flower's shoulder at the schedule. "Yes! There's Lien's name."

"See!" Flower turned to me. "You have 'cousins' here, too."

In December 1990, Flower and I moved the office to Lotus Pond Street. We hired the landlady's mother, Aunt Gentleness, as housekeeper and cook. In her mid-sixties, Aunt Gentleness had strong cheekbones and a high fore-head accented by a widow's peak. Out of respect, I called her "Senior Aunt"; in comparable regard, she called me "Older Sister." Aunt Gentleness adopted me. Soon every morning I joined her friends for badminton in Lenin Park.

I left the house before dawn, pushing my bicycle out into the dark and shuttered street. As I locked the house gate, a neighbor from several doors down tugged her noodle cart toward the corner. The cart's wooden wheels knocked against the cobblestones in a *cloppity* rhythm.

"Good morning, Older Sister," I said, walking my bike alongside her cart. I savored the aroma of the chicken broth steeped in cinnamon, gin-ger, and coriander. Soon she would pour the broth over rice noodles, serv-ing the neighborhood *pho,* a traditional Vietnamese breakfast.

"You're early today," she answered. At the corner, she removed a low table and four tiny stools from the back of her cart, transforming the side-walk into her noodle stand.

Across the street, another stall added the aroma of fresh-baked bread. The vendor, an older woman with hair wrapped around her head in the tradition of northern Viet Nam, pulled a tiny loaf from the warming oven she'd improvised from an old oil drum. "Older Sister!" she called to me. "Have some bread before you go to the park!"

"Thank you," I answered over my shoulder. "Please, Auntie, save me a loaf as always."

"You'll need it," she answered, clicking her tongue. "The uncles will run the meat off your bones!"

I turned onto Nguyen Du Street, named for the famous poet who had written Viet Nam's epic *The Tale of Kieu,* and pedaled along Thien Quang Lake. Two men in a small rowboat, their voices subdued, hauled in a net filled with silvery fish. Nearby, an elderly gentleman practiced tai chi on the grassy bank, his long white beard floating like the mist.

But as I passed Thien Quang pagoda, the quiet turned to uproar. The buses from the provinces had arrived. Cyclo drivers swarmed, yelling at the women lowering sides of pork and huge baskets of vegetables from the bus roofs. The bottom of one basket broke, its cabbages bouncing like soccer balls. A boy in a torn T-shirt snatched a rolling cabbage and tore off down the street.

"You're early today, Older Sister," a cyclo driver called.

I waved and pedaled through the gate of Lenin Park.

Gentleness was already playing badminton, her nape knot of long black hair bobbing with each shot. I shed my wool cap, scarf, and sandals. Choosing a badminton racket, I joined Gentleness and her friend Beloved. I missed shot after shot. I couldn't see the birdie against the grey, predawn sky. None of the others, all older than I, wore glasses, so I'd left mine at home.

"How can you see that thing?" I called to Beloved, finally hitting the birdie over our imaginary net.

"Pretend you're watching for bombers," she said, returning my volley.

One by one, Gentleness's friends took me on. After demure Beloved came gracious Dove who, like Aunt Gentleness, wore the traditional round-necked *ao ba ba* and black satin *quans*. The women rested in turn, but I kept playing until I shed down to my own *ao ba ba*.

"Are you tired yet?" Determination asked, stepping in front of me. He was a wiry man in his early sixties. Years before, rheumatism had crippled both Determination's arms. Then he took up badminton as therapy, first for his right arm, then for his left. Now, he played with two rackets. Clapping their handles, he twirled between shots like a circus acrobat between feats.

Rainbow, unusual in her plumpness, took Leader's place. Her touch was soft and her movements graceful.

"I used to have a Westerner's belly!" she announced, waddling in imitation of her former self.

"Beautiful," she said each time I returned the shuttlecock. The birdie floated between us like easy conversation.

The sky shifted to light grey and then to blue. Rainbow and I joined two men using a net. My partner, the only other person playing barefoot, wore his beret tilted at a rakish angle. He served the shuttlecock as if firing a bullet.

"*Chet!*—Dead!" he shouted each time he whipped a return over the net.

"So many deaths," I said, laughing at his vigor.

"Like the B-52s," he answered. He sizzled the birdie at Rainbow, who lobbed it back to me. "I lost my wife and child during the Christmas bombing," my partner added. "Are you French?"

My concentration snapped. The birdie landed at my feet. It lay there, lifeless.

"Uncle, I'm American."

The corner of his mouth quivered. "My only son. He was two."

"So many deaths," I said. "So much pain."

He picked at a racket string as if playing the plaintive one-stringed zither. "Sometimes," he said, "an old sorrow is sharper than yesterday's."

From the next court came the *plick, plick* of a birdie bandied. Nearby, a man with one leg snapped fallen branches into burnable lengths and loaded them into a handcart. A kiosk vendor turned on his radio, and the park filled with news of Baghdad and U.S. preparations for war.

"Uncle," I said, "can you forgive us?"

He twisted the sole of his bare foot against the asphalt, then turned to face me. "It was a long time ago."

"Yes," I said. "But time is slow in its solace."

"But look at us now," he said, tapping his racket against the asphalt. "You and I on the same side, and we just lost a point! It's their serve, Older Sister."

Rainbow served, and my partner whipped a return back to her; she responded with a graceful lob, which I sliced over the net. But her partner was equally quick. The birdie flew back and forth in an extended volley.

"What is she?" a bystander asked, pointing at me. Out of the corner of my eye, I could see that his jacket hung on him.

"Ask her," my partner answered. "She can talk."

"I'm American," I volunteered in Vietnamese. "What are you?"

"I'm Vietnamese," he answered in crystalline English. "I'll play you tomorrow!"

My partner and I played on until Uncle Strength arrived on his bicycle. At seventy, Uncle Strength's hair was as white as the feathers on a new birdie. He looked like a court jester in his bright blue sweat suit and baseball cap embroidered with THIS MEN, which I suppose was some local entrepreneur's flawed attempt at English.

"*Di, di!!*" Uncle Strength ordered, using on me the same expression— "Move it!"—that American GIs had once hurled at Vietnamese. He sent me racing, side to side. "Where are you?" he called out, laughing as he flicked the birdie. "Now where are you? You're stiff," he challenged. "Are you a tourist?"

"No, Uncle!" I said, diving for the birdie. "I'm not."

"Look!" said a bystander. "An American who knows how to run."

"But not in sandals," his companion added, looking at my bare feet.

I missed the shot.

"Bend like this," Uncle Strength said. Exaggerating his own grace, he crossed one leg in front of the other and, sweeping his racket, dipped so low that his knees rested on the pavement.

"We should book you into the Central Theater," I muttered. Sweat streamed down my arms even though it was so cold that my breath frosted into small clouds.

"Time for *pho*," Aunt Gentleness called.

Uncle Strength caught the birdie I returned. As we walked to my pile of sweaters, he patted the pouch of acupuncture needles in the pocket of his sweat pants.

"Any ailments today?" he asked.

"Creaky knees," I said.

"You need to grease your joints," Uncle Strength said. "Eat more pork fat." He laughed and mounted his bicycle. "See you tomorrow!" he called as he rode off.

It was 7 A.M. At daybreak, the park had been like the woods at home when the birds gather and burst into sound. By now, with full sunlight, it was quiet. The runners completed their last loop around the lake. Two fencers stopped to talk to soccer players gathering around their bicycles. My barefoot badminton partner unhooked his net. He waved as Aunt Gentleness and I passed by on our way to the park gate.

The Christmas bombing of 1972 that had shattered my badminton partner's life careened into every conversation I had in late 1990. The United States was preparing for combat. The Gulf War may have generated ebullience among many Americans, but for Vietnamese it sparked a minefield of memories. I constantly blundered into explosions of pain.

One day just before Christmas, Aunt Gentleness and I sat down to lunch. Flower had gone off to a wedding. Aunt Gentleness filled two bowls with steaming rice. I set the spring rolls and fish soup on the table. Sitting opposite me, Aunt Gentleness paired the chopsticks according to height and offered me a set. I had only just moved into the house on Lotus Pond. This was the first time Aunt Gentleness and I were alone together.

"Please," she said, inviting me to eat. She dipped her chopsticks in the soup and placed a morsel of fish on my rice.

Always shy with strangers, I wondered what to talk about. I settled on a safe topic. "Tell me about your grandchildren," I said.

"I have a granddaughter in America."

The fish stuck like a bone in my throat. From the street outside came the laughter of children jumping rope. The rope struck the cobblestones, *slap, slap.*

"A year ago," Aunt Gentleness continued, "my daughter-in-law took my granddaughter to America through the Orderly Departure Program. My granddaughter was thirteen. I had raised her since she was two, but then her mother came and took her away to America."

Aunt Gentleness set a spring roll on my rice; she toyed with her food. "When you return to the States, will you carry a package to my grand-daughter?"

"Of course."

The noon siren began with a low moan, then rose to the wail that had once announced American bombers.

"I went to Au Duong today," I said, changing the subject. An Duong had been the first site struck during Nixon's Christmas bombing in 1972 just as the Paris peace talks were ending. "They wanted an American to join their ceremony commemorating the people who were killed."

"That's when my husband died," Aunt Gentleness said, once again catching me by surprise. "During the last hour of the Christmas bombing."

What could I say?

Outside, the children skinned rope, *Slap! Slap! Slap! "Mot! Hai! Ba! Bon!*—One! Two! Three! Four!"

"I'm sorry," I murmured. "We Americans have never taken responsibil-ity for what we did."

Aunt Gentleness placed another spring roll on my rice. "Will they do it again?" she asked. "Bomb the Iraqis the way they did us?"

"I'm afraid so."

"But why?"

"Greed," I said. "Oil. Pride. We lost the American War in Viet Nam."

"But suppose Americans had lived under bombs . . ." Aunt Gentleness looked at her hands. "Could you bomb so easily?"

"Certainly not. Except for Pearl Harbor—and that was a military base—we can't remember war on our own land."

"We're so different," Aunt Gentleness said, touching her hair, which had strands of grey. "People my age, we've scarcely known peace."

A month later, when I left Ha Noi for the States, Aunt Gentleness gave me a Vietnamese cookbook to take to her granddaughter in America. For my father on his ninetieth birthday, she sent a youthful beret and lotus-seed candy. My gift was a photograph of her family taken on the anniversary of her husband's death.

In the photograph, Aunt Gentleness stands in the rice paddy where the fateful bomb exploded. She bends in prayer over a white crypt. Smoke from the incense sticks pressed between her palms drifts over her grown sons and daughters, their spouses and children. One grandchild is missing: She is somewhere in Massachusetts, far from her grandfather's grave.

Conversations during the fall of 1990 invariably came to silence. Always, out of the silence, came the same question.

"They won't bomb, will they?" Autumn asked at supper one evening at her house.

"Yes," I said. "They will."

"*Bom bi,*" her husband, Vigilance, muttered. "How can the Americans bomb again?!"

"*Hrmmmmmmmmmmmm,*" Autumn said, imitating a bomber. "*Boom!* And then the *bi* clatter." She held her thumb and forefinger an inch apart. "When the bombers came, we would jump into the manhole shelters. They had straw lids like the shield you tried on in Khanh Phu. Once, I found a piece of shrapnel stuck in the straw of my manhole lid. It had fallen from one of our own shells shot at a bomber." She held her thumb and forefinger two inches apart. "I was that far from death."

"Americans don't know about bombing," I said. "After all, I've never seen a *bi.*"

"Oh!" Vigilance said. "I'll show you." He left the table and, pulling a box from under the nearby bed, rummaged. He handed me a tiny package. "The baby bombs each burst into hundreds of these *bi.*"

Bi is the Vietnamese word for "marble," but what Vigilance set in my palm was no toy. Here was a dart the size of a straight pin but with flanges of steel.

"A baby bomb would kill you," Autumn said. "The *bi* wounded."

I nodded. I knew the tactic: Don't kill; instead, maim. An enemy buries its dead and moves on. But the maimed immobilize the enemy's resources by tying up medical staff and family members. I jabbed the dart against my fingertip, feeling its prick. "In the United States," I said, "we call this a 'flechette.' "

"Will they use flechettes on the Iraqis?" Vigilance asked.

"Yes," I said, "but this time, they'll use plastic."

"Plastic?" Autumn served me more rice and stir-fries. "Because it's cheaper?"

"No," I said. "X rays."

"X rays?" Autumn's brow furrowed. Then her eyes widened. "Oh! Then the arrows won't show up!"

"Exactly," I said.

"I have two flechettes," Vigilance said. "If you want, you can take that one back to America."

And so I did.

At home in the States, I carry Vigilance's flechette in my wallet as a reminder of how I, a taxpayer, bought and continue to pay for the American War.

Sometimes late at night I awaken from a recurring dream, where Americans and Vietnamese pluck those flechettes from earth and flesh, gathering them from the face of Viet Nam and from the faces of Vietnamese. Together the Americans and the Vietnamese lay the arrows side by side, end on end, until their flanges fuse into a span of steel strong enough to carry the silences that separate us.

By 1990, buying and selling had begun to dominate life in Ha Noi.

During the American War, women did much of the heavy industrial work. Many factories were evacuated to the countryside to escape American bombing. *(Ha Noi Women's Museum)*

General Vo Nguyen Giap, one of the architects of the victory against the French at Dien Bien Phu and of the Tet Offensive during the American War, in a military parade held in Ha Noi's historical Ba Dinh Square on May Day 1973. *(Ngo Vinh Long Collection)*

On May 15, 1975, two weeks after the fall of Sai Gon, there was a nationwide celebration of victory. *(Ngo Vinh Long Collection)*

Factory workers in Thai Binh,
North Viet Nam, in 1975, when I
visited during the war.

In 1975, workers were
still rebuilding Bach Mai
hospital, which was hit
during Nixon's
Christmas bombing in
1972.

A Ha Noi school
in 1975.

Flower (right) accompanied me around North Viet Nam during my wartime 1975 trip. Although I made numerous subsequent trips to Ha Noi, we did not see each other again until we both worked for Quaker Service in 1990. Here, Flower and a friend are entranced by the Ha Noi circus, a favorite wartime entertainment.

Ha Noi's Lake of the Redeemed Sword at the center of the city is a favorite gathering place.

For years
Ha Noi has
been a city of
bicycles.

The dramatic increase in motorcycles and cars and the change in consumer goods carried by cyclos signal the economic growth in Ha Noi since Renovation.

Dragon Dance at the funeral for the head of the Buddhist Church in December 1993. This was the largest funeral since the death of Ho Chi Minh.

During the American War, Mr. Huu Ngoc was editor in chief of North Viet Nam's Foreign Languages Publishing House, which printed books (and rhetoric) for overseas distribution. He now chairs the Advisory Committee for the press, which is allowed to publish works banned before Renovation. *(Photo by Diane Fox)*

XXIV

Nothing Is Born,
Nothing Dies

Nothing is born,
Nothing dies.
When one understands this,
Buddha appears—
The cycle of incarnation ends.

TENTH-CENTURY
BUDDHIST TEACHING

*I*t was dusk. Already the air had taken on its evening scent of kerosene and charcoal. The last of the daylight slanted through the dust that rose in small clouds from the bicycles and motorcycles surging along Trang Tien Street. Suddenly we all stopped, brakes squealing for the newly installed traffic lights. Ha Noi had joined the late twentieth century.

It was my last evening in the city. I had been there four months, and now winter had come, so I wore every sweater I had. I'd been in and out of Ha Noi so many times over the years that no one was paying much attention to my imminent departure. I was glad for this. I wanted to leave in my own way. I wanted to slip back into the quieter Ha Noi I remembered. That's why I was riding out toward Dragon Bridge, now restricted to the train and bicycles.

The bridge ramp, which was lined with vendors hawking bread, oranges, rice cakes, and flowers, felt like a ferry crossing. I parked my bike and bought a loaf of French bread from one vendor, an orange from another, and then continued on foot amidst the cyclists pushing their bikes up the ramp. They remounted and started pedaling across the bridge as I continued along the walkway.

One bike was stacked so high with baskets that I couldn't see the rider. Then came a family of four with the father pedaling. A toddler sat on the crossbar, holding his father's arms as if they were handlebars; the mother and a baby perched on the luggage rack. Behind them came a bike laden with sacks of rice. The young man pushed the bicycle, using a bamboo pole lashed to the handlebars and another lashed to the seat post just as his grandparents' and parents' generations had when supplying Dien Bien Phu and the Truong Son Trail.

Two women in the olive drab clothes often worn by factory workers pedaled past. Both women had hung their conical hats over their handlebars. One rested her hand on the other's sleeve as the two chatted. The breeze blew wisps of hair across her eyes. She brushed the hair aside and set her hand back on her friend's sleeve.

"He said we'd have a big order from Taiwan," she said, her voice melding with the next conversation between cyclists passing me.

I leaned over the rusty steel railing and looked out toward the Red River. In the distance, several women squatted in the hold of an open junk. They packed crockery into a huge basket. Using a shoulder yoke, two men in shorts hauled the basket down a narrow gangplank. Their work helmets fashioned from stitched leaves bobbed as they carried their load along a narrow foot dike lining a field where a farmer plowed.

"*Vat! Vat!*" the farmer called, telling his water buffalo to turn as he reset his marking stake in the mud. The stevedores continued on, passing a cone-shaped brick kiln before they entered a small stucco house. Soon they emerged with an empty basket, heading at a steady clip toward the junk. But this time they paused to chat with five middle-aged women packing mud into wooden forms. The woman added their wet clay cakes to the rows of bricks lined up like houses in a real estate development.

"You up there!" the oldest of the women called to me. She stood looking up, a fresh brick in both hands. A breeze blowing off the Red River fluttered the cuffs of her black satin *quans*. "Come join us, Westerner."

I know that making bricks, like raising rice, sends you to bed with a backache and wakes you with a charley horse. Still, if I could choose, I thought, I might live in that woman's stucco house by the Red River and spend my days packing red earth into a wooden mold. Something about those rhythms, like mine of driving a school bus twice a day for twenty years around the same rural route, gives life structure, community, and comfort. Standing there at the rusty railing, I knew that what lay below was my Ha Noi and that this life would fade quickly, like a conversation between two passing cyclists.

The low moan of a steam locomotive pulling up the grade to the bridge rose to a clean, shrill whistle. The engine, wheezing and huffing, entered the trestle, exhaling black smoke and sparks. The bridge shuddered as if once again racked by bombs. Then the shrieking whistle and the *clackety-clack* receded, and conversations between cyclists resumed.

I stayed on until the farmer unharnessed his buffalo and lifted the plow onto his shoulder and until the whir of evening traffic slipped into the isolated *whip-ti-whip* of an occasional bicycle.

From the bridge, I biked over to Rose's new house built of handmade bricks covered with stucco. Rose, her husband, and teenage son had lived for seventeen years in one room on Cotton Street. There, they shared the one water tap and toilet with eighteen other people. Now, with financing from a cousin working in Japan, Rose had designed her own house complete with a living room, dining area, and study.

I turned onto Rose's street and walked my bicycle through the "squatting market" that each evening blocked the mouth of the road the way a shifting shoal obstructs an estuary. Nodding to a vendor, I guided my front tire around a glistening pile of fish scales.

"You've come to say good-bye," the woman sitting behind a basket of carp said. She'd lost her husband in the Christmas bombing; she followed my visits to Rose with a neighbor's benign curiosity.

"Ly! Ly!" the woman next to her called. Her hair, wrapped in a black velvet turban, was as silver as the fish she held out. "Take our fish to America!"

"Here," the first woman said, tearing off a section of *Nhan Dan,* "some fish for your father. Insure his healthy old age!"

Her friend reached for a copy of *Cong An,* Ha Noi's version of the *National Enquirer.* "And fish for our American friends!"

"You're too kind," I said, "but Air Viet Nam pilots won't let me take fish. If you want, I can carry greetings."

"A thousand warm wishes to our friends in America!" the widow said.

"May your father live one hundred years!" the other vendor called as I lifted my bicycle up Rose's front steps and into her living room. I leaned the bike against others along the newly painted stucco wall, then climbed the stairs to Rose's study.

"You remember, Sister?" Rose said in English as we sat, bundled in overcoats at her desk. "*A Room of One's Own*. I couldn't imagine such a thing when you gave me that book, but you said, 'Yes, be patient, the time will come.' To think! I have a room! For books. To study. For my sister to stay in when coming to Ha Noi."

Rose peeled a mandarin orange. The rind sprayed, its pungent fragrance piercing the musty smell of books. She divided the orange, handing me half.

"So how do you feel, leaving?" she asked.

"Jealous." I was startled to hear that word pop from my mouth.

"Jealous?" Rose seemed equally surprised.

"Jealous of my replacements," I said. "I've been running so fast that I haven't had time to do anything, no time to gossip with the fishmongers outside your door or with the kids outside mine, no time just to be with you, no time for us to read books together."

"When you arrived," Rose said, "we thought we would have so much time."

I pinched an orange peel in hopes the spray stinging my nose would curb the anger in my voice. "I've thrown myself into getting projects into shape, finding a house, introducing my replacements to friends. Then I leave. Just when things are finally open, I hand it all over to them. *They* have time. So yeah, I'm jealous."

The electricity faltered, then failed. Rose lit the candle on her desk. The room with its stacked books softened. She peeled another orange, its loose skin falling off into her hands.

"It's like you plant an orchard of mandarin oranges," Rose said. "You choose the right spot and you dig big holes. You bring in the best soil. You plant small trees, and you cover the roots with that best soil. Year after year you carry water to the small trees. You prune their broken branches."

As she spoke, I thought of Senior Uncle in Ban Long, how he would climb his bamboo ladder to cut a rotten spot from a young jackfruit. I remembered planting a jujube tree with Mrs. Pearl in Khanh Phu's Garden of the Elders. By now, the jujube would be big enough to bear fruit.

"But then," Rose continued, "you leave us just when the orchard you care for begins to fruit. So you are sad."

"Yes," I said, feeling even more desolate.

"But don't you see?" Rose said, offering me another half of mandarin orange. "You'll come back again. When you come, you'll have this room of your own in Ha Noi. You will find your fruit trees healthy. Yes, you leave tomorrow. But when you return, we will serve you fruit."

As it turned out, the next morning I was given a brief reprieve. My plane originally scheduled for dawn was delayed until midday. The mail had come in the night before and, with it, word that the magnifying lamp for Mr. Pearl was on its way. And there was also good news for Viet Duc Hospital, Ha Noi's major surgical center.

Four years before in early 1987, I had been in Ha Noi when direct contact with Westerners was first allowed. Dr. Quang, the hospital director, asked me to help him join the International Society of Surgery. The application required a recommendation by three current members. However, the Vietnamese, isolated by the U. S. embargo, had no contacts.

By chance an honorary member of the Society was a Quaker whom I had taken around Quang Ngai during the war. At my request, he interceded. Now I had a letter announcing the acceptance into the Society of not only Dr. Quang but also three other surgeons whom he chose to nominate.

Dr. Quang and I celebrated over cups of rich, thick Vietnamese coffee. As I left the hospital, I recognized the gait and the greying hair of a man walking away from me. This is what I love about Ha Noi, I thought: its closeness, the way my past encircles me like a hand-stitched conical hat that still holds the scent of leaves.

Here now was Xuan Oanh who, with Flower, had first taken me across Dragon Bridge during the war. Even during the Years of Silence, when most Vietnamese spoke to me in rhetoric, Xuan Oanh never disguised the fact that he was foremost a musician, poet, and songwriter.

"I am an old man now," he said as we chatted under the flame trees. "I can retire to poetry."

I could have stayed forever on that corner of Nguyen Thai Hoc, chatting with Xuan Oanh, but I knew Flower would be loading my bags into the rented car. Sure enough, she was peering down Lotus Pond Street when I rounded the corner. Our neighbor had packed up her *pho* stall. She and I walked together, I pushing my bicycle, she pulling her tiny wooden cart over the cobblestones.

"Hurry up, Wanderer!" Flower said.

All too soon Flower was sitting in the front seat of the car. Aunt Gentleness and I sat in the back. I felt once again like a tourist. That car was a cage. The city I loved was outside, beyond reach. We passed the Central Theater and turned up the ramp to cross the Red River. I looked over at bombed-out Dragon Bridge and remembered the night before.

I wanted to disappear among the bicyclers on that bridge. I could almost taste the warm French bread I would buy, feel the bridge shaking beneath my feet, hear the cyclists' conversations, as soft as whirring spokes. It seemed that I could almost hear the family beneath the bridge calling out, "Come down here, American! Come make bricks. Come drink tea. Come sit and talk!"

As I looked out one window, Aunt Gentleness gazed out the other. She stroked the back of my hand. Perhaps Aunt Gentleness, looking deep into the past, saw her husband alive again. Maybe she looked to the future and saw her American granddaughter crossing the new bridge, returning to Ha Noi for a visit. She never looked at me. Still, I heard her voice, as quiet as a leaf falling from a mandarin orange tree in autumn.

"Don't forget us," Aunt Gentleness said.

Epilogue

Twilight

The wind hones its sword on the mountain rocks.
The trees are pierced with spears of cold.
A distant pagoda bell hastens the traveler's steps.
Children riding home on buffalos play their flutes.

FROM *A Prison Diary*
HO CHI MINH
1890–1969

X X V

At Rest

We will rebuild our country
Ten times more beautiful.

FROM HIS "Last Will and
Testament"
HO CHI MINH
1890–1969

*I*n the fall of 1993, I accepted a two-year assignment as Viet Nam field director for Quaker Service, returning once again to the house on Lotus Pond Street, to Flower and Aunt Gentleness and to predawn badminton with the elders. Once more, I worked with ethnic minorities in highland Son La province northwest of Ha Noi and with Vietnamese peasants in coastal Thanh Hao province south of the capital.

That fall, Second Harvest and Fifth Harmony traveled by the overnight Unification Express from Sai Gon to Ha Noi to visit Autumn and me. The wooden shutters on the houses of Lotus Pond Street were like eyelids closed in sleep when Autumn and I left before dawn to meet the train. Mist that was tinged with the soft smell of charcoal smoke hung over the empty streets.

But by the time we reached the train station, its plaza was alive with vendors hawking sticky-rice cakes, Chinese apples, and mandarin oranges. Autumn and I parked our bikes and slipped around the cyclos blocking the arrival gate, then dashed over the tracks and around the locomotive. Second Harvest hurried toward us. She lifted her conical hat.

"Do you know me?" she asked, laughing.

I would recognize Second Harvest's laughter anywhere just as I would know her face, as softly contoured as the full moon. But I was not prepared to see Second Harvest with short hair.

"Is it awful for a grown woman to cut her hair?" she asked as she ran her hand through the soft curls. She gestured toward the back of her neck. "My arm has grown so useless that I couldn't reach anymore to tie my nape knot, and I couldn't fan so much hair dry."

"Short hair makes you look younger!" Autumn said. She had cut hers many years before; after my trip to Ha Noi's first beauty parlor, mine had grown out enough that, if I wanted, I could tie it up in a respectable knot.

Soon Fifth Harmony joined us. She looked much the same, her gaunt cheeks accentuating her ears, which stood out attentive to every nuance. Sixth Sister, a northerner, had also come along. She'd married the younger brother of Second Harvest's husband after the two men went to the North for Regrouping in 1954. Like Fifth Virtue, Sixth Sister's husband had returned to the South on the Truong Son Trail.

As the three visitors climbed into cyclos, sitting among the baskets of grapes and candied bananas they'd brought from the south, I thought about how I had measured Ha Noi's transformation over the years by the change in cyclo loads. During the mid-seventies and early eighties, the cyclos carried people through streets devoid of private enterprise. But within a year after Renovation in late 1986, the cyclos were loaded with cassette players and TVs. These gave way to fans and video players, then to miniature pool tables in 1990 and on to refrigerators and washing machines in 1992. By 1993, the cyclo drivers were peering over stacks of foam mattresses and overstuffed chairs. Now, by late 1993, they were chatting with the first peasants to stay with a foreigner in Ha Noi.

Autumn and I led the cyclo drivers through the awakening city to Lotus Pond Street, where the aroma of chicken broth tinged the air. We pedaled by the half-dozen *pho* stalls lining one side of the street. On the other, a butcher quartered a pig, dividing the cuts among four women who, squatting on the sidewalk, sold the meat from huge, flat baskets. Nearby a young woman in a dark blue *ao ba ba* arranged cabbages, cauliflower, tomatoes, and carrots in a basket strapped to the back of her bicycle. With a florist's attention to color and form, she added red peppers and a spray of coriander to her display.

"Welcome to Ha Noi!" Autumn said as the cyclos drew to a stop in front of Quaker House.

I had anticipated a stressful visit. I was beginning a new job with two new Vietnamese colleagues in addition to Flower and Aunt Gentleness; I worried about fitting visitors into a jumbled work life. Now, with Sixth Sister, there was a third guest I scarcely knew. And so, when the women came down for lunch after resting from their all-night train trip, I tried to cover my anxiety as I introduced them around.

Aunt Gentleness and Flower filled our rice bowls as the rest of us squeezed around the kitchen table. *"Xin moi,"* we all said, inviting one another to eat. With her chopsticks, Aunt Gentleness clipped a sliver of beef and set it atop Sixth Sister's rice.

"So you are from Ha Bac," Aunt Gentleness said to Sixth Sister.

"How did you know that?" I asked.

Flower divided an omelette into bite-sized pieces, using the square ends of her chopsticks. "Ha Bac may be only twenty kilometers from Ha Noi," she said, "but nevertheless, people from Ha Bac have their own accent."

"I still have mine," Sixth Sister said, "even though I moved to Ha Noi thirty years ago to work in the Ministry of Construction."

"My husband worked in the Ministry of Construction," Aunt Gentleness said, adding his name.

"Oh!" Sixth Sister set down her rice bowl and chopsticks. "I remember him."

"See!" Flower said to me, joking. She dipped a piece of tomato into fish sauce and set it on my rice. "Ha Noi is still a village."

"And your husband now?" Sixth Sister was saying.

Aunt Gentleness held her chopsticks in midair. Her voice was thin, like the steam rising from the fish soup she had made for us. "He died in the Christmas bombing. The last hour."

Sixth Sister nodded. "I lost my husband, too. He went back south after Regrouping and died fighting in Tay Ninh." She glanced at Autumn. "When Autumn came to Ban Long," she said to Aunt Gentleness, "we figured out that she and my husband had taught in the same school when he was here in the North for Regrouping."

"Oh my," Flower said to me under her breath. "We really are one village."

More than anything else, Second Harvest and Fifth Harmony longed to pay their respects to Ho Chi Minh. Autumn was taking care of her grandson that day and Sixth Sister had gone to Ha Bac to visit her relatives. Second Harvest, Fifth Harmony, and I hailed a cyclo and set off for the Ho Chi Minh Mausoleum.

In his last will, Ho Chi Minh had asked that his body be cremated and that some of his ashes be sent to the "compatriots in the South" should he die before Viet Nam was reunited. He further requested that there be a plan for planting trees around the site(s) where his ashes were buried so that the trees could "multiply with the passage of time and form forests."

However, at the time of Ho's death at the height of the American War, Party leaders decided instead to preserve their leader's body. They built a stolid Soviet-styled mausoleum with granite, marble, and precious woods collected from all over Viet Nam. The Mausoleum was dedicated on September 2, 1975, thirty years to the day after Ho Chi Minh read Viet Nam's Declaration of Independence at that same site.

Some twenty-five hundred visitors pass through the Mausoleum each day. Second Harvest, Fifth Harmony, and I took our place ahead of a group of school children. At the entrance, we passed between two guards, their rifles held stiffly at attention. Then we stepped under the lintel inscribed with Ho Chi Minh's famous quotation, "Nothing is more precious than independence and freedom."

The air inside was bracing, as if winter had returned. I tightened around my neck the grey-checked peasant's scarf Second Harvest had brought me from the south. We followed a uniformed guard up the red-carpeted steps and entered the tomb. The huge room was silent except for the faint hum of the lights, which gave off a pink glow, adding color to Ho Chi Minh's cheeks.

I stared into Ho's face. It was delicate, the pale skin almost translucent. It seemed strange to gaze down upon a corpse but, standing there be-

tween Second Harvest and Fifth Harmony, I found the experience pro-
foundly moving. Both women had followed a vision of independence and
freedom long before they ever heard of Ho Chi Minh. But Ho, along with
Mao Tse-tung, had done something extraordinary among nationalist
leaders from the Third World. He had urged women to play a forceful role
in Viet Nam's Revolution. Women like Second Harvest and Fifth Harmony had listened to Ho's teachings, taking in his words as they would
those of a beloved uncle.

Now, as we three stood before Ho Chi Minh, Second Harvest and Fifth
Harmony's shoulders drooped as if bent by a generation of sorrow. Both
women wept. I wept, too.

Autumn and I wanted Second Harvest and Fifth Harmony to see parts of
their country they had never known. We took them to Ha Long Bay in the
Gulf of Tonkin four hours east of Ha Noi. Second Harvest peered out the
car window. "How beautiful!" she said, staring at the expanse of fields with
brown stubble left from the fall crop and, here and there, the iridescent
green seedling plots that promised another harvest.

"From the day my mother gave birth to me until now," Second Harvest
said, "I have longed to see this."

We let ourselves be tourists and rented a boat to ride among the islets
in Ha Long Bay. "Such funny mountains!" Fifth Harmony said. "Mountains should be on the land!"

One afternoon in Ha Noi, we wandered through the city's biggest
market, went out for *pho*, toured the Ho Chi Minh museum. Another day
Autumn took us to the Temple of Literature across from the house where I
had lived on Rice Soup Street. She pointed out her ancestor's name on the
oldest ceremonial tablet. One evening we took in the water puppets, an art
form unique to Viet Nam's Red River Delta. Another evening we walked
over to Autumn's house for supper. Each morning Aunt Gentleness accompanied Second Harvest and Fifth Harmony on an early-morning stroll
around Lenin Park.

Aunt Honesty, who ran a tea stall across Lotus Pond Street, took Second Harvest to see a traditional doctor about her hand. The two women
returned, carrying a basket filled with packets of "northern medicine,"
which is related to traditional Chinese medicine. Twice a day, Second Harvest brewed her herbs into a tea as dark as soy sauce, its smell as penetrat-

ing as that of *nuoc mam*. By then I'd come down with a racking cough that kept everyone awake at night. "I would make you some 'southern medicine,' " Second Harvest offered, pointing to the small Soviet electric cook stove, "but I don't know how to use that thing."

"Like this," I said, remembering that in Ban Long Second Harvest cooked with wood and water-palm branches. I inserted the plug into the wall socket and flipped on a burner. But I forgot to pull out a skillet. I was washing dishes and chatting with Autumn when I realized Second Harvest had set a lemon and a bulb of ginger directly on the burner. Using chopsticks, she rolled the spices around the red burner rings. The kitchen filled with a tangy aroma. Autumn coughed. Her bronchitis had already set in with the cool weather of fall.

"You should get away from this awful cold and humidity," Second Harvest said to Autumn. With a cleaver she shaved the ginger and lemon, dropping the blackened slivers into a glass. She added boiling water and sugar. "Autumn, why don't you move to the south with me when the weather is bad?" Second Harvest said, handing me the brew. "What do you think, Little One?"

Whew, I thought, this idea is more than I've bargained for. Autumn and Second Harvest had met through me, but they had long since developed their own friendship. I hedged. "It would be good for Autumn's bronchitis," I said, "but, well, maybe you'd want to broach the subject with your husbands."

The two women looked at each other, laughing with the abandon of teenagers.

"Oh my!" Second Harvest said. "I guess we should check with the men."

"But Last Child," Autumn added, "wherever we are, you'll always have a home with us."

During that fall visit from Second Harvest and Fifth Harmony, Arnold Schecter came by Quaker House. A medical doctor based at SUNY Binghamton, Arnold had been researching the effects of Agent Orange for ten years. Although he had conducted interviews arranged by the Ha Noi–based committee responsible for Agent Orange research, Arnold had never spoken informally with people who had been sprayed.

"Sure, we'll talk to him," Second Harvest said when I mentioned the possibility that Arnold might stop by.

That afternoon we sat with Arnold over tea. "Excuse me, Doctor," Second Harvest said, "I don't mean to be rude." She pulled up her trousers and pointed to small, circular scars on her legs.

Arnold leaned forward. "Yes," he said, examining the scars. "Those are from chloracne. The rash is often chronic."

Second Harvest stood up and bent to the floor, spreading her fingers across the tiles as if weeding. "Those are my souvenirs from working in a rice paddy," she said. "I didn't know the poison was in the paddy water, so I didn't scrub my legs afterwards with urine."

"Urine!" Arnold's lower jaw dropped.

"Yes!" Fifth Harmony said.

Second Harvest stood up again, touching her forehead and cheeks. "That's why I don't have scars on my face. When the Agent Orange rained on us, we had no clean water. Nothing to bathe with. We washed our faces in urine, but several days later I didn't think to wash my legs after I'd been working in the paddy." She pulled up her right trouser leg again and touched her knee. "This big scar," she added, "isn't from Agent Orange. That's from a baby bomb."

Arnold closed his eyes. From the street came the cry of a vendor hawking *banh chung* cakes. He opened his eyes again as Fifth Harmony began to describe "American rice," an overgrown and inedible mutant that appeared after the spraying. She talked about how the bananas had bloated and then died.

"Yes," Arnold said, looking at me. "That's the effect of the growth hormone. "Any effects on health?" he asked the women, his tone neutral.

Fifth Harmony told how the chickens, ducks, and pigs had died. She described the abnormal babies she'd delivered.

"Any such abnormalities before Agent Orange?" Arnold asked.

"None," she answered.

"It's all anecdotal information, Arnold," I added as I translated. "It's not verifiable or statistically significant."

"True," Arnold said. "But sometimes I need to put aside being a scientist and listen as a human being."

When it came time for Arnold to leave, I walked with him down Lotus Pond Street to find him a cyclo. When I returned to the house, Second Harvest was coaxing another nub of ginger around the stove rings. She moved to the table and began to slice the ginger. "Do you think Dr. Arnold believed me?" she asked. "What I told Dr. Arnold was true, but I didn't tell him everything."

I was still reeling from having heard Fifth Harmony describe once again the baby born with the face of an owl. I had been thinking of the stillborns I'd seen in the Sai Gon Ob/Gyn hospital. I shuddered, remembering again the extra arms, the eye in the middle of an abdomen.

Second Harvest added sugar and lemon to the ginger. She covered the mixture with boiling water. "I told you everything, Last Child," she said, offering me the drink, "because we've known each other such a long time. But not the doctor, no. Not the first time we meet. Can you understand? If I'd told Dr. Arnold everything, he would have been too sad."

One Saturday night, Aunt Honesty insisted we go out on the town. During the French War, she had worked as a nurse on one of the Resistance medical teams in the mountains; during the American War, four of her six children were evacuated to four different villages while the two youngest stayed with her in a fifth. Now that peace had come, Aunt Honesty tended her tea stall. Every morning at dawn she rode on the back of my bicycle to Lenin Park to play badminton.

Aunt Honesty, Second Harvest, Fifth Harmony, and I set out by foot. I had assumed we were going to the Lake of the Redeemed Sword in the center of Ha Noi, but Aunt Honesty had different ideas. Much to my surprise, she led us into the Central State Department Store.

The State Store, where goods made in the few remaining government factories were sold, was a vacuous remnant of socialism. Its wooden floors, worn smooth by bare feet and flip-flops, had the feel of generations past. We peered through dusty glass cases at TVs, plastic toys, and tiny ink bottles school children no longer used now that there were ballpoint pens. Like most of the other customers, we left without buying. Aunt Honesty turned toward home.

"Shouldn't we show them the park?" I suggested, glancing toward the Lake of the Redeemed Sword shimmering in the moonlight. According to legend, in the mid-fifteenth century, the Heavenly Creator gave Emperor Le Loi a magical sword to drive the Chinese out of Viet Nam. Later, while boating on the lake, the victorious Le Loi came upon a tortoise, who snatched the sword and, diving into the water, returned the magical weapon to the Heavenly Spirit.

The reflection of the full moon shimmered in the water near Tortoise Tower. We strolled along the brick path past lovers in tight clusters and small groups gathered around cards and checkers. A man in a Red Sox baseball cap pumped a pedal apparatus to spin cotton candy he made in an old fifty-five-gallon drum. The candy's sweet aroma mixed with the salty scent of the dried squid sold by the woman squatting at his feet.

As we walked back past a new one-hour photo shop, six preteens joined us. They were still giddy from their escapades during Teachers' Day, a holiday when schools close and children cruise the city on their bicycles, taking presents to their teachers. A tall girl with hair pulled into a ponytail tugged my sleeve.

"Westerner," she said, using the Vietnamese word for a Caucasian that had replaced "Soviet."

"Not true!" Aunt Honesty said, stopping in mid-step. She pointed to her own greying hair, as curly as mine. "Can't you see? We're mother and daughter, though it's true, her father's a Westerner."

"You're too big to have a Vietnamese mother," a boy with a Tiger-beer T-shirt said to me. He was tall and lean, like a bamboo sapling.

"Aren't you as tall as your parents but still growing?" I countered.

"Well, yes," he admitted.

"Come on, Daughter," Aunt Honesty said, taking my arm. "Time to take your old mother home."

Arm in arm, Aunt Honesty and I followed Second Harvest and Fifth Harmony. We passed a tea stall, where three old men shared a bong of *thuoc lao*. Across the street, traffic whirled around bicycles clustered outside a café. The café stereo was playing "A Drop of Rain on the Leaves," a song written by Trinh Cong Son, a famous Vietnamese songwriter living in Sai Gon, and sung by Khanh Ly, an equally famous singer living in the States. I stopped, letting the song's poignant yearning for peace in a troubled land wash over me.

During the war, the café outside Quaker House in Quang Ngai often played a tape with that same song. The Sai Gon government police would confiscate the tape, but several days later I'd invariably hear the same song playing once again. When I lived in Pulau Bidong, the Malaysian camp for Boat People, the Vietnamese camp police would also confiscated tapes because Trinh Cong Son was considered disloyal for choosing to stay behind in Ho Chi Minh City, as Sai Gon was then called. Meanwhile, in Ha Noi, the tapes were forbidden because Khanh Ly had fled to the States.

But all that was long ago. Now, the tape of the songwriter and singer who, for me, hold within their combined voices the sorrow of war played openly on a major Ha Noi street. I had to pause: In that moment, for me, the American War was finally over.

Aunt Honest tugged my sleeve. "What is it, Daughter?" she asked, her voice light with jest. "Did you forget something?"

"No, *Ma*," I said, "I won't forget." Suddenly I realized that Aunt Honesty must have thought I was talking nonsense. "I just had to listen, *Ma*," I explained. "That's all."

Aunt Honesty and I caught up to Fifth Harmony and Second Harvest at Quang Trung Street, named for the emperor who had hidden his junks up Roaring River and whose "citizens' war" at Tet had defeated Chinese invading Ha Noi. Motorcycles whipped by, their taillights merging into a red swirl. Second Harvest backed away from the curb.

"Scary," she muttered.

I put my hand on her shoulder. "Ha Noi's traffic is your monkey bridge," I said, teasing. Then I took her hand, feeling once again the calluses on her palm and the roughness of her fingertips.

"You can do it, Older Sister," I said.

In the moonlit darkness, led by an American, Second Harvest edged across.

One evening, Fifth Harmony left to visit a nephew, who had settled on one of the few remaining state farms. When Autumn left for home, Second Harvest and I were alone in the house. The radio carried news of Typhoon Six battering the coast. Rain rattled the glass in the windows. The wind shrieked. Next door, the metal roofing banged, each slap like a mortar exploding.

Second Harvest looked up the stairwell of the house on Lotus Pond. "Two people in two rooms on two floors," she said, toying with the light switch. "I'm afraid."

Here was a woman who had been imprisoned by the French when she was two. She had stood up against bombs, mortars, and Agent Orange. She'd suffered years of hunger and had lived with a bounty over her head sufficient to marry off a hundred daughters. She had faced armed GIs, her hands "loaded" only with birthing mucus. This was not a woman afraid of the dark.

But Second Harvest had always lived in the Mekong Delta, where the genies are kinder; she had never faced a typhoon raging like war itself. Still, I knew her expression of fear alluded to something more resonant than a typhoon. Vietnamese rarely sleep alone, for to be alone is to be unbearably sad. That's why in Khanh Phu, River would slip through the garden gate to sleep with Mrs. Spring Rain, and why in Ban Long, Third Success would come over to sleep with Senior Uncle.

"Would you feel better if I slept with you?" I asked Second Harvest.

"Yes."

That evening I had a report to finish writing. By the time I turned in, the storm had ebbed. The rain was steady and soft, as soothing as the sound of a Vietnamese zither. Second Harvest was already asleep, a blue quilt pulled up to her chin. I gazed at her face. She breathed deeply; with every breath, her black curls quivered against the white pillowcase. In the dim light, the lines around her eyes had softened.

She had been our enemy. Why?

Reaching up, I let down the mosquito net, taking care that it not touch her face. I tucked in the edges. Then I turned off the light and slipped inside.

Second Harvest stirred. "Last Child?" she whispered.

"Yes."

She turned toward me, her features further softened by the shadows. "We've known each other a long time," she said. "Seven years! You've made so many trips to visit me, and now I've come to see you." She reached under her pillow and retrieved a tiny red tin with a gold star on its lid. Opening it, she dabbed tiger balm onto her forefinger and then rubbed her temples. "Now we've finished our book," she said. She reached over and dabbed tiger balm onto my forehead. "Will our friendship stop?"

I inhaled the balm's pinching fragrance. "Not unless you want it to. Do you?"

"No." She raised up on her elbow. "When you write to your father, will you give him my greetings?" She paused. "Tell him my father treasures the picture he sent of his house by the river with sweet water the color of tea."

She lay back, staring at the netting, which wrapped us in the same cocoon. "When you next write a letter home," she added, "will you send my greetings to all the American women, and to the men, too?"

"Yes," I said.

Second Harvest settled her hand onto mine. "Have we done enough for today?" she asked.

"I think so."

"Then we can rest," she said.

In memory of

Uncle Last Gust
Pham Ngoc Lan

Uncle Beautiful
Dinh Van My

and

Mrs. Beautiful
Vu Thi My

DESCRIPTION OF TERMS

Agent Orange	One of several defoliants the United States sprayed on 46 percent of South Viet Nam's forests and 10 percent of the cropland to destroy jungle cover and paddy land used by the Viet Cong. Agent Orange contains dioxin, which is also toxic to wildlife, livestock, and humans.
American War	Vietnamese expression for the Viet Nam War. According to Vietnamese, the American War began with the 1954 Geneva Accords and ended with the Sai Gon government's collapse on April 30, 1975.
ARVN	Army of the Republic of Viet Nam (U.S.-backed Sai Gon government).
B-52	High-flying American plane famous for "carpet" or "harrow" bombing of both North Viet Nam and South Viet Nam during the American War.
baby bomb, or bom bi	An American antipersonnel weapon that explodes into pellets, called flechettes, designed to embed in the flesh.
Christmas bombing	President Richard Nixon's surprise December 1972 bombing of North Viet Nam and particularly Ha Noi at the end of the Paris peace talks. Because signing of the Paris Agreement was imminent, Ha Noi children who during earlier bombing attacks had been evacuated to the countryside to escape American bombs were back living in the city. Casualties from the surprise bombing were high, destruction massive.
CIA	U.S. Central Intelligence Agency. The CIA supplied the French War, staged covert operations to subvert the 1954 Geneva Accords, engaged in a clandestine

war in Laos, facilitated the Phoenix Program to elimi-
nate Viet Cong leaders, and staged Operation CHAOS
in the U.S. to stifle antiwar critics.

Dien Bien Phu

Famous battle ending the French War in 1954. Soldiers
and peasants hauled matériel by foot and bicycle, each
trip to the site taking three months. During the American War, the Vietnamese would repeat many of the
same tactics they had used at Dien Bien Phu.

Doi Moi *(Renovation)*

Policy adopted by the Sixth Congress of the Vietnamese Communist Party in December 1986. *Doi
Moi* included a move to a free-market economy, more
personal freedom, and openness to the world.

Dong Khoi

1960 Southern Uprising of Vietnamese peasants
against the U.S.-backed Diem government.

French Wars

Vietnamese wars of independence from the French.
The Vietnamese Resistance began with the French in-
vasion of Viet Nam in the 1850s. The First French War
ran from 1860 until Ho Chi Minh declared independence in 1945. The Second French War ran from 1945
to 1954. American personnel from the CIA were involved in the second war. The U.S. was paying 75 percent of the French costs by the end of the second war.

Geneva Accords

Agreement signed on July 20, 1954 ending the French
War. The Accords provisionally divided Viet Nam into
two zones—North and South—at the 17th parallel.
They also provided for the withdrawal of French troops
and for general elections in 1956 to reunify the country.
The U.S., a participant at the negotiations, refused to
sign the Accords. CIA teams under Col. Edward Lansdale's direction began immediately to subvert the
Accords in both North Viet Nam and South Viet Nam.

Ho Chi Minh

(1890–1969). Affectionately referred to by Vietnamese as "Senior Uncle," Ho helped found the Vietnamese Communist Party and the Viet Minh. He led
the Resistance struggle against French colonialism
and then against American intervention in the South.

Ho Chi Minh Trail

American name for the network of trails and roads
through the Truong Son Mountains. The trail was
used by North Viet Nam to supply the NVA and PLAF
in the South.

Indochina	The southeast Asia region comprising Viet Nam, Laos, and Cambodia, all of which were once French colonies.
Khe Sanh	One of the bloodiest battles of the American War, Khe Sanh involved 50,000 U.S. troops, 60,000 tons of napalm, and 40,000 tons of regular ordnance. The NVA-PLAF attack on Khe Sanh was a tactic to divert attention from Vietnamese preparations for the Tet Offensive.
Nam Ky Khoi Nghia	1940 Southern Uprising against the French. Organized by the Communist Party, *Nam Ky Khoi Nghia* was to be a major uprising all across southern Viet Nam. However, the French arrested Communist Party leaders just before the Uprising, which did occur but mostly in Chau Thanh district of what is now Tien Giang province.
napalm	Jellied gasoline supplied by the United States to France for the French War and also used by the U.S. during the American War. When napalm canisters were dropped from airplanes, the gasoline exploded, sticking to anything it hit and burning with intense heat.
Ngo Dinh Diem	(1901–1963). A Catholic, anti-Communist nationalist selected by the Americans and brought from self-exile in the U.S. to be prime minister of South Viet Nam just before the Geneva Accords were signed. Backed by the U.S., Diem refused to hold the elections stipulated by the Geneva Accords. His forces imprisoned family members of former Resistance fighters then in the North for Regrouping, referring to them as "Viet Cong." Diem was deposed by a U.S.-backed coup on November 1, 1963. The next day, he was found murdered.
Nguyen Van Thieu	(1923–). Member of the military junta that, with U.S. backing, overthrew Ngo Dinh Diem. Thieu was president of South Viet Nam from 1967 until shortly before the collapse of the Sai Gon government on April 30, 1975.
NLF	National Liberation Front of South Viet Nam. Also known as the Viet Cong, the NLF was a coalition of nationalists and Communists formed in 1960 to oppose Diem's repressive policies.

north; center; south	The northern region of Viet Nam includes Ha Noi, Hai Phong, and the Red River Delta. The central region includes Hue, Da Nang, and Quang Ngai. The southern region includes Sai Gon and the Mekong Delta.
the North	North Viet Nam, formally the Democratic Republic of Viet Nam, a separate country from 1954 until 1975. During the American War, the Chinese and the Soviets supplied the North.
NVA	North Vietnamese Army (the American term for the People's Army of Viet Nam).
Paris Peace Accords	The agreement signed on January 25, 1973, after lengthy and intermittent talks between North Viet Nam, the Sai Gon government, the PRG, and the U.S. The Accords stipulated a cease-fire, withdrawal of U.S. troops, and an exchange of prisoners. However, the Accords allowed Vietnamese troops from both sides to remain in place.
Phoenix Program	A CIA-backed Sai Gon government program of payments to identify and "neutralize" members of the Viet Cong infrastructure through defection, arrest, torture, and assassination.
PLAF	Peoples Liberation Armed Forces, the army of the NLF in South Viet Nam; the "Viet Cong."
PRG	Provisional Revolutionary Government of South Viet Nam formed from the NLF in 1969.
Regrouping (tap ket)	Between 150,000 and 200,000 Vietnamese Resistance fighters went to the North for Regrouping in 1954 in compliance with the Geneva Accords. They expected to return in July 1956 for the elections stipulated by the Accords in reunify Viet Nam.
the South	South Viet Nam, formally the Republic of Viet Nam, a separate country from 1954 until 1975. During the American War, the U.S. supplied the South. The U.S., South Korea, Australia, Philippines, Thailand, and New Zealand provided the South with troops.
Tet	The Lunar New Year and Viet Nam's major holiday. Tet involves weeks of preparation, all-night firecrackers on Tet Eve, and at least three days of feasting.

Tet Offensive	NVA and PLAF offensive at Tet in early 1968. The U.S. intelligence system failed to predict the offensive. NVA and PLAF forces staged coordinated attacks on a hundred cities and towns across South Viet Nam. They captured Hue and My Tho and penetrated the United States embassy in Sai Gon.
tiger cages	Prison cells on Con Son (Poulo Condore) Island off the coast of southern Viet Nam. Measuring 5 x 9 feet and open on the top to the weather, the tiger cages were used by the French and by the American-backed Sai Gon government for political prisoners during the French and American wars.
Truong Son	Mountain range running the length of Viet Nam; Vietnamese name for "Ho Chi Minh Trail."
VC	American GI slang for "Viet Cong," originally a pejorative, now commonly used by Vietnamese to refer to southern Resistance fighters during the American War.
Viet Cong	Literally "Vietnamese Communist," a pejorative coined by Ngo Dinh Diem in the 1950s; used by Americans and only recently by Vietnamese for southern Resistance fighters (many of whom were not Communists) during the American War.
Viet Minh	Short for *Viet Nam Doc Lap Dong Minh Hoi,* or League for an Independent Viet Nam, formed under Ho Chi Minh's leadership in 1941; term used for Vietnamese who resisted the French from 1941 until the Vietnamese victory at the end of the Second French War in 1954.
Vo Nguyen Giap	(1912–). Vietnamese general who was commander-in-chief of the Vietnamese army during the Resistance against the French and the Americans.
William Westmoreland	(1914–). American general who was commander of the Military Assistance Command, Vietnam (MACV) in Viet Nam from 1964 to mid-1968. General Westmoreland predicted "some light at the end of the tunnel" at the National Press Club in Washington on November 21, 1967, and then was caught off guard by the Tet Offensive two months later.

OUTLINE OF VIETNAMESE HISTORY

I
Resistance to the Chinese

1st Millennium B.C.	Period of the Hung Kings; Bronze Age.
2nd Century B.C.	Annexation by the Han Chinese Empire.
40 A.D.	Trung Sisters defeat the Chinese and restore Viet Nam's independence.
43	Chinese reassert domination.
544	Ly Nam De's insurrection.
939	Ngo Quyen defeats the Chinese and sets up an independent Vietnamese state.
1009–1225	Ly dynasty.
1010	Thang Long (Ha Noi) becomes the capital.
1225–1400	Tran dynasty.
1225–1288	Resistance against three Mongol invasions.
1407–1427	Ming Chinese invade and occupy Viet Nam.
1418–1427	Le Loi and Nguyen Trai lead Vietnamese nationalists against the Chinese.
1427–1789	Le dynasty.
17th–18th centuries	Struggle between Trinh (north) and Nguyen (south) lords; peasant insurrections.
1785	Nguyen Hue defeats the Thais on Roaring River in the Mekong Delta.
1789	Nguyen Hue (Quang Trung) defeats the Chinese in Ha Noi.
1802	Gia Long branch of the Nguyen dynasty begins.

II
First French War

1858	French attack Da Nang.
1867	French annex southern Viet Nam.
1875	French attack Ha Noi.
1884	French impose protectorate status on Viet Nam.
1860–1900	Popular uprisings led by scholars against the French.
1904–1908	Patriotic movements led by Phan Boi Chau and Phan Chu Trinh.
1920	Nguyen Ai Quoc (Ho Chi Minh) votes at Tours to establish the French Communist Party.
1930	Ho Chi Minh and others found the Vietnamese Communist Party; popular uprisings against the French.
1940	Germany occupies France; Japan seizes French holdings in Viet Nam; Southern Uprising (*Nam Ky Khoi Nghia*); uprisings in Bac Son and Do Luong.
1941	Viet Minh founded.
1941–1945	Guerrilla actions against Japanese and French occupying Viet Nam.
1945	Japanese force peasants to grow jute; between one and two million peasants die from starvation; Viet Minh take Ha Noi, Hue, and Sai Gon; Vietnamese emperor Bao Dai presents imperial sword and seal to Viet Minh.
September 2, 1945	Ho Chi Minh reads Viet Nam's Declaration of Independence in Ha Noi's Ba Dinh Square.

III
Second French War

September 23, 1945	French troops arriving on U.S. carriers attack southern Viet Nam; Vietnamese Resistance begins.
November–December 1946	French attack northern Viet Nam; Vietnamese Resistance begins; U.S. gives France $160 million in credit for the war.

1950–1954	U.S. aid for French War rises from 60 to 75 percent of French costs; CIA personnel and airplanes supply the French; Chinese assist Viet Nam.
1954	Vietnamese People's Army defeats the French at Dien Bien Phu.

IV
American War

June 1954	Ngo Dinh Diem brought to South Viet Nam from the United States to be prime minister.
July 1954	Geneva Accords provisionally divide Viet Nam at the 17th parallel into North Viet Nam (under Ho Chi Minh) and south Viet Nam (under Ngo Dinh Diem) with elections to reunify the country scheduled for July 1956; French troops to leave Viet Nam; Vietnamese Resistance fighters in the south to go north for Regrouping for two years.
	The U.S. refuses to sign the Accords; Secretary of State John Foster Dulles and CIA head Allen Dulles recruit Edward Lansdale to begin immediate covert operations to subvert the Accords in both the North and the South; nearly one million Catholics, many organized by Lansdale's team, flee to the South; the U.S. provides military assistance in the form of advisors and matériel to Diem.
1954–1960	Ngo Dinh Diem refuses to hold elections; imprisons family members of the Vietnamese former Resistance fighters in the North for Regrouping; land reforms in the North include leftist abuses with many killed.
1960	Southern Uprising (*Dong Khoi*) against the U.S.-backed Diem government; formation of the National Liberation Front.
1961–1963	American military advisors authorized to return fire.
1964	The U.S. begins embargo against North Viet Nam; Gulf of Tonkin incident; Gulf of Tonkin Resolution.

1965	American ground combat troops begin offensive operations in the South; United States bombs the North; antiwar protests in the U.S. and Europe; China and Soviet Union supply the North.
1968	Soviet Union becomes the major supplier of North Viet Nam; North Vietnamese siege of Khe Sanh; Tet Offensive by the NVA and PLAF forces against a hundred cities and towns across South Viet Nam; American troops kill over four hundred civilians at My Lai; Paris peace talks begin.
1969	American troop strength preaches 543,300; "Vietnamization" of the war begins; massive antiwar demonstrations in the United States; Ho Chi Minh dies; My Lai massacre story breaks.
1970	U.S. invades Cambodia; massive antiwar demonstrations in the U.S.; four Kent State students and two Jackson State students killed during antiwar protests.
1972	U.S. détente with China; Chinese assistance to North Viet Nam withdrawn; NVA and PLAF offensive against American and Sai Gon troops; the U.S. blockades North Vietnamese coast; surprise "Christmas bombing" of the North as the Paris peace talks end.
1973	Paris Peace Agreement signed; withdrawal of American ground troops; return of prisoners from both sides; Vietnamese troops from both sides remain in place.
1973–1975	War continues; the U.S. supports the Sai Gon government; Soviet Union supports the North.
Spring 1975	NVA and PLAF offensive.
April 30, 1975	Sai Gon government collapses; Viet Nam is reunified.

V
Cambodian and Chinese Wars and Peace

1976	Nationwide elections in Viet Nam; the U.S. tries to keep Viet Nam out of the United Nations.

Christopher Reynolds Foundation
Foreign Press Center of Viet Nam
Ohio Arts Council
Vietnamese Union of Friendship Organizations
William Joiner Center for the Study of War and Social Consequences
Women's Museum of Ha Noi
Women's Union of Viet Nam